K. Eileen Allen

Professor Emerita
University of Kansas

Lynn R. Marotz,
RN, Ph.D

University of Kansas

Developmental Profiles

Pre-birth through Twelve

6TH EDITION

WADSWORTH
CENGAGE Learning

AUSTRALIA
BRAZIL
JAPAN
KOREA
MEXICO
SINGAPORE
SPAIN
UNITED KINGDOM
UNITED STATES

WADSWORTH
CENGAGE Learning

Developmental Profiles

Pre-birth through Twelve, 6th Edition

K. Eileen Allen | Lynn R. Marotz

Executive Editor: Marcus Boggs

Acquisitions Editor: Chris Shortt

Developmental Editor: Shelley Murphy

Assistant Editor: Caitlin Cox

Editorial Assistant: Linda Stewart

Media Editor: Mary Noel

Marketing Manager: Kara Parsons

Marketing Assistant: Dimitri Hagnere

Marketing Communications Manager: Martha Pfeiffer

Content Project Manager: Samen Iqbal

Creative Director: Rob Hugel

Art Director: Maria Epes

Print Buyer: Paula Vang

Rights Acquisitions Account Manager, Text: Bob Kauser

Rights Acquisitions Account Manager, Image: Leitha Etheridge-Sims

Production Service: Elm Street Publishing Services

Cover Designer: Irene Morris

Cover Image: © Coco Masuda/Stock Illustration Source/ Getty Images

Compositor: Integra Software Services Pvt. Ltd.

For product information and technology assistance, contact us at Cengage Learning Customer & Sales Support, 1-800-354-9706.

For permission to use material from this text or product, submit all requests online at www.cengage.com/permissions.

Further permissions questions can be e-mailed to permissionrequest@cengage.com.

Library of Congress Control Number: 2008943482

Student Edition
ISBN-13: 978-1-4354-1294-1
ISBN-10: 1-4354-1294-X

Wadsworth
10 Davis Drive
Belmont, CA 94002-3098
USA

Cengage Learning is a leading provider of customized learning solutions with office locations around the globe, including Singapore, the United Kingdom, Australia, Mexico, Brazil, and Japan. Locate your local office at www.cengage.com/ international.

Cengage Learning products are represented in Canada by Nelson Education, Ltd.

To learn more about Wadsworth, visit **www.cengage.com/wadsworth**

Purchase any of our products at your local college store or at our preferred online store www.ichapters.com.

CONTENTS

CHAPTER 3   Prenatal Development   47

CHAPTER 4   Infancy: Birth to Twelve Months   71

CHAPTER 5   Toddlerhood: Twelve to Twenty-four Months   111

PREFACE

Developmental Profiles opens with a brief overview of major child development theories and principles. These chapters (1 and 2) serve as a refresher of basic concepts and provide background material on age-level expectancies for the chapters that follow. Chapter 3 is devoted to maternal practices that are important for promoting healthy fetal development. Detailed word pictures of children's development across six domains, including typical daily routines, safety alerts, developmental alerts, and learning activities are described in Chapters 4 through 8. Chapter 9 focuses on when and where to seek help if there are concerns about a child's developmental progress. Extensive checklists and resource material of interest to families and individuals who work with young children are provided in the appendixes.

Developmental Profiles is designed for:

- Child-development and early-childhood students and preservice teachers.
- Teachers in home-based settings, early-childhood centers, Head Start programs, schools, before- and after-school programs, and caregivers in the child's own home.
- Allied health professionals from fields such as nursing, nutrition, audiology, social work, physical and occupational therapy, psychology, medicine, and language and speech therapy as well as other disciplines providing services for children and their families.
- Families, the most important contributors to a child's optimum development.

Developmental Profiles provides nontechnical information about:

- What to expect of young children at each succeeding stage of development.
- The ways in which all areas of development are intertwined and mutually supportive.
- The unique pathway that each child follows in a developmental process that is alike, yet different, among children of similar age.

- Sequences, not age, being the critical concept in evaluating developmental progress.
- The use of developmental norms in teaching, observing, and assessing children and in designing individualized as well as group learning experiences.

Developmental Profiles includes a number of special features:

- A chapter that briefly defines and describes the most commonly encountered terms and concepts in the child development literature.
- Concise profiles of developmental domains at various age levels from pre-birth through age twelve.
- Developmental Connections, a technology feature linked to the CD-ROM accompanying this book. This feature allows students and instructors to relate important chapter content to the video clips provided on the CD-ROM. Critical Thinking Questions tie concepts presented in the book with video footage of children in naturalistic settings to provide ample opportunities for reflection, application, and professional development.
- Developmental alerts for each level that might suggest a possible delay or problem that warrants further evaluation.
- Descriptions of daily activities and routines typical of children at each level.
- Where and how to get help if there is concern about a child's development.
- Annotated Websites at the end of each chapter for ease in locating professional organizations and additional resource information.
- Objectives and key terms to draw the reader's attention to important points in each chapter.
- Suggested activities for promoting children's curiosity and learning.
- Developmental checklists for use in observing and screening children's developmental progress (Appendix B).
- Safety alerts for each developmental stage to help families and teachers create safe environments, maintain quality supervision, and encourage children's safety awareness.
- Developmental sketches and related questions to help readers link chapter content to real-life situations.
- Color photographs to illustrate key concepts described throughout the book.
- Annotated descriptions for additional readings on child development, screening and assessment, diversity, parenting, and referral and information resources (Appendix F).
- A sample child health history form (Appendix C).
- Examples of frequently used screening and assessment instruments designed for evaluating children from six months through twelve years (Appendix D).
- Additional information resources for families and professionals (Appendix E).

Developmental Profiles is designed as a concise, user-friendly resource for teachers, families, caregivers, and practitioners. It is *not* intended to provide readers with an in-depth perspective on classic and contemporary theories of children's development. We believe this format will encourage individuals who work with children to be vigilant and proactive in promoting children's development and identifying delays in their earliest stage.

ANCILLARIES

Video Connections CD-ROM

The CD-ROM contained in this book includes all new video clips of infants and toddlers, preschoolers, and school age children in naturalistic settings and at different developmental stages. Designed to integrate technology and early-childhood education, this valuable resource provides instructors and students with ample opportunities for personal reflection, practical application, and professional development. The technology tie-in boxes embedded in each chapter can be used to connect material presented in the text to corresponding segments on the CD-ROM.

Instructor's Manual

The instructor's manual includes an outline of content material and objectives for each chapter as well as answers to the developmental sketch application and review questions. A series of discussion questions and suggested student activities that correspond to each chapter have also been added to reinforce learning and facilitate continued dialogue.

e-Resource

The e-resource component is designed to provide instructors with all the classroom tools they need on one convenient CD-ROM. Instructors will discover that this resource offers a turnkey solution to course development and teaching by offering Microsoft® PowerPoint® slides, a computerized test bank (ExamView), an electronic version of the Instructor's Manual, and other text specific resources. The computerized test bank comprises true/false, multiple-choice, short-answer, and completion questions for each chapter. Instructors can use the computerized test bank software to create their own unique quizzes for students. Refer to the ExamView User's Guide for more information on how to prepare and post quizzes to your school's Internet or intranet server. Students may also access sample quizzes from the Book Companion Website to accompany this sixth edition of *Developmental Profiles: Pre-birth through Twelve*.

Book Companion Website

Book Companion Website to accompany the sixth edition of *Developmental Profiles: Pre-birth through Twelve* is your link to early-childhood education on the Internet.

The Companion Website includes many features and resources to help focus and enhance an understanding of child development. You will find the Companion Website at www.cengage.com/education/allen. The authors and Wadsworth Cengage Learning make every effort to ensure that all Internet resources are accurate at the time of printing. However, due to the fluid, time sensitive nature of the Internet, we cannot guarantee that all URLs and Web site addresses will remain current for the duration of this edition.

WebTutor™

The WebTutor™ to accompany *Developmental Profiles: Pre-birth through Twelve*, sixth edition, enables you to take learning beyond the classroom. This online courseware is designed to complement the text and benefits students by enabling them to manage better their time, prepare for exams, organize their notes, and more. Special features include:

- *Chapter Learning Objectives* Correlate with textbook chapter objectives.
- *Online Course Preparation* List what students should have read or done prior to using online content.
- *Study Sheets* Outline the content of each chapter and contain notes. Study Sheets can be printed to help students learn, review, and remember important points.
- *Glossary* Provides definitions for terms in each chapter or in the course as a whole.
- *Flash Cards* Allow students to test themselves on word definitions.
- *Discussion Topics* Allow questions to be posted to encourage use as a threaded bulletin board and as assignments to develop critical thinking skills.
- *FAQs* Provide questions and answers that students might have about specific content.
- *Online Class Notes* Provide additional information about the chapter content.
- *Online Chapter Quizzes* Provide, in various formats, matching exercises, true-false quizzes, short-answer questions, and multiple-choice questions with immediate feedback for correct and incorrect answers. Multiple-choice questions also include rationales for right and wrong choices.
- *Web Links* Provide students with practice searching the Internet for information. Learners choose from a variety of Web links and report findings to their instructor through e-mail.

A benefit for instructors as well as for students, the WebTutor™ enables online discussion with the instructor and other class members, real-time chat to enable virtual office hours and encourage collaborative learning environments, a calendar of syllabus information for easy reference, e-mail connections to facilitate communication among classmates and between students and instructors, and customization tools that help instructors tailor their course to fit their needs by adding or changing content. WebTutor™ extends your reach beyond the classroom and is available on either WebCT or Blackboard platforms.

INTRODUCTION

This sixth edition of *Developmental Profiles: Pre-birth through Twelve* has been expanded and updated. At the same time, it maintains the authors' original intent to provide a comprehensive yet nontechnical, easy-to-follow guide to children's development. Major characteristics of each developmental domain for each age level are in the original point-by-point format (Chapters 4 through 8). This arrangement has proven invaluable for teachers, students, families, and practitioners in readily accessing needed information. The Daily Routines for each age are easily located in uniquely designed boxes. The new design quickly distinguishes the Daily Routines from Learning Activities, Developmental Alerts, and Safety Alerts, which are also noted. Glossary words are highlighted in boldface type throughout the text, with each term defined at the bottom of the page on which it is used as well as in a comprehensive glossary at the end of the book.

Features of the Sixth Edition

This new edition of *Developmental Profiles* continues to bring readers important features designed to support learning and provide current information in a format that is efficient to use. For, it is teachers—caregivers, families, and professionals—who, through their understanding of the critical importance of the early years, creation of enriched learning opportunities, and modeling of desirable behaviors, ultimately make a difference in children's lives.

New Full-Color Edition

The sixth edition is the first to be printed in full color. Line sketches and black-white photos that appeared in previous editions have been replaced throughout the book with contemporary color photographs to improve its visual appeal. Photographs have been selected to enhance the reader's ability to relate descriptive content to everyday settings and experiences with children.

Objectives and Key Terms

These pedagogical features draw the reader's attention to important concepts the authors have addressed in each chapter. Objectives are designed to provoke critical thinking. Key terms are highlighted in bold in the text, defined on the page where they first appear, listed at the end of the chapters, and included in a comprehensive glossary at the end of the book.

Developmental Sketches

Brief developmental sketches are presented in shaded boxes at the beginning of each chapter to improve an understanding of sometimes complex information. Their placement is intended to set the stage and encourage readers to analyze and synthesize content as it is presented. Questions at the end of the chapter provide readers with an opportunity to apply what they have learned to real life situations.

Safety Alerts

Because children are always at greater risk of injury, the authors felt strongly that more information on safety promotion should be included. Safety concerns draw attention to some of the most important safety considerations at each developmental stage. For example, important recommendations for reducing the risk of SIDS in infants are addressed in Chapter 4. Safety guidelines are based on the rapidly occurring changes in children's growth and development that, in turn, have a direct effect on the nature of adult awareness and supervision necessary.

Prenatal Development (Chapter 3)

A mother's health and lifestyle, before and during pregnancy, have a direct impact on her child's developmental potential and long-term well-being. Because this is such a critical period, new information has been added to reflect current research findings. Month-by-month fetal development is described in a concise visual format. Information on nutrition, maternal infections, drugs, and practices that can potentially interfere with healthy fetal development has been updated. New information on maternal depression and labor and delivery has been included in this edition.

Child Development Theory and Principal Concepts

Those who have used previous editions of this book will notice that the first two chapters have been reorganized and rewritten to improve students' understanding of important material. Chapter 1 now includes an expanded discussion of classic child development theories and describes authentic data-gathering strategies based on observation. Chapter 2 focuses on the basic principles and concepts that help us understand and explain children's development.

Chapter 9

Information on when and how to seek help for children who are suspected of having developmental disabilities has been updated. Major legislative acts supporting children's healthy development, including information on the Individuals with

Disabilities Education Improvement Act (IDEA) of 2004, have been added to Chapter 9. An annotated sampling of commonly used screening and assessment instruments has also been updated and included in Appendix D. Additional resources for families and professionals, including listings of organizations and special-interest Websites, is now available in Appendix E for easier location and use.

Additional Reading Resources

An annotated listing of additional books on topics such as child development, diversity, parenting, observation and assessment, and children with special needs has been included in Appendix F. The authors acknowledge that many excellent books are available on these topics but have included only a limited selection due to space considerations.

Annotated Web Links

Web addresses for many professional organizations and resources are provided for readers who are interested in accessing additional information about topics discussed in each chapter. Links to other valuable resources can often be found on these sites.

PHILOSOPHICAL NOTES

The common practice of dividing infancy and childhood into age-related units of months and years can distort the realities of human development. However, when describing developmental expectations, developmental progress, and delays, other systems seem to work even less well. Let it be stressed here, as it is again and again throughout the text, that the age specifications are only approximate markers derived from *averages* or *norms*. In a way, they can be thought of as midpoints not intended to represent any one child. Age expectations can be thought of also as summary terms for skills that vary from child to child in form and time of acquisition. The truly important consideration in assessing a child's development is *sequence*. The essential question is not chronological age but whether the child is moving forward step by step in each area of development. *Developmental Profiles* proves itself an invaluable resource in addressing this issue.

As in the previous editions of *Developmental Profiles*, the early days, weeks, and months of infancy are examined in great detail. New research findings on brain and early development clearly support the critical importance of this relatively short time span. What is now known about the infant's capacity for learning is indeed amazing given conventional wisdom, which suggests that young babies simply flounder around in a booming, buzzing confusion. Far from it! With more and more infants entering infant programs at ever earlier ages, it is most important for teachers to be knowledgeable about infant development and learning. It is also crucial for families to hold appropriate expectations and can describe to teachers what they want and believe is best for their infants.

The first year of life is critical in terms of building a foundation of learning in every area of development. The vast array of new and complex behaviors that toddlers and preschoolers must learn in three or four short years is also monumental. At no other period in a lifetime will so much be expected of an individual in so short a time. With other-than-parent child care being the norm rather than the exception, it is essential for teachers and families to have a thorough knowledge of how young children grow, develop, and learn. Thus, an underlying theme of *Developmental Profiles* continues to be partnerships with families. No matter how many hours a day the child is with care-givers or in school, family members still play the most significant role. They need to be encouraged to talk about their child and to share their observations and concerns. Such information is integral to the well-being of each child. When family members talk, professionals need to listen with focused attention and respond with genuine interest and respect.

Partnerships with families become even more critical when an infant or older child is suspected of having a developmental problem or irregularity. The Developmental Alerts following each age section can be especially useful to families and teachers for initiating a discussion about their concerns. Let it be emphasized, however, that under no circumstances should this book or any other book be seen as an instrument for diagnosing a developmental problem. That is the job of professional clinicians and child-development specialists.

Thus, the purposes of this text can be summed up as follows:

- To provide a concise overview of developmental principles
- To provide easily accessible information about what to expect at each developmental level
- To suggest appropriate ways for adults to facilitate learning and development during the early years
- To pinpoint warning signs of a possible developmental problem
- To suggest how and where to get help
- To describe cultural and ethnic diversity in terms of its impact on the developmental process
- To emphasize the value of direct observation of children in their natural settings, whether in a classroom, a child care program, or the child's own home
- To help adults encourage every child to achieve his or her potential, develop a positive sense of self esteem, and to feel loved and respected

ACKNOWLEDGMENTS

First and foremost, we wish to recognize Wadsworth Cengage Learning's long-standing commitment to the field of early childhood education. Their vision and dedication have contributed to an improved understanding of children and families and continues to help teachers, in all types of settings, provide meaningful learning experiences that support and realize children's developmental potentials. Recent organizational changes will only strengthen and improve what is already an outstanding early childhood division.

The preparation of this sixth edition reflects the collaborative efforts of many behind the scenes people. We welcome Chris Shortt on board and look forward to collaborating for a long time. We appreciate his vision and support and are indebted to him for using whatever magical powers he possesses to bring this edition out in full color. Thank you, Chris! We also recognize Anne Orgren for her initial guidance and prompt response in getting things started. It is never easy taking over responsibilities in the middle of a project, but Shelley Murphy has done a terrific job of picking up the pieces, getting us back on track, and seeing us through until the very end. A special thank you to Shelley! There are also many others we would like to thank for their innumerable contributions: the editorial, production, and marketing staff of the Early Childhood division—thank you.

We are also grateful to our reviewers and want to express our sincere appreciation for their insightful critiques, suggestions, and ability to help us see issues from multiple perspectives:

- Barbara Pavel-Alvarez, West Virginia University
- Elizabeth M. Blunk, Texas State University-San Marcos
- Marlene A. Bumgarner, Gavilan College
- Bronwyn Fees, Kansas State University
- Lisa Fuller, Cerro Coso Community College
- Kay Gillock, Owner/Provider, Gillock Gang's Home Child Care, Opelika, Alabama
- John Kesner, Georgia State University
- Stephanie Miller, Austin Community College
- Dianne Waller, Seminole Community College

Finally, we would like to thank our readers for their dedication and commitment to improving the quality of life for children and families everywhere.

About the Authors

K. Eileen Allen, professor emerita, was a member of the Early Childhood faculty at the University of Washington in Seattle and at the University of Kansas in Lawrence. For a total of thirty one years, she taught a variety of courses: child development, developmental disabilities in young children, parenting, early education, and an interdisciplinary approach to early intervention and inclusion. She also trained teachers and supervised research-focused classrooms at both schools and has published seven college textbooks as well as numerous research articles and position papers in major professional journals. During her retirement, she continues to write, jury research articles, consult in both the private and public sector, and actively advocate on behalf of children and families.

Lynn R. Marotz is a member of the Department of Applied Behavioral Sciences faculty and serves as the Associate Director of the Edna A. Hill Child Development Center at the University of Kansas. She brings her nursing background, training in education, and years of experience with children to the field of early education. Her primary interests include teacher training and administration, policy development, parent education, early identification and intervention, and the promotion of children's wellness. She teaches undergraduate courses in child development, parenting, administration, health, and nutrition. Her experience also includes extensive involvement in state policy development, health screenings, professional development training, working with families and allied health professionals, and the referral process. She has made numerous professional presentations at state, national, and international conferences and has authored a variety of publications on children's health, environmental safety, and nutrition. In addition, she also serves on a number of state and local advisory boards.

Child Development Theories and Data Gathering

Objectives

After reading this chapter, you should be able to:

- Discuss how Gesell and Piaget would explain why infants learn to feed themselves.

- Discuss how environment shapes a child's development, according to Vygotsky and Bronfenbrenner.

- Explain what effect reinforcement has on behavior.

- Identify and describe several methods to gather information for authentic assessments.

- Explain why we should consider developmental theories that might offer conflicting viewpoints.

MEET FOUR-YEAR-OLD JAMAL

Jamal was an undernourished and severely neglected nine-month-old when first placed in foster care. As a four-year-old, he is now in his fifth foster home, where he has been for almost one year. His foster parents, Berta and Doug Clay, have two little girls, ages four and six, of their own and three other foster children ranging in age from four to nine. All of the children are vigorous and outgoing except for Jamal, who seems to tire easily. Berta took him in early for his well-child checkup because she was concerned. When Jamal was weighed and measured, he was only in the thirtieth percentile for height and weight, despite the fact that he eats far more than the other children.

Berta and Clay have also noted that Jamal rarely plays with the other children and seldom converses with anyone. However, they have overheard him holding lengthy and comprehensible conversations between himself and an imaginary friend, Honey, at times when he thinks he is alone. The talk is usually about things he fears, possibly the root of recurring bad dreams from which he often wakes up screaming. Yet, despite his problems, Jamal is a kind and lovable child. He often seizes any opportunity to curl up in Berta's or Doug's lap, suck his thumb, and snuggle his free hand into one of theirs. The Clays have come to love Jamal as one of their own. Fully aware of the challenges that his current development presents, they are in the process of formally adopting him.

Child development has been a major research focus of psychology for decades, (Figure 1-1). Throughout the years, theorists have studied children and offered their viewpoints on everything from growth to behavior. In some instances, their explanations are consistent whereas, on other points, there is considerable disagreement. For example, Arnold Gesell thought that all learning is determined by a biological readiness, whereas Jean Piaget believed that it is due to a combination of genetics and environmental conditions.

Figure 1-1

Children's development has been the subject of study for decades.

At first glance, these multiple theoretical frameworks for understanding children's growth and development might appear confusing and in conflict with one another. However, it is unlikely that any one theory adequately explains the complexity of children's behavior. Each offers a somewhat different interpretation of the factors that shape development and, thus, encourages us to consider behavior from multiple perspectives. It should also be remembered that theories reflect the ideas and conditions accepted at a given point in time. As new research is conducted, previous ideas are often revisited and revised. Thus, as societies change, ideas about children's behavior and development are also likely to change.

Contemporary Theories

Interest in studying children's behavior peaked during the twentieth century, when many influential theories were developed. Early studies were based primarily on researchers' observations and personal interpretations. As a result, subsequent studies often contradicted or rejected previous conclusions. However, each theory has given us another valuable piece of information that has increased our collective understanding of children's cognitive, socioemotional, and biological development.

A long-standing controversy in the field has centered on whether heredity or environment is responsible for children's development. This argument is commonly referred to as the **nature vs. nurture** controversy (Santrock, 2006; Horowitz, 1995). Coming from both sides of the issue, a long line of researchers has provided us with the principal concepts related to how children learn, how they grow, and how they mature. Most of our current knowledge stems from research related to several fundamental theories: maturational, psychoanalytic and psychosocial, cognitive-developmental, behaviorism and social learning, bioecological and essential needs. Brief descriptions of each theoretical approach follow and include the names of early dominant figures.

MATURATIONAL THEORY

Maturational theory focuses on a biological or *nature* approach to human development. It explains all behavior in terms of genetics and biological changes that occur as an individual ages. For example, maturational theory would argue that a baby learns to walk only when the neurological system has matured sufficiently to permit this activity, regardless of any other factors.

Arnold Gesell's historical work is still significant in this area of developmental research. He believed that all development is governed primarily by internal forces of

---

nature/nurture—refers to whether development is primarily due to biological–genetic forces (heredity–nature) or to external forces (environment–nurture).

Figure 1-2

Gesell described children's development in terms of biological maturation.

biologic and genetic origin (Dalton, 2005; Gesell & Ilg, 1949) (Figure 1-2). He was also one of the first to describe children's achievements according to age and to explain his findings in ways that parents could understand and use.

Few scientists would disagree that genetics exert a strong influence on human development and, in some cases, even a limiting effect. For example, a child's height, eye color, shoe size, and other distinguishing features are the direct result of genes inherited from his or her biological parents. Chromosomal abnormalities that cause Down syndrome or fetal alcohol syndrome are also likely to result in a range of lifelong learning and physical disabilities. New research is also looking at possible links between genetics and personality traits such as shyness, aggressiveness, and predisposition to certain mental health problems (Leckman, 2007; Whittle et al., 2006). Although the genetic contribution to human development is well understood, most experts do not accept that it is solely responsible for all human behavior.

Gesell's contributions continue to apply in the early-childhood field. His observations have been translated into **norms**, or benchmarks, that have proven useful for assessing and monitoring the range of children's developmental skills and abilities. Although his original conclusions were based on observations of middle-class, Caucasian children, scientists have updated the standards to reflect today's population diversity more accurately.

norms—age-level expectancies associated with the achievement of developmental skills.

PSYCHOANALYTIC AND PSYCHOSOCIAL THEORY

Psychoanalytic and psychosocial theory postulates that much of human behavior is governed by unconscious processes, some of which are present at birth, others that develop over time. Sigmund Freud is the acknowledged originator of psychoanalytic theory. He believed that children's behavior is a reflection of their inner thoughts and conflicts and that these vary according to stages. The way in which these emotional problems are resolved gradually forms the child's basic personality, especially during the first five years of life.

Psychosocial theory is based on the work of Erik Erikson, who expanded on Freud's ideas about personality development. He, too, believed that each developmental stage is characterized by certain conflicts that must be resolved. After a successful resolution has been achieved, a person is then motivated to undertake the next challenge.

However, unlike Freud, Erikson's theory acknowledges the influence of environment and social interactions. He coined the term *ego identity* to describe a person's conscious awareness of self (who I am in relation to others) and the lifelong changes that occur as a result of social interactions. Erikson was also the first to describe development across the life span by introducing his eight universal stages of human development (Erikson, 1950). The first four stages address the early years; the remaining four cover the span from adolescence to the later years:

- **Trust vs. mistrust (0–12 months)** Establishing a sense of trust with caregivers
- **Autonomy vs. shame and doubt (1–3 years)** Learning to gain control over some behaviors (e.g., eating, toileting, sleeping) and developing a sense of autonomy or independence
- **Initiative vs. guilt (3–5 years)** Using social interaction to gain control over one's everyday world
- **Industry vs. inferiority (5–12 years)** Developing a sense of competence and pride through successful accomplishments
- **Identity vs. confusion (12–20 years)** Learning about self in relationship to others
- **Intimacy vs. isolation (early adulthood)** Exploring and forming intimate relationships
- **Generativity vs. stagnation (middle adulthood)** Focusing on family, career, and ways of contributing to society
- **Integrity vs. despair (old age)** Reflecting on one's life and forming a sense of satisfaction or dissatisfaction

Psychoanalytic and psychosocial theories have contributed to our understanding of personality and socioemotional skills and their influence on all aspects of children's development. They have also helped us understand better the universal challenges children face at each stage and how to create environments that support children's social and emotional needs along a developmental continuum. Although these theories are not as popular as they once were, they continue to foster research in areas such as caregiver consistency, attachment, morality, and sibling relationships.

COGNITIVE-DEVELOPMENTAL THEORY

Cognitive-developmental theory is attributed to Piaget, who theorized that children construct knowledge and form meaning through active exploration of their environment (Figure 1-3). The term **constructivism** is often used today in reference to this style of learning. According to Piaget, children progress through four major stages of intellectual development, beginning in infancy and continuing into the late teens (Piaget, 1954):

- **Sensorimotor (birth–2 years)** Reflexive behavior gives way to intentional behavior; children use their senses to discover the world around them. Example: The child sees an object and reaches for it.

- **Preoperational (2–7 years)** Children begin thinking in symbols about things in their immediate environment. Example: The three year old picks up a long stick and calls it a fishing pole. This illustration also shows a second aspect of the preoperational stage, the emergence of language, which is another form of symbolic usage.

- **Concrete operational (7–11 years)** Children now are in the process of comprehending and formulating ideas about their immediate world. They are

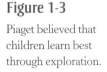

Figure 1-3

Piaget believed that children learn best through exploration.

constructivism—a learning approach in which a child forms his or her own meaning through active participation.

learning to think logically, to anticipate outcomes, to classify objects, and to problem-solve. These emerging *schema* (Piaget's term) lead to understanding such things as basic math and spatial concepts.

- **Formal operational (11–15 years)** During these years, the child develops complex thinking skills related not only to objects and experiences but also to abstract thoughts and ideas and the ability to solve problems.

Piaget's ideas are evident today in many early-childhood programs where developmentally appropriate learning centers and discovery learning are practiced.

Lev Vygotsky offered a somewhat different perspective on children's cognitive development. Although he agreed with Piaget's notion that development follows a unique pattern, Vygotsky believed that social and cultural environments (e.g., values, beliefs, and practices) played an active and influential role in shaping the learning process (Vygotsky, 1986). For example, he explained that children initially learn how to behave through a series of adult directives: "Don't touch," "Come here," "Eat this," "Stop that." As children begin to internalize social rules and cultural expectations and to develop self-control, the nature of these directives gradually changes. Adults stop telling children what to do and instead shift to encouraging and assisting their active involvement in learning new skills. Vygotsky referred to this as the *Zone of Proximal Development*.

Vygotsky also considered children's acquisition of speech and language an important step in this process. He believed that young children spend significant time learning new words and thinking about their meanings and uses. Vygotsky observed that some children hold conversations with themselves as a way of thinking out loud. He referred to this stage as "self-talk," or inner speech, and suggested that the process gives children an opportunity to rehearse the meanings of words and their uses as communication tools (Vygotsky, 1986). Later, children begin to internalize their ideas and are able to recall them for future use.

Marie Montessori's ideas have also contributed to our understanding of cognitive-developmental theory. Trained as a pediatrician, she later became interested in educating children who were considered ineducable. She was convinced that all children had potential but that traditional instructional methods might not always be effective. Her observations led to her belief that children learned best through a process of self-directed exploration. She designed sensory-based materials that were self-correcting and that required limited adult intervention. She also developed educational programs based on a philosophy that emphasized children's natural curiosity and self-directed involvement in learning experiences.

Cognitive-developmental theorists have enhanced our understanding of how children learn and construct meaning. They have made us aware that children differ in their learning styles and that instructional approaches must be individualized to address each child's unique developmental needs. Application of these findings is evident in the National Association for the Education of Young Children's (NAEYC) position statement on Developmentally Appropriate Practice (DAP) and those of other early-childhood organizations (NAEYC, 2004). Knowledge of cognitive-developmental theory has also influenced the concept and delivery of early-intervention services. Children's cognitive development continues to intrigue researchers, particularly as it relates to curriculum, instructional methods, family involvement, the influence of culture, and social interaction and is likely to serve as a source of study for decades to come.

BEHAVIORISM AND SOCIAL LEARNING THEORY

In its modern form, behaviorism and social learning theory stems from the work of B. F. Skinner and John B. Watson, who formulated a *nurture*, or environmental, approach to learning (Skinner, 1938). They argued that development, for the most part, involves a series of learned behaviors based on an individual's positive and negative interactions with his or her environment (Figure 1-4). For example, reinforcing a behavior typically causes it to be repeated. In other words, telling a child that he has done a great job on his spelling test is likely to motivate him to study even harder for the next one. However, the opposite is also true: giving in to a crying child's demands for a much-wanted toy can encourage the child to repeat the behavior the next time he or she wants something. Ignoring the child's demands will eventually extinguish the behavior because there is no reinforcement.

Skinner also explained how the association between two events (stimulus-response) results in learning. For example, a toddler bumps her head (stimulus) when she stands up under the table, so she abruptly ends the activity (response). A preschooler touches a hot pan (stimulus) and is careful to avoid repeating the behavior again (response).

Figure 1-4

Social learning theory explains development as behavioral change that results from observation and imitation.

You promise to read a favorite book to your daughter (stimulus) if she picks up her toys quickly (response).

Albert Bandura modified some of these earlier ideas when he formulated his own theory of social learning (Bandura, 1977). He viewed behavior as a combination of environmental influences (nature) and cognitive abilities (nurture). He also believed that children learned both positive and negative behaviors through observation and modeling, or imitation. However, unlike Skinner, he did not agree that reinforcement was necessary to motivate or change behavior. He felt that children learned, for example, not to hit another child or not to take away a toy after observing another child being punished for the same act.

Families and teachers employ the principles of behavioral theory on a daily basis. They expect children to comply with requests and then reward or punish accordingly. They model behavior that children are likely to imitate. They provide encouragement and, thus, reinforce or increase the child's efforts. Behavioral procedures are also used to address serious developmental problems, such as aggression, feeding disorders, anger management, and obesity (Cornell & Hamrin, 2008; Tompson et al., 2007).

BIOECOLOGICAL THEORY

There is little dispute today that environment exerts a direct influence on children's development (Plomin, Asbury, & Dunn, 2001). Urie Bronfenbrenner, a noted psychologist, alleged that environment shaped a person's development. He proposed an ecological model that describes environment as being multilayered—from the settings in which a person participates (family, school, church, teams), relationships within these groups, and experiences in other social settings (media, neighbors, social agencies) to the shared beliefs and values of one's culture (Bronfenbrenner, 1979).

Bronfenbrenner later modified his original ideas to include the influence of biological factors. His revised bioecological model offers several unique perspectives on human development. First, it recognizes environment as having multiple and often complex layers versus being treated as a single entity. It also acknowledges that a person's behavior is not determined by any one layer alone but rather by interactions that occur on multiple levels. For example, poverty by itself might not limit a child's development if effective social services, good schools, and a nurturing family are in place. Bronfenbrenner also recognized the interactive nature of environment—that environment not only affects an individual, but that a person's behavior, age, and interactions are continually changing the nature of that environment.

The bioecological theory has had a significant impact on early-childhood practice. It has raised awareness of diversity issues. This, in turn, has led to the development of antibias curricula, assessment procedures, play materials, and teacher education programs that reflect sensitivity and respect for individual differences. It has helped us to understand better how environment and relationships help shape a child's development and why family involvement and collaboration are essential in early-childhood programs.

ESSENTIAL NEEDS

All children, those who are developing normally or typically, those who have developmental disabilities, and those who are **at risk** for developing problems, have essential physical and psychological needs in common (Maslow, 1968). These needs must be met if infants and children are to survive, thrive, and develop to their best potential. Developmental psychologists have long considered the early years to be the most critical in the entire life span (Shonkoff, 2000). Data obtained from brain research have documented their assumptions. Never again will the child grow so rapidly or change so dramatically. During these very early years, children learn all the many behaviors that characterize the human species—walking, talking, thinking, and socializing. It is truly amazing, all of that within the first two or three years! Never again will the child be so totally dependent on parents, caregivers, and teachers to satisfy the basic needs of life and to provide opportunities for learning.

To discuss **essential needs** in an orderly and logical fashion, they can be separated into physical, psychological, and learning needs. However, it must be understood that they are mutually interrelated and interdependent. Meeting a child's physical needs while neglecting psychological needs can lead to developmental problems. The opposite also is true—a child who is physically neglected can experience difficulty in learning and getting along with others. Addressing children's essential needs in all areas improves their chances of developing to their full potential (Jacobs et al., 2008; Raver, 2004).

Physical Needs

- Adequate shelter and protection from harm: violence, neglect, and preventable injuries
- Sufficient food that is nutritious and appropriate to the child's age
- Clothing and shoes suitable to the climate and season
- Access to preventive health and dental care; treatment of physical and mental conditions as needed; immunizations as prescribed for childhood illnesses
- Personal hygiene: washing hands, brushing teeth, and bathing
- Rest and activity, in balance; space for indoor and outdoor play

Psychological Needs

- Affection and consistency: **nurturing** families and teachers who can be depended on to "be there" for the child
- Security and trust: familiar surroundings with parents and teachers who respond reliably to the needs of the infant and child

---

at risk—term describing children who may be more likely to have developmental problems due to certain predisposing factors such as low birth weight (LBW), neglect, or maternal drug addiction.

essential needs—basic physical needs such as food, shelter, and safety as well as psychological needs, including love, security, and trust, which are required for survival and healthy development.

nurturing—qualities of warmth, loving, caring, and attention to physical needs.

- **Reciprocal** exchanges: beginning in earliest infancy, give-and-take interactions that promote responsiveness in the child (Swain et al., 2007)

- Appropriate adult expectations of what the child can and cannot do at each level of development

- Acceptance and positive attitudes toward whatever cultural, ethnic, language, or developmental differences characterize the child and family

Learning Needs

- Play as an essential component of early learning. Infants and young children need unlimited opportunities to engage in play in all its many forms, with freedom to explore and experiment, with necessary limits clearly stated and consistently maintained (Ranz-Smith, 2007; Stegelin, 2005) (Figure 1-5)

- Access to **developmentally appropriate** experiences and play materials (Honig, 2007)

- An appropriate match between a child's skill levels and the materials and experiences available so the child is challenged but not excessively frustrated

- Treatment of errors and delays in achieving a skill as important steps in the learning process, never as reasons for criticizing or ridiculing a child

- Adults who demonstrate in their everyday lives the appropriate behaviors expected of the child, especially in language, social interactions, or ways of

Figure 1-5

Children are continually learning through exploration and play.

reciprocal—exchanges between individuals or groups that are mutually beneficial (or hindering).

developmentally appropriate—a term describing learning experiences that are individualized based on a child's level of skills, abilities, and interests.

handling stress. Remember that adults serve as important models of behavior for children; children learn far more from what adults do than from what they say

- A literacy-rich environment and inclusion in an active language "community" in which children can learn to communicate through sounds, gestures, signs, and, eventually, words and sentences (spoken, signed, or written)

Need for Respect and Self-Esteem

- A supportive environment in which the child's efforts are encouraged and approved: "Thank you for picking up your crayons without being asked!"
- Respect for accomplishments whether small or large, for errors as well as for successes: "Look at that! You laced your shoes all by yourself" (no mention of the eyelet that was missed).
- Recognition that accomplishment and the "I can do it" attitude is the major and most essential component of a child's **self-esteem**: "You're really getting good at pouring the juice!"
- Sincere attention to what the child is doing well; using **descriptive praise** to help the child recognize and respect his or her own accomplishments: "You got your shoes on the right feet all by yourself!"
- Awareness of the effort and concentration that go into acquiring basic developmental skills; providing positive responses to each small step as a child works toward mastery of a complex skill such as self-feeding with a spoon: "Right! Just a little applesauce on the spoon so it stays on."

Only when children's basic needs are satisfied can we expect them to be ready and able to learn (Marotz, 2009). Researchers continue to demonstrate the critical nature of this relationship (AAP, 2008; Fu et al., 2007). These findings have prompted support for numerous programs that assist families in meeting children's needs for nutritious food, health care (mental, physical and oral), safe and nurturing homes, and learning opportunities. Examples include Head Start, School Breakfast, Parents as Teachers, and State Children's Health Insurance Program (SCHIP). Early-childhood educators also understand this critical connection and devote considerable time and attention to making sure children's needs are being met.

Data Gathering

What we know about children—how they grow and develop, how they learn, and how they interact with others—stems from firsthand observation. For decades, psychologists and educators have observed the daily activities of hundreds of infants and young children. They recorded what they saw and heard as children learned to walk, communicate, grasp basic science and math concepts, play with other children, reason,

---

self-esteem—feelings about one's self-worth.

descriptive praise—words or actions that describe to a child specifically what she or he is doing correctly or well.

and solve problems. Their observations have provided the foundation for what we now know about child development, effective teaching practices, curriculum models, and the significance of family–child relationships.

Early-childhood educators continue to recognize the importance of gathering information about children's behavior and development (Figure 1-6). Despite increasing pressures for standardized testing, documentation, and accountability issues in schools, teachers understand the value of observing young children in their **naturalistic settings**. This approach, referred to as **authentic assessment**, is considered the most effective and developmentally appropriate method for evaluating young children (Bagnato, 2007). Performance-based information about children's developmental progress is collected in the context of everyday settings and activities. Samples of children's products, family input, and teacher observations are collected continuously and systematically to document evidence of learning. This information provides an ongoing, well-rounded picture of the child and reduces the bias that results when only one evaluation source is used. Authentic assessment also helps teachers understand children's skills, abilities, and special needs against a background of environmental factors that shape their development (Gallant & Moore, 2008; Brassard & Boehm, 2007). The results of authentic assessment can be used to design learning goals, interventions, and responsive environments that effectively meet children's individual needs (Hallam et al., 2007).

Figure 1-6

Behavioral data yields useful information for assessing children's developmental progress.

naturalistic settings—environments that are familiar and part of children's everyday experiences, such as classrooms, care arrangements, and home.

authentic assessment—a process of collecting and documenting information about children's developmental progress; data is gathered in children's naturalistic settings and from multiple sources.

TEACHERS AS CLASSROOM OBSERVERS

Regularly scheduled observations and assessments of children's developmental progress are benchmarks of high-quality early-childhood programs (Downs & Strand, 2006). Watching and recording what children actually do in the classroom and during outdoor play gives teachers insight into their progress, strengths, and limitations. Information acquired through observational methods can also be helpful for identifying children who have special talents, developmental delays, or behavior problems. In addition, teachers can use this information to design activities, instruction, and environments that are developmentally appropriate and support effective learning.

The ability to conduct and interpret meaningful observations requires teachers to be familiar with children's development and know what expectations are appropriate. They must understand that family, culture, and linguistic differences can account for variations in what children know and are able to do. With time and practice, teachers can become proficient at identifying specific behaviors for observation, knowing what to look for, recording observations in an objective manner, and using the results to address children's individual needs.

FAMILIES AS OBSERVERS

Families should always be welcomed in their child's classroom, whether as scheduled observers or on a drop-in basis. They have a right to see and question everything that occurs in the classroom. When family members arrange for a scheduled observation, they can be given a clipboard and paper on which to note points of interest or questions they might have about learning materials, teacher responses or what seems to please or bother the child. Teachers should arrange a follow-up meeting to learn the family's thoughts about the program, to point out the child's positive qualities, and to share mutual concerns about the child's progress.

Observations made by family members at home or at school are invaluable. Families know and understand their child better than anyone else and see him or her behaving in almost every imaginable circumstance. They are aware of the child's likes and dislikes, joys and anxieties, and positive and negative qualities. Most important, they often have particular goals and objectives they want their child to achieve and care deeply about their child's well-being.

Observation Methods

Recorded observations take many forms: anecdotal notes, running records and logs, time and event sampling, frequency and duration counts, checklists, rating scales, and portfolios (Figure 1-7). Each method is described briefly in the section that follows. Additional information on assessment is available in Chapter 9, "When and Where to Seek Help," and Appendix D, "Selected Screening and Assessment Instruments."

Figure 1-7

A variety of methods can be used to collect and record observational data.

ANECDOTAL NOTES

Several times each day, the teacher takes a minute or less to write down a few relevant words about what they see happening. Anecdotal notes can be recorded on a small notebook or pad (3×5 inches) carried in a pocket. The teacher makes brief, dated entries about the **discrete behaviors** observed for a given child: "Played in block area for 5 minutes without hitting another child," "Initiated conversation with teacher." Anecdotal notes are useful for tracking development in one or more **domains** or for gathering information about a specific concern.

Over time, these notes yield a running record, or composite picture, of the child's progress. They can reveal a need for special guidance or changes in instructional strategies. If so, continued note taking can help teachers determine whether the child is actually benefiting from a planned intervention. When anecdotal notes are filed chronologically by developmental domains, they also become valuable for the purposes of placement, writing progress reports, evaluating lessons, or preparing for family conferences.

TIME OR EVENT SAMPLING

Sampling techniques enable a teacher to collect behavioral data on one or more children simultaneously during a given time frame or activity. For example, a teacher might be interested in learning which behaviors children use to resolve conflicts during free

---

discrete behaviors—behaviors that can clearly be observed and described: hitting, pulling hair, spitting.

domains—a term describing an area of development such as physical, motor, socioemotional, or speech and language.

Figure 1-8

Time sampling form.

	_____ date								Activity: Free Play		

Code:
  pa – physical aggression
  va – verbal aggression
  cps – cooperative play/problem solving

Child	8:30			8:40			8:50			9:00		
	pa	va	cps	pa	va	cps	pa	va	cps	pa	va	cps
LaShauna												
Jose												
Markie												
Winston												

Total: pa ___   va ___   cps ___

play: physical aggression (pa), verbal aggression (va) or cooperative problem solving (cps) skills. A simple score sheet can be developed, for recording purposes, with children's names listed along one axis, the times and behavioral codes and categories identified across the other (Figure 1-8). A new sheet is dated and used for recording each day's observations.

A sampling approach is often used to obtain information about children's language development. An observer writes down every utterance a child makes, exactly as the child says it. One purpose of the samplings, which are usually recorded for ten to fifteen minutes at a time over a month-long period or so, is to track the child's speech and language progress. Another purpose is to see whether the child's language works. Is the child communicating effectively? Does the child get what he or she needs and wants by using language? No other behavior (except communicative gestures or facial grimaces) is recorded, although brief notations might be made, for example, that other children rarely respond to the child's verbal overtures. Language samples are invaluable in planning individualized programs. They also are effective for recalling quips or insightful statements the child has made.

FREQUENCY AND DURATION COUNTS

When concerns about a specific aspect of a child's behavior arise, teachers must first determine how often the behavior actually occurs (frequency) or how long it continues (duration) (Figure 1-9). Observations are made and data recorded while teachers go about their tasks. One form of frequency count simply requires the teacher to make a tally

Figure 1-9

Sample frequency and duration counts.

Child's name: <u>Nicholas J.</u>
Week of: <u>June 4–9, 2008</u>
Observer: <u>Juanita M.</u>
Behavior observed: <u>Not attending/distracting other children</u>

Activity:	Mon	Tues	Wed	Thurs	Fri	Comments
Morning circle	II	0	II	I	III	
Afternoon circle	III	II	IIII	0	III	

mark every time the child engages in the specified behavior. A count might reveal that a two-year-old who was said to cry or hit "all the time" was actually doing so only once or twice per morning and some mornings not at all. For behaviors that occur at a high rate, teachers sometimes use a golf stroke or handheld counter. Frequency counts give teachers objective information that can help them decide whether a "problem" is indeed a problem.

A duration count measures the amount of time a child engages in particular behavior. For example, a teacher might simply jot down the time when a child enters and leaves an area or activity. Another example would be penciling (unobtrusively) on a corner of a painting or collage the time the child started and finished the project. Or, the teacher might note when a child's tantrum began and ended. Duration counts are helpful for deciding whether actions are needed to increase or decrease a specific behavior.

CHECKLISTS AND RATING SCALES

Checklists permit a teacher or other observer to record quickly the occurrence of certain skills or behaviors. For example, in infant centers, many firsts can be checked off: the day Josie first smiled, rolled over, or walked alone. In preschools, a checklist can be an effective method for monitoring children's skill acquisition. The date can be inserted as teachers check off when, for example, Carmella correctly identified and matched her primary colors; when Jayson built a tower of eight one-inch cubes; and when Sophia zipped her jacket by herself. Checklists often are constructed by teachers to reflect program objectives. The lists, whether teacher-made or commercial, can be simple or detailed, depending on the need (see Appendix B, "Developmental Checklists").

Rating scales, like checklists, are usually designed to target specific behaviors (Figure 1-10). They provide an efficient method for recording teacher observations and later retrieving information in a meaningful way.

PORTFOLIOS

Representative examples of a child's work—drawings, photographs of block structures that have been built, notes describing manipulative activities completed, and audiotapes of conversations and language samples—offer another effective method

Figure 1-10

Sample rating scale form.

Child's name: <u>Nicholas J.</u>

Date: _____

Task:	Not Yet	Attempts/ Not always accurate	Usually accurate	Proficient	Comments (observer/date):
Identifies numbers 1–10					
Arranges numbers 1–10 in correct order					
Counts from 1–10 with prompting					
Counts from 1–10 without prompting					
Writes numbers 1–10					

for tracking children's developmental progress. Teachers select materials that reflect a child's learning across all developmental domains and assemble them in an individual portfolio for each child. Children should also be given an opportunity to choose items for inclusion. Information obtained from teacher and family observations should also be a part of this collection as they often provide additional insight and meaning.

Materials in a child's portfolio should be reviewed periodically to monitor changing interests, mastery of specific skills, and need for additional instruction. Teachers can also use these items when preparing for parent conferences, for illustrating discussion points and for sharing with families. In addition, children's portfolios often reveal important information about the effectiveness of a curriculum or teaching methods and can, thus, be beneficial for program improvement.

VIDEO CONNECTIONS

Clip 1

Learning Theories Infants are wired and programmed to learn. Everything an infant experiences yields information that is stored and used in the future for more complex learning.

Critical Thinking Questions:

1. Infants learn about the environment through their sensory systems. Explain this statement. What examples from the video illustrate this concept?

2. After watching the children in this video, would you agree or disagree with the maturation theory?

3. Which infant behaviors illustrated in the video support Bronfenbrenner's bioecological theory of child development?

VIDEO CONNECTIONS

Clip 2

Sensory Development Vision plays an important role in early development. Infants spend considerable time gathering visual information to learn about their environment.

Critical Thinking Questions:

1. What behaviors can be observed to determine whether an infant's visual system is intact and functional?
2. Which stage of Piaget's developmental theory are the infants in this video illustrating?
3. What is depth perception? What purpose does it serve?
4. How might blindness or low vision affect other areas of an infant's development, such as motor skills and social skills?

S U M M A R Y

Today's knowledge of child development is a composite of human development theories: maturational, psychoanalytic, psychosocial, cognitive-developmental, behaviorism and social learning, bioecological, and essential needs. All theories agree that meeting the fundamental physical and psychological needs of infants and children is a powerful determinant of optimum development. For the first time, actual changes within the brain have been documented as a result of addressing these needs. Paramount among these are adequate physical care, responsive nurturing, abundant learning experiences, and opportunities for developing positive self-esteem.

Current explanations about how children grow and develop rarely rest on any one theory exclusively. Each approach has made major contributions to our understanding of children's behavior. The majority of today's researchers dismiss the nature vs. nurture question as an improbable either–or proposition; human development is not that simplistic. Instead, it is generally viewed as a complex series of interactions involving environmental and biological characteristics.

Teachers and families continue to play an important role in gathering information about children's growth and development. Their observations contribute to a better understanding of children's unique interests, abilities, talents, and needs. The process of documenting children's behavior enables teachers to make necessary adjustments in curriculum and instructional methods to improve learning.

KEY TERMS

at risk
authentic assessment
constructivism
descriptive praise
developmentally appropriate
discrete behaviors
domains

essential needs
naturalistic settings
nature vs. nurture
norms
nurturing
reciprocal
self-esteem

APPLY WHAT YOU KNOW

A. Apply What You Have Learned

Reread the developmental sketch about Jamal at the beginning of the chapter. How might you answer the following questions?

1. As foster parents, which essential physical needs are Berta and Doug presumably providing for Jamal?

2. What are some of Jamal's fundamental psychological needs, and how are his foster parents attempting to meet them?

3. Could Jamal's early months of living in an impoverished environment have any effect on his current development? Explain your answer based on the theories described in this chapter.

4. Although Jamal's motor skill development might be delayed, he has learned to sit up, crawl, stand, walk, and eventually run. Which is more important to consider in his case, the fact that he was older than is typical when he learned these skills or that he has developed them in this particular order? Explain.

5. Based on the brief description of Jamal and his family, what reciprocal effect might you anticipate when Jamal crawls up onto his father's lap? How would Skinner and Bandura explain this response?

B. Review Questions

1. What is the nature vs. nature controversy, and how does it contribute to our understanding of children's development?

2. What behaviors would children be likely to exhibit during each of the first four stages of Erikson's developmental theory?

3. In what ways does the maturational theory differ from the cognitive-developmental theory?

4. What is behaviorism, and how does it explain why a child might continue to refuse eating despite repeated warnings from his mother?

5. If you were concerned about a child's attention span and wanted to know whether he was able to remain engaged in a specific task, what type of data would you want to gather? Describe the method(s) you would select for this purpose.

HELPFUL
WEBSITES Visit the book companion website at *www.cengage.com/education/allen* for links to these websites and additional resources.

REFERENCES

American Academy of Pediatrics Committee (AAP) on Early Childhood, Adoption, and Dependent Care and Council on School Health. (2008). School readiness. *Pediatrics, 121*(4), e1008–1015.

Bagnato, S. (2007). *Authentic assessment for early childhood intervention best practices.* New York: Guilford Press.

Bandura, A. (1977). *Social learning theory.* New York: General Learning Press.

Brassard, M., & Boehm, A. (2007). *Preschool assessment: Principles and practices.* New York: Guilford Press.

Bronfenbrenner, U. (1979). *The ecology of human development: Experiments by nature and design.* Cambridge, MA: Harvard University Press.

Cornell, T., & Hamrin, V. (2008). Clinical interventions for children with attachment problems. *Journal of Child & Adolescent Psychiatric Nursing, 21*(1), 35–47.

Dalton, T. (2005). Arnold Gesell and the maturation controversy. *Integrative Psychological and Behavioral Science, 40*(4), 182–204.

Downs, A., & Strand, P. (2006). Using assessment to improve the effectiveness of early childhood education. *Journal of Child & Family Studies, 15*(6), 671–680.

Erikson, E. (1950). *Childhood and society.* New York: Vintage.

Fu, M., Cheng, L., Tu, S., & Pan, W. (2007). Association between unhealthful eating patterns and unfavorable overall school performance in children. *Journal of the American Dietetic Association, 107*(11), 1935–1943.

Gallant, D., & Moore, J. (2008). Assessing ethnicity: Equity for first-grade male students on a curriculum-embedded performance assessment. *Urban Education, 43*(2), 172–188.

Gesell, A., & Ilg, F. (1949). *Child development.* New York: Harper.

Hallam, R., Grisham-Brown, J., Gao, X., & Brookshire, R. (2007). The effects of outcomes-driven authentic assessment on classroom quality. *Early Childhood Research & Practice, 9*(2), 316–326.

Honig, A. (2007). Play: Ten power boosts for children's early learning. *Young Children, 62*(5), 72–78.

Horowitz, F. D. (1995). The nature-nurture controversy in social and historical perspective. In F. Kessel (Ed.), *Psychology, science, and human affairs,* (pp. 89–99). Boulder, CO: Westview Press.

Jacobs, R., Black, M., Casey, P., Cook, J., Cutts, D., Chilton, M., Heeren, T., Levenson, S., Meyers, A., & Frank, D. (2008). Household food insecurity: Associations with at-risk infant and toddler development. *Pediatrics, 121*(1), 65–72.

Leckman, J. (2007). Genes and behavior: Nature-nurture interplay explained. *Journal of Child Psychology and Psychiatry, 48*(2), 219–220.

Marotz, L. (2009). *Health, safety & nutrition for the young child.* Clifton Park, NY: Delmar Cengage Learning.

Maslow, A. (1968). *Toward a psychology of being* (2nd ed.). New York: Van Nostrand Reinhold.

NAEYC. (2004). Where we stand on curriculum, assessment, and program evaluation. Accessed on April 6, 2008, from *http://www.naeyc.org/about/positions/pdf/standlcurrass.pdf.*

Piaget, J. (1954). *The construction of reality in the child.* New York: Basic Books.

Plomin, R., Ashbury, K., & Dunn, J. (2001). Why are children in the same family so different? *Journal of Family Therapy, 29*(2), 114–130.

Ranz-Smith, D. (2007). Teacher perception of play: In leaving No Child Behind are teachers leaving childhood behind? *Early Education and Development, 18*(2), 271–303.

Raver, C. (2004). Placing emotional self-regulation in sociocultural and socioeconomic contexts. *Child Development, 75*(2), 346–353.

Santrock, J. (2006). *Children* (8th ed.). Boston: McGraw-Hill.

Shonkoff, J. (2000). *From neurons to neighborhoods: The science of early childhood development.* Washington, DC: National Academies Press.

Skinner, B. F. (1938). *The behavior of organisms: An experimental analysis.* New York: Appleton-Century.

Stegelin, D. (2005). Making the case for play policy: Researched-based reasons to support play-based environments. *Young Children, 60*(2), 76–85.

Swain, J., Lorberbaum, P., Kose, S., & Strathearn, L. (2007). Brain basis of early parent-infant interactions: Psychology, physiology, and *in vivo* functional neuroimaging studies. *Journal of Child Psychology and Psychiatry, 48*(3–4), 262–287.

Tompson, M., Pierre, C., Haber, F., Fogler, J., Grof, A., & Asarnow, J. (2007). Family-focused treatment for childhood-onset depressive disorders: Results of an open trial. *Clinical Child Psychology & Psychiatry, 12*(3), 403–420.

Vygotsky, L. (1986). *Thought and language* (2nd ed.). Cambridge, MA: MIT Press.

Whittle, S., Allen, N., Lubman, D., & Yucel, M. (2006). The neurobiological basis of temperament: Towards a better understanding of psychopathology. *Neuroscience & Biobehavioral Reviews, 30*(4), 511–525.

BOOK COMPANION WEBSITE

The book-specific website at *www.cengage.com/education/allen* offers students a variety of study tools and useful resources such as chapter overviews and notes, tutorial quizzes, web links, frequently asked questions, discussion questions, glossary/flashcards, internet exercises, references and more. To register or purchase access to the premium resources for this text including video clips tied to chapter content, go to *www.cengage.com/login*.

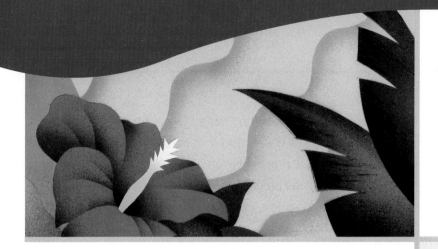

CHAPTER 2

Principles of Growth and Development

Objectives

After reading this chapter, you should be able to:

- Define growth and development as separate concepts and provide at least two examples of each.

- Identify the six major developmental domains that are the focus of this text.

- Describe the role of the environment in early brain development.

- Explain the importance of using sequences of development rather than chronological age in assessing developmental progress.

- Discuss what is meant when an infant or child is said to be at risk, listing at least five factors that lead to high-risk early development.

- Defend this statement: "Sequence, not age, is the important factor in evaluating a child's progress."

MEET THE TWINS EMMA AND ETHAN

The twins, Emma and Ethan, soon to be three years old, weighed in at a little over four pounds each at birth. Although they were born two months early and considered to be low birth-weight babies, they are now strong and healthy. They look similar, with dark brown eyes, thick eyelashes, and high cheekbones. Although they behave alike in many ways, there are also marked differences. Since early infancy, Emma has been more physically active. She slept less, ate more, sat up, crawled, and walked alone weeks before Ethan or other babies her age. She also has been more adventuresome in trying out new experiences such as slides and climbing equipment. Ethan, however, was the first to smile, play peek-a-boo, and say recognizable words. He now uses complete sentences and has considerable letter, word, and number recognition skills. He likes to "read" to Emma and acts as her interpreter when she can't make herself understood. In turn, Emma is first to comfort Ethan when he is hurt or frightened. Recently, the two were enrolled in an early-childhood program to which they adjusted easily but still needed to stay close to one another throughout the day.

Basic Patterns and Concepts

Groups of children of approximately the same age appear to be remarkably similar in size, shape, and abilities. However, closer observation reveals a wide range of individual differences (Figure 2-1). Both similarities and differences depend on a child's unique patterns of growth and development. What defines this complementary process of *growth and development*? Why do children experience this progression differently? Many terms are used, sometimes interchangeably, to explain these concepts, but they are not describing identical concepts.

GROWTH

Growth refers to specific physical changes and increases in the child's actual size. Additional numbers of cells, as well as enlargement of existing cells, are responsible

Figure 2-1

Children's development includes a wide range of differences.

growth—physical changes leading to an increase in size.

for the observable increases in a child's height, weight, **head circumference**, shoe size, length of arms and legs, and body shape. Changes in growth also lend themselves to direct and fairly reliable measurement.

The growth process continues throughout most of the life span, although the rate varies according to age. For example, growth occurs rapidly during infancy and adolescence but is typically much slower and less dramatic in the school-age child. Even into old age, the body continues to repair and replace its cells, although much less vigorously.

DEVELOPMENT

Development refers to an increase in complexity—a change from the relatively simple to the more complicated and detailed. The process involves an orderly progression along a continuum, or pathway. Little by little, knowledge, behaviors, and skills become increasingly refined and expanded. The sequence is basically the same for all children. However, the rate of development shows great variability from child to child. The rate and level of development are closely related to physiological maturity of the nervous, muscular, and skeletal systems. Development is also influenced by heredity, environmental factors, culture, and family values unique to each individual (Figure 2-2). These collective factors account for the wide range of variations observed in individual

Figure 2-2

Many factors collectively influence a child's development.

head circumference—measurement of the head taken at its largest point (across the forehead, around the back of head, returning to the starting point).

development—refers to an increase in complexity, from simple to more complicated and detailed.

children's developmental progress. For example, families in many cultures encourage their children to begin crawling and walking at an early age, whereas in other cultures the early acquisition of motor skills is not highly valued or supported.

Developmental Milestones

Major markers or points of accomplishment are referred to as developmental milestones in tracking the emergence of motor, social, cognitive, and language skills. They represent behaviors that appear in somewhat orderly steps and within fairly predictable age ranges for typically developing children. For example, almost every child begins to smile socially by ten to twelve weeks and to speak a first word or two around twelve months. These achievements (social smile, first words) are but two of the many significant behavioral indications that a child's developmental progress is on track. When children do not achieve one or more developmental milestones within a reasonable time frame, they should be monitored carefully and systematically by a child development specialist or health care provider.

Sitting, walking, and talking are examples of developmental milestones that depend on biological maturation, yet these skills do not develop independently of the environment. For example, learning to walk requires muscle strength and coordination. It also requires an environment that encourages practice, not only of walking as it emerges, but also of the behaviors and skills that precede walking such as rolling over, sitting, and standing.

Sequences of Development

A sequence of development is composed of predictable steps along a developmental pathway common to the majority of children. Children must be able to roll over before they can sit and sit before they can stand. *The critical consideration is the order in which children acquire these developmental skills, not their age in months and years.* The appropriate sequence in each area of development is an important indication that the child is moving steadily forward along a sound developmental continuum (Figure 2-3). For example, in language development, it does not matter how many words a child speaks by two years of age. What is important is that the child has progressed from cooing and babbling to jabbering (inflected **jargon**) to syllable production. The two- or three-year-old who has progressed through these stages usually produces words and sentences within a reasonable period of time.

Developmental progress is rarely smooth and even. Irregularities, such as periods of **stammering** or the onset of a **food jag**, often characterize children's development. Regression, or taking a step or two backward now and then, is perfectly normal. For example, a child who has been toilet trained for some time might begin to have "accidents" when starting preschool or child care; an older child might resort to hitting or become verbally aggressive following a family move.

---

jargon—unintelligible speech; in young children, it usually includes sounds and inflections of the native language.

stammering—to speak in an interrupted or repetitive pattern; not to be confused with stuttering.

food jag—a period when only certain foods are preferred or accepted.

Figure 2-3

Typical sequence of motor development.

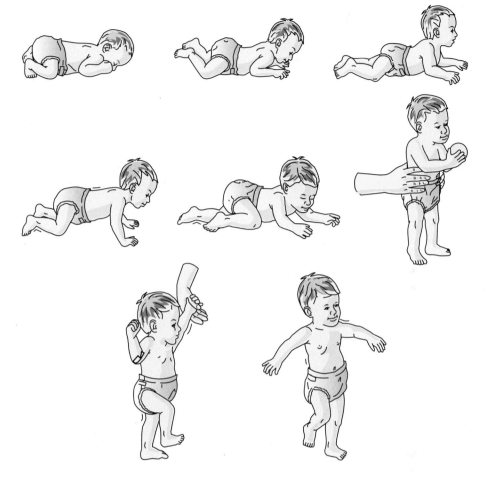

AGE-LEVEL EXPECTANCIES OR NORMS

Age-level expectancies can be thought of as **chronological**, or age-related levels of development. Psychologists, including Gesell, Piaget, and Erikson, conducted hundreds of systematic observations of infants and children of various ages. Analyses of their findings represent the average or typical age at which many specifically described developmental skills are acquired by most children in a given culture (Gesell & Ilg, 1949; Piaget, 1954). This average age is often referred to as the norm. Thus, a child's development may be described as at the norm, above the norm, or below the norm. For example, a child who begins walking at eight months is ahead of the norm (twelve to fifteen months), while a child who does not walk until twenty months is considered to be below the norm.

Age-level expectancies *always represent a range and never an exact point in time* when specific skills are most likely to be achieved. Profiles in this text (age expectancies for specific skills) should always be interpreted as approximate midpoints on a range of

---

chronological—events or dates in sequence in the passage of time.

months (as in the example on walking, from eight to twenty months with the midpoint at fourteen months). Once again, a reminder: It is *sequence* and *not age* that is the important factor in evaluating a child's progress (Plomin, 2003). In real life, there is probably no child who is truly typical in every way. The range of skills and the age at which skills are acquired show great variation. Relevant again is the example of walking, one infant starting at eight months and another not until twenty months (many months apart on either side of the norm). No two children grow and develop at exactly the same rate, nor do they perform in exactly the same way. There are a half dozen ways of creeping and crawling. Most children, however, use what is referred to as *contralateral locomotion*, an opposite knee–hand method of getting about prior to walking. Yet, some normally walking two-year-olds never crawl, indicating a distinct variation in typical development.

ORGANIZATION AND REORGANIZATION

Development can be thought of as a series of phases. Spurts of rapid growth and development often are followed by periods of disorganization. The child then seems to recover and move into a period of reorganization. It is not uncommon for children to demonstrate behavior problems or even regression during these phases. The reasons vary. Perhaps a new baby has become an active and engaging older infant who is now the center of family attention. Three-year-old brother might revert to babyish ways about the same time. He begins to have tantrums over minor frustrations and might, for the time being, lose his hard-won bladder control. Usually, these periods are short-lived. The three-year-old will almost always learn more age-appropriate ways of getting attention if given adequate adult support and understanding.

BRAIN GROWTH AND DEVELOPMENT

Brain maturation lays the foundation for all other aspects of a child's development. Growth and development of the fetal brain is rapid, exceedingly complex, and influenced by a combination of maternal environment (see Chapter 3, "Prenatal Development") and genetics. Children's brains continue to increase in size and composition as a direct result of experiences (Durston & Casey, 2006; Nelson, Thomas, & Haan, 2006). Health care providers measure an infant's head circumference during well-baby checkups to monitor the brain's continued growth (not too fast, not too slow).

Early on, there are many more brain cells (neurons) than the child will need. Connections between cells continue to form as the result of new and repetitive learning experiences. Gradually, through a natural process called **pruning**, active cells and neural connections are strengthened by allowing those that are unused to drop away. This explains, for example, why a child learns to speak in his or her own native language but not in one that is different; or, why one child becomes an outstanding pianist while other children excel at playing sports. Thus, it is important to remember that both genetic

---

pruning—elimination of neurons and neural connections that are not being used; this process strengthens developing connections the child is using.

Figure 2-4

Growth and development are shaped by genetics and learning opportunities.

factors and learning experiences play a significant role in fostering brain growth and development (Figure 2-4).

Current research also reveals amazing information about the relationship between the brain and language development (Zubrick et al., 2007). For example, infants not only take in the sounds of the language they are hearing, but they replicate them complete with a dialect. Furthermore, the dialect is maintained without change for years to come. It is as if, in the case of language development, the brain will not easily sever connections made in the earliest months and years of life, regardless of subsequent changes in language environments. Other findings from brain research will be discussed throughout the text as they relate to particular aspects of development.

TYPICAL GROWTH AND DEVELOPMENT

The terms **typical** and *normal* development are often used interchangeably to describe the acquisition of certain skills and behaviors according to a predictable rate and sequence. However, as previously stated, the range of typical behaviors within each developmental domain is broad and includes mild variations and simple irregularities

---

typical—achievement of certain skills according to a fairly predictable sequence, although with many individual variations.

such as the three-year-old who stutters or the twelve-month-old who learns to walk without having crawled. The use of these terms also oversimplifies the concept. Normal or typical development implies:

- An integrated process governing change in size, **neurological** structure, and behavioral complexity

- A cumulative or building-block process in which each new aspect of growth or development includes and builds on earlier changes; each accomplishment is necessary to acquisition of the next set of skills

- A continuous process of give and take (reciprocity) between the child and the environment, each changing the other in a variety of ways. For example, the three-year-old drops a cup and breaks it, and the parent scolds the child. Both events, the broken cup and the adult's displeasure, are environmental changes that the child triggered. From this experience, the child might learn to hold on more firmly next time, and this constitutes a change in both the child's and the adult's behavior—fewer broken cups, thus less adult displeasure.

INTERRELATEDNESS OF DEVELOPMENTAL DOMAINS

Discussions about development usually focus on several major domains: physical, motor, perceptual, cognitive, social-emotional, and language. However, no single area develops independently of the others. Every skill, whether simple or complex, requires a mix of developmental abilities. Social skills are a good example. Why are some young children said to have good social skills? Often the answer is because they play well with other children and are sought out as playmates. To be a preferred playmate, a child must have many skills, all of them interrelated and interdependent. For example, a four-year-old should be able to:

- Run, jump, climb, and build with blocks (good motor skills).
- Ask for, explain, and describe what is going on (good language skills).
- Recognize likenesses and differences among play materials and so select appropriate materials in a joint building project (good perceptual skills).
- Problem-solve, conceptualize, and plan ahead in cooperative play ventures (good cognitive skills).

Every developmental area is well represented in the preceding example, even though social development was the primary area under consideration.

TEMPERAMENT

The term *temperament* refers to the genetic component of an individual's personality (Rothbart, 2007). It describes the characteristic nature of a person's emotional responses

---

neurological—refers to the brain and nervous system.

such as the intensity, disposition or mood, focus, and ability to adjust. Infants and young children differ in their activity levels, alertness, irritability, soothability, restlessness, and willingness to cuddle. Such qualities often lead to labels—the "easy" child, the "difficult" child, and the "slow-to-warm" child (Henderson & Wachs, 2007). These characteristics (and labels) tend to affect how family and teachers respond to the child (Figure 2-5). Their responses, in turn, reinforce the child's self-perceptions. For example, a slow-to-warm child might evoke few displays of affection from others and so perceive this as rejection, making it even more difficult for the child to act warm and outgoing.

GENDER ROLES

Early in life, young children learn gender roles appropriate to their culture (Brody, 2000). Each boy and girl develops a set of behaviors, attitudes, and commitments that

Figure 2-5

A child's temperament can affect the nature of adult responses.

are defined, directly or indirectly, as acceptable male or female attributes. In addition, each child plays out gender roles according to everyday experiences. The child's sense of maleness or femaleness is also influenced by genetics, playmates and play opportunities, toys, media exposure, cultural expectations and, especially, adult role models (families, neighbors, teachers).

ECOLOGICAL FACTORS

Beginning at conception, **ecology**—the environmental influence of family and home, community, and society—affects all aspects of development (Noble, McCandliss, & Farah, 2007). The following are examples of powerful ecological factors.

- Income level; adequacy of food and shelter
- Cultural values and practices
- General health and nutrition; availability of prenatal and postnatal care for mother and child
- Families' education level (mother's level of education is a major predictor of a child's school achievement) (Melhuish et al., 2008; Farver, 2006)
- Families' understanding of obligations and responsibilities before and after the infant's birth
- Family communication and child-rearing practices (loving or punishing, nurturing or neglectful); family stress
- Family structure—single- or two-parent, blended, or extended family; grandparent with primary parenting role; nontraditional household; foster homes

Differences in the way each of these factors are experienced ultimately results in a child being unlike any other child. For example, the child born to a single, fifteen-year-old mother living in poverty will have life experiences different from those of a child born and reared in a two-parent professional family.

TRANSACTIONAL PATTERNS OF DEVELOPMENT

From birth, children influence the behavior of their adult caretakers (e.g., families, teachers). In turn, these same adults exert a strong influence on children's behavior and development. For example, a calm, cuddly baby expresses his or her needs in a clear and predictable fashion. This infant begins life with personal–social experiences that are quite different from those of a tense, colicky infant whose sleeping and eating patterns

---

ecology—in terms of children's development, refers to interactive effects between children and their family, child care situation, school, and everything in the wider community that affects their lives.

are highly irregular and often stressful to parents. This complex **transactional process** of give and take between children and their families and daily events is ongoing and continually changing and results in developmental experiences and outcomes that are often quite different for each child.

Infants and young children thrive when adults respond promptly and positively, at least a fair share of the time, to appropriate things a child says and does. Research indicates that children develop healthier self-concepts as well as earlier and better language, cognitive, and social skills when raised by responsive adults (Dalton, Frick-Horbury, & Kitzmann, 2006).

CHILDREN AT RISK

Some children are born into situations that might be harmful to their development or interfere with its typical progress. These children are often described as being *at risk*. Premature birth and low birth weight are examples of two conditions that increase a child's vulnerability and chances of developing physical problems, learning disabilities, behavioral problems, or all three (Wolke et al., 2008; Atkinson & Braddick, 2007). They are typically associated with poor maternal health, inadequate prenatal care, substance abuse during pregnancy, poverty, or maternal age outside the "normal" range (very young teenagers and women in their early forties and older). Children who live in poverty or are exposed to abusive or neglectful treatment are also considered to be at higher risk for experiencing developmental problems (Rose-Jacobs et al., 2008; Fantuzzo et al., 2007).

ATYPICAL GROWTH AND DEVELOPMENT

The term *atypical* describes children with developmental differences, deviations, or marked delays—children whose development appears to be incomplete or inconsistent with typical patterns and sequences. There are many causes of atypical development, including genetic errors, poor health and nutrition, injury, and too few or poor-quality opportunities to learn.

Abnormal development in one area might or might not interfere with development in other areas. However, the child with developmental delays might perform in one or more areas of development like a much younger child. For example, the three-year-old who is still babbling with no recognizable words is an example of a child with delayed development. This condition need not be disabling unless the child never develops **functional language**. The term *developmental deviation* describes an aspect of development that is different from what is expected in typical development (Figure 2-6). For example, the child born with a missing finger or a profound hearing

---

transactional process—the give-and-take relationship between children, their primary caregivers, and daily events that influences behavior and developmental outcomes.

functional language—language that allows children to get what they need or want.

Figure 2-6

A vision problem is an example of a developmental deviation.

loss has a developmental deviation. The child with a missing finger is not likely to be disabled. In contrast, the child who is deaf will have a significant, lifelong disability without early and intensive intervention.

In any event, the concepts and principles described in this chapter apply to the child with developmental differences as well as to the child who is said to be developing typically. However, one must always be cautious not to make judgments about a child's development without first being sensitive to cultural, ethnic, socioeconomic, language, and gender variations that might indeed account for any differences (Foster, 2007; Trawick-Smith, 2003). It must also be remembered that a child who experiences any type of developmental problem is, most important and foremost, a child with the same basic needs as all other children.

Developmental Domains

A framework is needed to describe and accurately assess children's developmental progress. In this book, we focus on six major domains, or developmental areas: physical, motor, perceptual, cognitive, speech and language, and social-emotional. Each domain includes the many skills and behaviors that will be discussed in the developmental profiles that are the major focus of this book (Chapters 4 through 8). Although these developmental areas are separated for the purpose of discussion, they cannot be separated from one another in reality. Each is integrally related to and **interdependent** with each of the others in the overall developmental process.

Developmental profiles, or word pictures, are useful for assessing both the immediate and ongoing status of children's skills and behavior. It is important to remember that the rate of development is uneven and occasionally unpredictable across areas. For example, the language and social skills of infants and toddlers are typically less well developed than is their ability to move about. Also, children's individual achievements can vary across developmental areas: a child might walk late but talk early. Again, an important reminder: Development in any of the domains is dependent in a large part on children having appropriate stimulation and adequately supported opportunities to learn. Additionally, the types of learning experiences children encounter are highly variable and often reflect cultural, socioeconomic, and family values.

PHYSICAL DEVELOPMENT AND GROWTH

This domain governs the major tasks of infancy and childhood. Understanding the patterns and sequences of physical development is essential to being effective parents, teachers, and caregivers. It is healthy growth and development, not adult pressure or coaching, that makes new learning and behavior possible. Adult pressure cannot hurry the process and, in fact, is more likely to be counterproductive. A seven-month-old infant cannot be toilet trained; the **sphincter** muscles are not yet developed sufficiently to exert such control. Nor can the majority of kindergartners catch or kick a ball skillfully; such coordination is impossible given a five- or six-year-old's stage of physical development, yet most of us have seen a coach or family reduce a child to tears for missing a catch or a kick.

Governed by heredity and greatly influenced by environmental conditions, physical development and growth is a highly individualized process (Gottlieb, 2004). It is responsible for changes in body shape and proportion as well as for overall body size. Growth, especially of the brain, occurs more rapidly during prenatal development and the first year than at any other time. Growth is also intricately related to progress in other developmental areas. It is responsible for increasing muscle strength necessary for movement, coordinating vision and motor control, and synchronizing neurological and muscular activity in gaining bladder and bowel control. A child's growth is closely linked to nutritional status and ethnicity (Lunde et al., 2007). Thus, the state of a child's physical development serves as a reliable index of his or her general health and well-being. Physical growth and development also exert a direct influence on determining whether children are likely to achieve their full cognitive and academic potential.

---

interdependent—affecting or influencing development in other domains.

sphincter—the muscles necessary to accomplish bowel and bladder control.

MOTOR DEVELOPMENT

The child's ability to move about and control the various body parts are the major functions of this domain. Refinements in motor development depend on maturation of the brain, input from the *sensory system*, increased bulk and number of muscle fibers, a healthy nervous system, and opportunities to practice. This holistic approach contrasts markedly with the way early developmentalists such as Gesell viewed the emergence of motor skills. They described a purely maturational process, governed almost entirely by instructions on the individual's genetic code (nature). Today's psychologists consider such an explanation misleading and incomplete. Their research suggests that when young children show an interest, for example, in using a spoon to feed themselves, it is always accompanied by improved eye–hand coordination (to direct the spoon to the mouth), motivation (*liking* and *wanting* to eat what is in the bowl), and the drive to imitate what others are doing. In other words, the environment, that is, experience, plays a major role in the emergence of new motor skills (nurture).

Motor activity during very early infancy is purely **reflexive**, although that type of movement and gradually disappears as the child develops **voluntary** control over his or her movements. If these earliest reflexes do not phase out at appropriate times in the **developmental sequence**, it might be an indication of neurological problems (see Chapter 4, "Infancy"). In such cases, medical evaluation should be sought. Three principles govern motor development:

1. **Cephalocaudal** Bone and muscular development that proceeds from head to toe (Figure 2-7). The infant first learns to control muscles that support the head and neck, then the trunk, and later, those that allow reaching. Muscles for walking develop last.

Figure 2-7

Cephalocaudal development proceeds from head to toe.

reflexive—movements resulting from impulses of the nervous system that cannot be controlled by the individual.

voluntary—movements that can be willed and purposively controlled and initiated by the individual.

developmental sequence—a continuum of predictable steps along a developmental pathway of skill achievement.

cephalocaudal—bone and muscular development that proceeds from head to toe.

2. **Proximodistal** Bone and muscular development that begins with improved control of muscles closest to the central portion of the body, gradually extending outward and away from the midpoint to the extremities (arms and legs) (Figure 2-8). For example, control of the head and neck is achieved before the child is able to pick up an object with thumb and forefinger (pincer grasp or finger–thumb opposition).

3. **Refinement** Muscular development that progresses from the general to the specific in both **gross motor** and **fine motor** activities. In the refinement of a

Figure 2-8

Proximodistal development proceeds outward from the trunk.

proximodistal—bone and muscular development that begins closest to the trunk, gradually moving outward to the extremities.

refinement—progressive improvement in ability to perform fine and gross motor skills.

gross motor—large muscle movements such as locomotor skills (walking, skipping, swimming) and nonlocomotive movements (sitting, pushing and pulling, squatting).

fine motor—also referred to as manipulative skills; includes stacking blocks, buttoning and zipping, and toothbrushing.

gross motor skill, for example, a two-year-old might attempt to throw a ball but achieves little distance or control. The same child, within a few short years, might pitch a ball over home plate with speed and accuracy. As for a fine motor skill, compare the self-feeding efforts of a toddler with those of an eight-year-old who is motivated (for whatever reason) to display good table manners.

PERCEPTUAL DEVELOPMENT

This is the increasingly complex way the child uses information received through the senses—sight, hearing, touch, smell, taste, and body position (Santrock, 2007). It might be said that perception is a significant factor that determines and orchestrates the functioning of the various senses, singly or in combination. The perceptual process also enables the individual to focus on what is relevant at a particular moment and to screen out whatever is irrelevant: Which details are important? Which differences should be noted? Which should be ignored? Three aspects of perceptual development are important:

1. *Multisensory* Information is generally received through more than one sense organ at a time. For example, when listening to a speaker, we use sight (watching facial expressions and gestures) and sound (listening to the words) (Pollak & Sinha, 2002).

2. *Habituation* This term refers to a person's ability to concentrate on a specific task while ignoring everything else. For example, a child might be focused on reading a book of interest and be completely unaware of classmates' conversation or background music. In other words, he or she is able to tune out things around him or her and devote full attention to what is most important to the immediate situation (Casasola & Bhagwat, 2007).

3. *Sensory integration* This process involves translating **sensory information** into functional behavior. For example, the five-year-old sees and hears a car coming and waits for it to pass before crossing the street.

The basic perceptual system is in place at birth. Through experience, learning, and maturation, it develops into a smoothly coordinated operation for processing complex information from multiple senses. Because of this mechanism, children can sort shapes according to size and color and make fine discriminations or hear and distinguish the difference among initial sounds in rhyming words such as rake, cake, and lake. The sensory system also enables each of us to respond appropriately to all kinds of messages and signals, such as smiling in response to a smile or keeping quiet in response to a frown.

COGNITIVE DEVELOPMENT

This domain addresses the expansion of a child's intellect or mental abilities. Cognition involves recognizing, processing, and organizing information and then using the

---

sensory information—information received through the senses: eyes, ears, nose, mouth, touch.

information appropriately (Charlesworth, 2007). The cognitive process includes such mental activities as discovering, interpreting, sorting, classifying, and remembering. In preschool-aged and school-aged children, it means evaluating ideas, making judgments, solving problems, understanding rules and concepts, thinking ahead, and visualizing possibilities or consequences. Cognitive development is an ongoing process of interaction between the child and his or her perceptual view of objects or events in the environment (Piaget, 1954). It is probably safe to say that neither cognitive nor perceptual development can proceed independently of each other.

VIDEO CONNECTIONS

Clip 3

Emotional Development: Temperament is considered one component of an individual's personality. Infants, for example, differ in terms of their emotional perceptions and responses to caregivers and the environment.

Critical Thinking Questions:

1. What determines a child's temperament?
2. Which adjectives did parents in the video use to describe their child's temperament?
3. How does a child's temperament influence the transactional process of parenting?
4. How would you describe your own temperament?
5. Do you think there are cultural differences in temperament? Explain.

The development of cognition begins with the primitive or reflexive behaviors that support survival and early learning in the healthy newborn. One example of very early learning is when a mother playfully sticks out her tongue several times and the baby begins to imitate her. This and other early behaviors led developmental psychologists to ponder the many striking similarities in how infants and children learn. Based on repeated observations of such similarities during the 1950s, the Swiss psychologist Jean Piaget formulated his four stages of cognitive development: sensorimotor, preoperational, concrete operations, and formal operations (see Chapter 1, "Child Development Theories and Data Gathering").

Cognitive skills always overlap with both perceptual development and motor involvement. Early in the second year, the emergence of speech and language adds yet another dimension.

LANGUAGE DEVELOPMENT

Language is often defined as a system of symbols, spoken, written, and gestural (waving, smiling, scowling, cowering), that enables us to communicate with one another.

Normal language development is regular and sequential and depends on maturation as well as on learning opportunities (Huttenlocher et al., 2007). The first year of life is called the prelinguistic or prelanguage phase. The child is totally dependent on body movements and sounds such as crying and laughing to convey needs and feelings. This is followed during the second year by the linguistic or language stage, in which speech becomes the primary mode for communicating. Over the next three or four years, the child learns to put words together to form simple and then compound sentences that make sense to others because the child has learned the appropriate grammatical constructions. Between five and seven years of age, most children have become skilled at conveying their thoughts and ideas verbally. Many children at this age have a vocabulary of 14,000 words or more, which can double or triple during middle childhood, depending on a child's language environment.

Most children seem to understand a variety of words, concepts, and relationships long before they have the words to describe them (Owens, 2007). This ability is referred to as **receptive language**, which precedes **expressive language** (the ability to speak words to describe and explain). Speech and language development is closely related to the child's general cognitive, social, perceptual, and neuromuscular development. Language development and the rules that address how it is to be used are also influenced by the type of language children hear in their homes, schools, and community (Bowerman, Levinson, & Levinson, 2001) (Figure 2-9).

Figure 2-9

A child's home environment exerts a strong influence on language development.

receptive language—understanding words that are heard.

expressive language—words used to verbalize thoughts and feelings.

SOCIAL AND EMOTIONAL DEVELOPMENT

This is a broad area that covers how children feel about themselves and their relationships with others (Lane, Stanton-Chapman, & Jamison, 2007; Turner & Brown, 2007). It refers to children's behaviors, the way they respond to play and work activities, and their attachments to family members, caregivers, teachers, and friends. Gender roles, temperament, independence, morality, trust, acceptance of rules, and social expectations are also important components of this developmental area.

In describing personal and social development, it must also be remembered that children develop at different rates. Individual differences in genetic and cultural backgrounds, health status, living arrangements, family interactions, and daily experiences within the larger community continuously shape and reshape children's development. Consequently, no two children can ever be exactly alike, not in social and emotional development or in any other developmental area.

VIDEO CONNECTIONS

Clip 4

Gender: Children's concept of gender refers to the qualities and behaviors considered appropriate for one's gender. Many factors exert a collective influence on what children believe it means to be a girl or a boy.

Critical Thinking Questions:

1. On what dimensions did children in the video segment distinguish a person as being either male or female?
2. Which additional terms are often used to describe male or female children?
3. Is gender identity a product of nature or nurture? Explain.
4. Do you think children growing up in single-parent families would respond differently to questions such as "Who takes care of the children?" or "Who goes to work?" Explain.

Age Divisions

The following age divisions, used throughout this book, are commonly referred to by many child developmentalists when describing significant changes within developmental areas:

Infancy	birth to one month
	1–4 months
	4–8 months
	8–12 months

Toddlerhood	12–24 months
	24–36 months
Early Childhood	3–5 years
	6–8 years
Middle Childhood	9–12 years

Age divisions are to be used with extreme caution and great flexibility when dealing with children. They are based on the average achievements, abilities, and behaviors of large numbers of children at various stages in development. As stated again and again, there is great variation from one child to another. It is the sequential acquisition of developmental tasks, *not age*, that is the major index to healthy development.

The step-by-step development that we detail in Chapters 4 through 8 speaks to the importance of understanding that it is sequence and not age that indicates developmental progress in each domain and in the overall development of each child.

S U M M A R Y

Growth and development are influenced by a child's unique genetic makeup and the quality of the everyday environment, which includes nurturing, health care, and opportunities to learn the vast range of skills that are evidence of developmental progress. Each child's well-being depends on acquiring the necessary skills in six developmental domains: physical, motor, perceptual, cognitive, language, and socioemotional. Although the six domains are separated for discussion purposes, they are interwoven and interdependent during the developmental years and throughout life.

Although age-level expectations (*norms*) are of some value in assessing an individual child's developmental status, they must be used cautiously. The accepted range of normalcy is broad and recognizes that each child is unique. Thus, the more important factor is not age but sequence—is the child progressing through each step in each developmental area even though it might be somewhat later (or earlier) than most children of similar age? Atypical development is characterized by marked delays or characteristics not seen in typical development. Nevertheless, it must be remembered that all children have the same basic needs regardless of their special abilities, limitations, or challenges.

KEY TERMS

cephalocaudal	fine motor
chronological	food jag
development	functional language
developmental sequence	gross motor
ecology	growth
expressive language	head circumference

interdependent	reflexive
jargon	sensory information
neurological	sphincter
proximodistal	stammering
pruning	transactional process
receptive language	typical
refinement	voluntary

APPLY WHAT YOU KNOW

A. Apply What You Have Learned

Reread the brief developmental sketch about Emma and Ethan at the beginning of the chapter. How might you answer the following questions?

1. From the brief descriptions of Emma and Ethan, which characteristics can be attributed solely to genetic makeup?

2. In what ways do Emma's and Ethan's motor skill development differ?

3. What is refinement? Give an example of this developmental principle from the descriptions of Emma and Ethan.

4. How do Emma and Ethan differ in terms of their personal–social development? Given that they are twins, what factors might explain these differences?

5. According to Piaget, which stage of cognitive development are the twins, who are almost three, currently experiencing? Give an example of this concept from the descriptions of Emma and Ethan.

6. Just because Emma and Ethan are twins, should you expect them to grow and develop in exactly the same way and at exactly the same rate? How would developmental theorists account for these differences (see Chapter 1)?

B. Review

1. How do the concepts of growth and development differ?

2. Identify and discuss three factors that might contribute to atypical development.

3. What is meant by the term *perceptual information*? Give three examples to illustrate this concept.

4. Why would you not be concerned about a toddler who was learning to walk but now insists on crawling instead? Explain.

5. Define the terms *cephalocaudal* and *proximodistal* development. Give an example of each.

6. What are developmental milestones and what purpose do they serve?

7. Identify three ecological factors and describe how they might influence children's early development.

HELPFUL
WEBSITES

Visit the book companion website at *www.cengage.com/education/allen* for links to these websites and additional resources.

REFERENCES

Atkinson, J., & Braddick, O. (2007). Visual and visuocognitive development in children born very prematurely. *Progress in Brain Research, 164,* 123–149.

Bowerman, M., Levinson, C., & Levinson, S. (2001). *Language acquisition and conceptual development (Language, culture, & cognition).* New York: Cambridge University Press.

Brody, L. (2000). The socialization of gender differences in emotional expression: Display rules, infant temperament, and differentiation. In A. Fischer (Ed.), *Gender and emotion: Social psychological perspectives,* (pp. 24–47). New York: Cambridge University Press.

Casasola, M., & Bhagwat, J. (2007). Do novel words facilitate 18-month-olds' spatial categorization? *Child Development, 78*(6), 1818–1829.

Charlesworth, R. (2007). *Understanding child development* (7th ed.). Clifton Park, NY: Delmar Cengage Learning.

Dalton, W., Frick-Horbury, D., & Kitzman, K. (2006). Young adult's retrospective reports of parenting by mothers and fathers: Associations with current relationship quality. *Journal of General Psychology, 133*(1), 5–18.

Durston, S., & Casey, B. (2006). What have we learned about cognitive development from neuroimaging? *Neuropsychologia, 44*(11), 2149–2157.

Fantuzzo, J., Bulotsky-Shearer, R., McDermott, P., McWayne, C., Frye, D., & Perlman, S. (2007). Investigation of dimensions of social-emotional classroom behavior and school readiness for low-income urban preschool children. *School Psychology Review, 36*(1), 44–62.

Farver, J., Xu, Y., Eppe, S., & Lonigan, C. (2006). Home environments and young Latino children's school readiness. *Early Childhood Research Quarterly, 21*(2), 196–212.

Foster, E., & Kalil, A. (2007). Living arrangements and children's development in low-income White, Black, and Latino families. *Child Development, 78*(6), 1657–1674.

Gesell, A., & Ilg, F. (1949). *Child development.* New York: Harper.

Gottlieb, G. (2004). Normally occurring environmental and behavioral influences on gene activity. In C. G. Coll, E. L. Bearer, & R. M. Lerner (Eds.), *Nature and nurture.* Mahwah: Erlbaum.

Henderson, H., & Wachs, T. (2007). Temperament theory and the study of cognition-emotion interactions across development. *Developmental Review, 27*(3), 396–427.

Huttenlocher, J., Vasilyeva, M., Waterfall, H., Vevea, J., & Hedges, L. (2007). The varieties of speech to young children. *Developmental Psychology, 43*(5), 1062–1083.

Lane, K., Stanton-Chapman, T., & Jamison, K. (2007). Teacher and parent expectations of preschoolers' behavior: Social skills necessary for success. *Topics in Early Childhood Special Education, 27*(2), 86–97.

Lunde, A., Melve, K., Gjessing, H., Skjaerven, R., & Irgens, L. (2007). Genetic and environmental influences on birth weight, birth length, head circumference, and gestational age by use of population-based parent-offspring data. *American Journal of Epidemiology, 165*(7), 734–741.

Melhuish, E., Phan, M., Sylva, K., Sammons, P., Siraj-Blatchford, I., & Taggart, B. (2008). Effects of the home learning environment and preschool center experience upon literacy and numeracy development in early primary school. *Journal of Social Issues, 64*(1), 95–114.

Nelson, C., Thomas, K., & Haan, M. (2006). *Neuroscience of cognitive development: The role of experience and the developing brain.* New York: Wiley.

Noble, K., McCandliss, B., & Farah, M. (2007). Socioeconomic gradients predict individual differences in neurocognitive abilities. *Developmental Science, 10*(4), 464–480.

Owens, R. (2007). *Language development: An introduction* (7th ed.). Boston: Allyn & Bacon.

Piaget, J. (1954). *The construction of reality in the child.* New York: Basic Books.

Pollak, S., & Sinha, P. (2002). Effects of early experience on children's recognition of facial displays of emotion. *Developmental Psychology, 38*(5), 784–791.

Plomin, R. (2003). 50 years of DNA. *American Psychological Society, 16,* 7–8.

Rose-Jacobs, R., Black, M., Casey, P., Cook, J., Cutts, D., Chilton, M., Heeren, T., Levenson, S., Meyers, A., & Frank, D. (2008). Household food insecurity: Associations with at-risk infant and toddler development. *Pediatrics, 121*(1), 65–72.

Rothbart, M. (2007). Temperament, development, and personality. *Current Directions in Psychological Science, 16*(4), 207–212.

Santrock, J. (2007). *Children* (9th ed.). New York: McGraw-Hill.

Trawick-Smith, J. (2003). *Early childhood development: A multicultural approach.* Upper Saddle River, NJ: Merrill/Prentice Hall.

Turner, K., & Brown, C. (2007). The centrality of gender and ethnic identities across individuals and contexts. *Social Development, 16*(4), 700–719.

Wolke, D., Samara, M., Bracewell, M., & Marlow, N. (2008). Specific language difficulties and school achievement in children born at 25 weeks of gestation or less. *Journal of Pediatrics, 152*(2), 256–262.

Zubrick, S., Taylor, C., Rice, M., & Slegers, D. (2007). Late language emergence at 24 months: An epidemiological study of prevalence, predictors, and covariates. *Journal of Speech, Language and Hearing Research, 50*(6), 1562–1592.

BOOK COMPANION WEBSITE

The book-specific website at *www.cengage.com/education/allen* offers students a variety of study tools and useful resources such as chapter overviews and notes, tutorial quizzes, web links, frequently asked questions, discussion questions, glossary/flashcards, internet exercises, references and more. To register or purchase access to the premium resources for this text including video clips tied to chapter content, go to *www.cengage.com/login*.

Prenatal Development

Objectives

*After reading this chapter,
you should be able to:*

- Describe how implantation exposes the embryo to environmental risks.

- Discuss the functional roles of the placenta.

- Explain why medical supervision is important during pregnancy.

- Identify nutrients that are required in greater amounts during pregnancy.

- Discuss how a mother's age influences fetal development.

- Identify five teratogens and describe their preventive measures.

MEET ANNA AND MIGUEL

Anna and Miguel were elated when they learned that she was 7 weeks pregnant. Six months earlier, Anna had experienced a miscarriage during her third month of pregnancy. At the time, Anna's doctor advised her to stop smoking before attempting future pregnancies. Although she was not able to quit, she did significantly reduce the number of cigarettes she was smoking each day. Anna also made an effort to improve her diet by eating more fruits and vegetables and eliminating alcohol consumption.

When Anna and Miguel shared their exciting news with family members, everyone had advice for preventing another miscarriage. Her mother insisted that Anna rest and avoid any type of activity, including cleaning the house and cooking. Miguel's aunt advised Anna not to drink milk and to eat all she could "because she was now eating for two." Her sister discouraged Anna from continuing to work at the bank because she had heard that stress could cause miscarriage. However, Anna's job was the only way she and Miguel could maintain their health insurance coverage. Anna appreciated her family's suggestions, but she was convinced that everything would be okay this time around.

Each of the approximately 266 days of prenatal development (from **conception** to birth) is critical to producing a healthy newborn. **Genes** inherited from the baby's biological mother and father determine all physical characteristics as well as many abnormalities. Studies have suggested that **temperament** can also have a biological basis (Henderson & Wachs, 2007). However, because it is the mother who provides everything physically essential (as well as harmful) to the growing fetus, she plays a major role in promoting its healthy development. Her personal health, nutritional status, and lifestyle before and during pregnancy strongly influence the birth of a healthy baby. Researchers have recently determined that a father's health and personal habits and his caring support for the mother throughout the pregnancy also contribute to the unborn infant's development (Macarthur et al., 2008; Martin et al., 2007). Thus, it is important for every potential parent to be familiar with the patterns of normal prenatal development as well as with practices that support and interfere with this process (Figure 3-1).

Figure 3-1

A mother's and father's lifestyles have a direct effect on their baby's development.

conception—the joining of a single egg or ovum from the female and a single sperm from the male.

genes—genetic material that carries codes, or information, for all inherited characteristics.

temperament—an individual's characteristic manner or style of response to everyday events, including degree of interest, activity level, and regulation of behavior.

The Developmental Process

The prenatal period is commonly divided into stages. In obstetrical practice, pregnancy is described in terms of trimesters, each consisting of 3 calendar months:

- First trimester—conception through the third month
- Second trimester—fourth through the sixth month
- Third trimester—seventh through the ninth month

Pregnancy can also be discussed in terms of fetal development (Table 3-1). This approach emphasizes the critical changes that occur week by week and encompasses three stages as well:

- Germinal
- Embryonic
- Fetal

Table 3-1 Characteristics of Fetal Development

2 weeks	• Cell division results in an embryo consisting of 16 cells.
3–8 weeks	• Structures necessary to support the developing embryo have formed: placenta, chorionic sac, amniotic fluid, and umbilical cord.
	• Embryonic cell layers begin to specialize, developing into major internal organs and systems as well as external structures.
	• First bone cells appear.
	• Less than 1 inch (2.54 cm) in length at eight weeks.
12 weeks	• Weighs approximately 1 to 2 ounces (0.029–0.006 kg) and is nearly 3 inches (7.6 cm) in length.
	• Sex organs develop; baby's gender can be determined.
	• Kidneys begin to function.
	• Arms, legs, fingers, and toes are well defined and movable.
	• Forms facial expressions (e.g., smiling, looking around) and is able to suck and swallow.
16 weeks	• Weighs about 5 ounces (0.14 kg) and is 6 inches (15.2 cm) in length.
	• Sucks thumb.
	• Moves about actively; mother may begin to feel baby's movement (called "quickening").
	• Has strong heartbeat that can be heard.
20 weeks	• Weighs nearly one pound (0.46 kg) and has grown to approximately 11 to 12 inches (27.9–30.5 cm) in length (approximately half of baby's birth length).
	• Experiences occasional hiccups.
	• Eyelashes, eyebrows, and hair forming; eyes remain closed.
24 weeks	• Weight doubles to about 1.5 to 2 pounds (0.68–0.90 kg) and length increases to 12 to 14 inches (30.5–35.6 cm).

(continued)

Table 3-1 Characteristics of Fetal Development *(continued)*

	• Eyes are well formed, often open; responds to light and sound.
	• Grasp reflex develops.
	• Skin is wrinkled, thin, and covered with soft hair called *lanugo* and a white, greasy, protective substance called *vernix caseosa*.
28 weeks	• Weighs about 3 to 3.5 pounds (1.4–1.6 kg); grows to approximately 16 to 17 inches (40.6–43 cm) in length.
	• Develops a sleep/wake pattern.
	• Remains very active; kicks and pokes mother's ribs and abdomen.
	• Able to survive if born prematurely, although lungs are not yet fully developed.
32 weeks	• Weighs approximately 5 to 6 pounds (2.3–2.7 kg) and is 17 to 18 inches in length (43–45.7 cm).
	• Baby takes iron and calcium from mother's diet to build up reserve stores.
	• Becomes less active due to larger size and less room for moving about.
36–38 weeks	• Weighs an average of 7 to 8 pounds (3.2–3.6 kg) at birth; length is approximately 19 to 21 inches (48–53.3 cm).
	• Moves into final position (usually head down) in preparation for birth.
	• Loses most of lanugo (body hair); skin still somewhat wrinkled and red.
	• Is much less active (ha s little room in which to move).
	• Body systems are more mature (especially the lungs and heart), thus increasing baby's chances of survival at birth.

The *germinal stage* refers to the first 14 days of pregnancy. The union of an ovum and sperm produces a **zygote**. Cell division begins within 24 hours and gradually forms a pinhead-size mass of specialized cells called a *blastocyst*. Around the fourteenth day, this small mass attaches itself to the wall of the mother's uterus. Successful attachment (**implantation**) marks the beginning of the **embryo** and the embryonic stage. Approximately two thirds of zygotes will survive this phase and continue to develop.

The *embryonic stage* includes the third through the eighth week of a pregnancy and is a critical period for the developing fetus. Cell division continues and forms specialized cell layers that are responsible for all major organs and systems, such as the heart, lungs, digestive system, and brain. Many of these structures will be functional near the end of this period. For example, embryonic blood begins to flow through the fetus's primitive cardiovascular system (heart and blood vessels) in the fourth to the fifth weeks.

zygote—the cell formed as a result of conception; called a zygote for the first 14 days.

implantation—the attachment of the blastocyst to the wall of the mother's uterus; occurs around the twelfth day.

embryo—the cell mass from the time of implantation through the eighth week of pregnancy.

During this time, other important changes are also taking place. When implantation is completed, a **placenta** begins to form. This organ serves four major functions, including:

- Supplying nutrients and hormones to the fetus.

- Removing fetal waste products throughout the pregnancy.

- Filtering out many harmful substances as well as viruses and other disease-causing organisms. (Unfortunately, many drugs can get through the placenta's filtering system.)

- Acting as a temporary immune system by supplying the fetus with the same antibodies the mother produces against certain infectious diseases. (In most instances, the infant is protected for approximately 6 months following birth.)

An umbilical cord, containing two arteries and one vein, develops as the placenta forms and establishes a linkage between the fetus, its mother, and the outside world. From this point on, the fetus is affected by the mother's health and lifestyle and begins to share everything the mother experiences and takes into her body via the placenta. During this early stage, the fetus is especially vulnerable if exposed to certain chemical substances such as alcohol, cigarette smoke, medications (see Table 3-2), or infectious illnesses (see Table 3-3) that enter the mother's body. Exposure to any of these substances potentially can cause damage to developing fetal organs and systems. As we note in a later section, the risk of irreversible birth defects, ranging from mild to severe, can result.

The *fetal stage* refers to the period between the ninth week and the onset of labor and delivery (around the thirty-eighth week). Most fetal systems and structures are now formed, and this final and longest period is devoted to continued growth and maturity. By 7 months, a fetus is capable of surviving birth. During the final 2 months, few developmental changes occur. Instead, the fetus undergoes rapid and important gains in weight and size by adding layers of fat. For example, a seven-month-old fetus who weighs 2 to 3 pounds (0.9–1.4 kg) will gain approximately 1/2 pound (0.23 kg) per week until birth. Body systems also are maturing and growing stronger, thus improving the fetus's chances of surviving outside of the mother's body.

Promoting Healthy Fetal Development

Critical aspects of development are taking place during the earliest days of pregnancy, often before pregnancy has even been confirmed. Therefore, it is important for both mother and father to follow healthy lifestyle practices throughout their reproductive

---

placenta—a specialized lining that forms inside the uterus during pregnancy to support and nourish the developing fetus.

years. Current research provides information about many factors that can improve a mother's chances of having a healthy baby, including:

- The importance of early prenatal care
- Eating a healthful diet
- Maintaining a moderate weight gain
- Obtaining sufficient rest
- Avoiding excessive stress
- Having a positive emotional state
- Planning pregnancies when a mother is in her twenties to thirties and in good health
- Participating in daily physical activity
- Limiting exposure to teratogens such as drugs, alcohol, tobacco, and environmental chemicals
- Spacing pregnancies at least 2 years apart (Lu et al., 2006).

PRENATAL CARE

Medically supervised prenatal care is critical for ensuring the development of a healthy baby (Cramer et al., 2007) (Figure 3-2). Arrangements for such care should be made as soon as a woman suspects that she is pregnant. Women should not rely solely on home pregnancy tests before seeking medical care because the results are not always accurate, especially during the early days and weeks of pregnancy. During the initial visit to a health care provider, pregnancy can be confirmed (or refuted), and any medical problems the mother might have can be evaluated and treated. The parents-to-be can also be

Figure 3-2

Routine prenatal care is essential for a healthy pregnancy and baby.

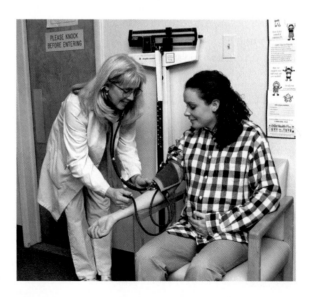

counseled on practices that influence fetal development. For example, mothers can be encouraged to participate in a program of regular noncontact exercise. (As long as there are no complications, regular exercise can improve weight control, circulation, muscle tone, and elimination and is believed to contribute to an easier labor and delivery.)

Although nearly 84 percent of pregnant women in the United States currently receive prenatal care during the first trimester of pregnancy, this figure still leaves considerable room for improvement (National Center for Health Statistics, 2007) (Figure 3-3). A lack of prenatal care is often associated with an increased rate of preterm births, **low birth weight (LBW)** infants, fetal death, and disabilities (Figure 3-4). Poverty can limit a mother's access to medical care as well as her understanding about its importance (Park, Vincent, & Hastings-Tolsma, 2007). Language barriers, differences in cultural beliefs, being a teen mother, and ethnicity have also been identified as restricting factors (Johnson et al., 2007; Tough, Siever, & Johnston, 2007). Consequently, continued efforts must be made to improve mothers' awareness of government-sponsored nutrition programs such as the national WIC program (Supplemental Food for Women, Infants & Children), low-cost medical insurance, and community-sponsored health clinics.

NUTRITION

A mother's nutritional status, determined by what she eats before and during pregnancy, has a significant effect on her own health as well as on that of the developing

Figure 3-3

Percentage of mothers' receiving prenatal care.

(*Source:* Centers for Disease Control and Prevention, National Center for Health Statistics, National Vital Statistics System).

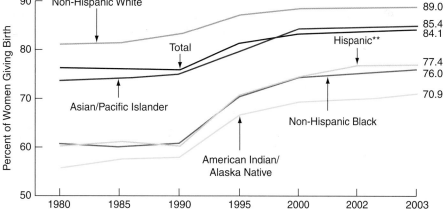

*2003 data are preliminary.
**May be of any race.

low birth weight (LBW)—an infant who weighs less than 5.5 pounds (2500 grams) at birth, regardless of age.

Figure 3-4

Percent of low birth weight infants in the United States by mother's age.

(*Source:* National Vital Statistics Reports, Vol. 56, No. 6, December 5, 2007).

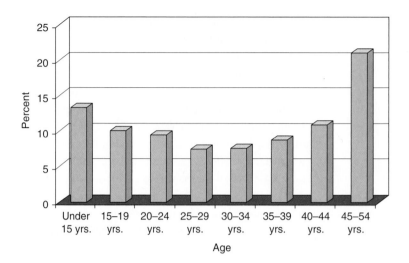

fetus. Consuming a healthy diet lessens the risk of having a low birth weight or **premature infant**, two conditions often associated with serious developmental problems (Ricciotti, 2008).

It is important for pregnant women to continue to follow the Food Guide Pyramid recommendations to ensure an adequate intake of essential nutrients and calories (*www.mypyramid.gov*) (Figure 3-5). Pregnancy increases a woman's dietary need for calories (energy); proteins, fluids; and certain vitamins such as folacin (folic acid), B_6, B_{12}, C, and D; and minerals such as iron and calcium. Breast-feeding further increases a mother's need for these nutrients as well as for calories. Studies have established a critical link between folic acid intake (taken before and during pregnancy: 400 micrograms daily for nonpregnant women, 600 micrograms daily for pregnant women) and the reduced incidence of neural tube defects (i.e., **spina bifida**, **anencephaly**), and **cleft lip/cleft palate** deformities (Pitkin, 2007; Badovinac et al., 2006). Folic acid is a B vitamin found in many foods, especially raw leafy green vegetables, dried beans, lentils, orange juice, and fortified whole grain products such as pastas, breads, and breakfast cereals.

Although vitamin supplements are generally prescribed, they must not be considered a substitute for a nutritious diet. They lack the essential proteins, calories, and other important nutrients found in most foods that are required for healthy fetal development and that aid the body in using the vitamins and minerals taken in tablet form. Herbal preparations are usually not recommended due to a lack of sufficient information about their safety during pregnancy (Dugoua et al., 2008a; Dugoua et al., 2008b).

premature infant—an infant born before 37 weeks following conception.

spina bifida—a birth defect caused by a malformation of the baby's spinal column.

anencephaly—a birth defect resulting in malformation of the skull and brain; portions of these structures might be missing at birth.

cleft lip/cleft palate—incomplete closure of the lip, palate (roof of the mouth), or both, resulting in a disfiguring deformity.

Figure 3-5

The interactive Food Guide Pyramid allows you to track nutrient intake and physical activity.

Several groups, including the U.S. Environmental Protection Agency (EPA), have advised women contemplating pregnancy, pregnant women, nursing mothers, and young children to limit their intake of certain fish and seafood due to potential mercury and pesticide contamination (University of Wisconsin-Madison, 2007; Xue et al., 2007; EPA, 2004). However, because fish are low in calories and a good source of high-quality protein and essential fats, researchers suggest that the benefits of including them in one's diet can outweigh the potential risks. Thus, women and young children are encouraged not to consume more than 12 ounces of seafood such as shrimp, salmon, pollock, catfish, and canned light tuna (not albacore tuna which has a higher mercury content) per week. Fish such as shark, swordfish, tilefish, and mackerel should be avoided. Consumers are also encouraged to check with authorities before eating fish that are caught in local rivers and lakes to determine whether mercury contamination is a concern. Additional information about mercury and seafood is available at *www.epa.gov/waterscience/fish/advisory.html*.

WEIGHT

What is the optimum weight gain during pregnancy? Most medical practitioners agree that a woman of normal weight should ideally gain between 25 and 30 pounds (10–11.4 kg) over the 9-month period (American College of Obstetricians & Gynecologists, 2008). Gains considerably under or over this range can pose increased risks for both the mother and child during pregnancy and at birth.

Following a diet that is nutritionally adequate helps ensure optimum weight gain. Including the recommended servings of a wide variety of fruits and vegetables also ensures that vitamins critical for fetal growth (vitamins A and C) and fiber to decrease constipation are supplied. Choosing low-fat dairy products and lean meats and plant proteins (e.g., dried beans, legumes, whole grains) is helpful for moderating caloric intake while providing key minerals (e.g., iron and calcium) required for the infant's and mother's health. Consuming too many empty calories, such as those found in junk foods, sweets, and alcohol, can lead to excessive weight gain and deprive both mother and fetus of critical nutrients found in a well-balanced diet.

REST AND STRESS

Pregnancy places added strain on the mother's body and often increases her sense of fatigue. Adequate nighttime sleep and occasional daytime rest periods often help ease these problems. Pregnancy can also induce or increase emotional stress. Prolonged or excessive stress can adversely affect the mother's health, contributing to sleep and eating disorders, high blood pressure, depression, headaches, lowered resistance to infections, and backaches (Black, 2007; Borders et al., 2007). It can also have harmful effects on the fetus by reducing weight, breathing rate, heartbeat, and activity level. Although it might not be possible for a pregnant woman to avoid all stress, strain, and fatigue, the ill effects can be lessened with proper rest, nutrition, and exercise.

AGE AND GENERAL HEALTH

A woman's age at the time of conception is an important factor in fetal development. Numerous studies conclude that the early twenties to early thirties are the optimum years for childbearing (Cleary-Goldman et al., 2005). Teenage mothers experience a rate of premature births, low birth weight babies, infant deaths, and babies born with developmental disabilities that is nearly double that for all mothers (Chen et al., 2007). These problems are often the result of inadequate prenatal care, poor nutrition and housing, substance abuse, or all three. In addition, the immaturity of a teen mother's reproductive system and her basic lack of knowledge about how best to care for her own personal needs often place these infants at increased risk.

Pregnancy in older women (late thirties and beyond) presents a different set of concerns (Caughey et al., 2007). Genetic material contained in the ova gradually deteriorates as a woman ages, thus increasing the probability of certain birth defects such as Down syndrome. It has been suggested that the quality of a male's sperm might also lessen with age and exposure to environmental hazards, thus increasing the risk of transmitting damaged chromosomes that can cause birth defects (Wyrobek et al., 2006). Older women also tend to experience a higher incidence of medical problems during pregnancy. However, greater awareness of healthful nutrition, exercise, and medical supervision can improve an older mother's chances of having a healthy baby (Figure 3-6).

Figure 3-6

Mother's age at the time of birth.

(*Source:* www.cdc. gov/nchs/data/nvsr/ nvsr56/nvsr56_06. pdf).

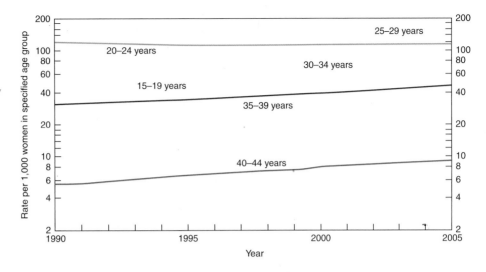

Increased knowledge and improved technology are also contributing to a reduction in fetal risk for mothers of all ages. Genetic counseling, ultrasound scanning (**sonogram**), **CVS** (chorionic villus sampling), **amniocentesis**, and new maternal blood tests enable medical personnel to monitor fetal growth closely and detect specific genetic disorders earlier. These procedures are especially beneficial for many women who are electing to delay childbearing until their late thirties and early forties (Luke & Brown, 2007).

Although the risks of pregnancy are undeniably greater for older women and teenagers, the problems often have as much to do with lack of knowledge and poverty as with age. (Exceptions are the chromosomal abnormalities such as Down syndrome.) Regardless of maternal age, a significant number of fetal problems are closely associated with a lack of medical care, poor nutrition, substandard housing, substance abuse, and limited education, all often closely associated with poverty. Allowing an interval of at least 24 months between pregnancies also improves the mother's health and ability to carry another pregnancy to full-term (Conde-Agudelo, Rosas-Bermudez, & Kafury-Goeta, 2007).

sonogram—visual image of the developing fetus, created by directing high-frequency sound waves.

CVS—chorionic villus sampling; a genetics-screening procedure in which a needle is inserted and cells removed from the outer layer of the placenta; performed between the eighth and twelfth weeks to detect some genetic disorders such as Down syndrome.

amniocentesis—genetics-screening procedure in which a needle is inserted through the mother's abdomen into the sac of fluids surrounding the fetus to detect abnormalities such as Down syndrome or spina bifida; usually performed between the twelfth and sixteenth weeks.

Clip 5

Prenatal Development: Several procedures can be used during pregnancy to detect some genetic abnormalities. Each test has its advantages and disadvantages and might present the family with a difficult decision if genetic conditions are detected.

Critical Thinking Questions:

1. How is a sonogram performed and for what purpose is it used?
2. What is an amniocentesis and what risks are associated with this procedure?
3. How common are genetic abnormalities?
4. For a period of time, business offered on-the-spot sonograms in local shopping malls. Do you think this is a good idea? Why or why not?

Threats to Optimum Fetal Development

Much is known about lifestyle practices that improve a mother's chances of having a healthy infant. However, there is also evidence to suggest that some environmental substances can have negative consequences on the unborn child (Lumeng et al., 2007). These factors are called **teratogens**. Some are especially damaging during the earliest weeks, often before a woman realizes that she is pregnant. It is during these sensitive or critical periods that various fetal structures and major organ systems are rapidly forming and, thus, are most vulnerable to the effects of any harmful substance. The length of these critical periods varies, for example, heart: third to sixth weeks, palate: sixth to eighth weeks. Extensive research has identified a number of major teratogens, including:

- Alcohol consumption.
- Maternal smoking.
- Addictive drugs (e.g., cocaine, heroin, amphetamines).
- Hazardous chemicals (e.g., mercury, lead, carbon monoxide, polychlorinated biphenols [PCBs]), paint solvents.
- Pesticides and insecticides.
- Some medications (Table 3-2).

teratogens—harmful agents that can cause fetal damage (e.g., malformations, neurological, behavioral problems) during the prenatal period.

- Maternal infections (Table 3-3).
- Radiation such as X rays.

Researchers continue to study other potential links between environmental factors and birth defects. To date, many findings are still considered to be inconclusive, controversial, or both (Browne et al., 2007). Some of the factors being investigated include:

- Prolonged exposure to high temperatures (hot baths, saunas, hot tubs).
- Secondary smoke.
- Some herbal supplements and over-the-counter medications.
- Electromagnetic fields such as those created by heating pads and electric blankets.
- Caffeine.
- Hazardous waste sites.

The relationship between teratogen exposure and fetal damage is not always clear or direct. Several factors can influence a teratogen's harmful effect on fetal development, including the amount of exposure (dose), fetal age (timing), and genetic makeup of the mother and fetus. Thus, women who are contemplating pregnancy should avoid unnecessary contact with known teratogens because many of these substances are capable of crossing the placental barrier. As noted earlier, fetal organs and body systems are especially vulnerable to such agents during the early weeks following conception. This is not to suggest that there is ever a completely safe period. Even during the later months, fetal growth can be seriously affected by maternal exposure to or use of substances mentioned here and in the following sections. There is also new evidence suggesting that teratogens can influence an individual's health throughout his or her lifetime (Lumeng et al., 2007; Penner & Brown, 2007).

ALCOHOL

Alcohol consumption during pregnancy can have serious consequences for both the mother and the developing fetus (Streissguth, 2007). Warnings to this effect now appear on the labels of all alcoholic products. Mothers who consume alcohol during pregnancy have a greater risk of miscarriages, stillbirths, premature infants, and low birth weight infants. The incidence of fetal death is also significantly higher. Because alcoholic beverages contain only calories and no nutrients, drinking them on a regular or binge basis limits the mother's dietary intake of essential proteins, vitamins, and minerals necessary for her well-being and that of her infant.

Alcohol is also a potentially toxic teratogen that can have a wide range of irreversible effects on fetal development (Lawrence et al., 2008). Because mother and baby share a common circulatory system (through the placenta and umbilical cord), both are affected by any alcohol that is consumed. However, alcohol remains in the fetal circulatory system twice as long as in that of the mother. Alcohol is particularly damaging to the fetus during the critical first trimester of pregnancy when most body structures and organs, especially the brain, heart, and nervous system are being formed.

Prenatal exposure to alcohol can result in conditions commonly referred to as fetal alcohol spectrum disorders (FASDs). Heavy or binge drinking is associated with a preventable condition known as fetal alcohol syndrome (FAS), which causes mental and growth retardation, behavior and learning problems (hyperactivity), poor motor coordination, heart defects, characteristic facial deformities (eyes set wide apart, shortened eye lids, flattened nose), and speech impairments (Moore et al., 2007). Mothers who consume moderate amounts of alcohol during pregnancy can give birth to children with a milder form of this condition called fetal alcohol effect (FAE). These children often exhibit a range of learning and behavior disorders. When consumed later in the pregnancy, alcohol typically interferes with proper fetal growth.

Precisely how much alcohol might be damaging to an unborn child is difficult to determine. Most likely, the relationship between alcohol and fetal damage is more complex than it might initially appear. *Thus, no amount of alcohol is considered safe to consume during pregnancy* (Iveli et al., 2007; U.S. Department of Health & Human Services, 2005).

SMOKING

Fetal malformations and birth complications have also been linked to maternal smoking (Hindmarsh et al., 2007) (Figure 3-7). Thus, warnings to this effect have been issued by the U.S. Surgeon General and are printed on all tobacco products. Cigarette smoke contains substances, including nicotine, tars, and carbon monoxide, that cross the placental barrier and interfere with normal fetal development. Carbon monoxide reduces the amount of oxygen available to the fetus. This early oxygen deprivation seems to correlate with learning and behavior problems, especially as exposed children reach school age. Mothers who smoke during pregnancy are more likely to experience miscarriage, premature births, stillborn infants, and low birth weight infants. Their babies are also at higher risk for developing sudden infant death syndrome (SIDS) and a range of acute and chronic respiratory problems (e.g., allergies, asthma, colds). Some studies have also shown that attention deficit disorders are more common among children whose mothers smoked during their pregnancy (Schmitz et al., 2007).

Figure 3-7

Percentage of mothers who smoke during pregnancy.

(*Source:* National Vital Statistics Reports, Vol. 56, No. 6, December 5, 2007).

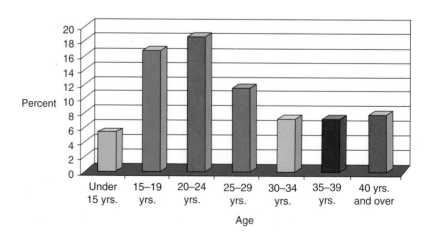

CHEMICALS AND DRUGS

Numerous chemicals and drugs are also known to have an adverse effect on the developing fetus. These substances range from prescription and nonprescription medications to pesticides, fertilizers, and street drugs (Chiriboga, Kuhn, & Wasserman, 2007; Weiss, St. John-Seed, & Harris-Muchell, 2007) (Table 3-2). Some cause severe malformations such as missing or malformed limbs or facial features. Others can lead to fetal death (spontaneous abortion), premature birth, or lifelong behavior and learning disabilities. Not all exposed fetuses will be affected in the same manner or to the same degree. The nature and severity of an infant's abnormalities seem to be influenced by the timing of exposure during fetal development, the amount and type of substance, the mother's general state of health, and maternal and fetal genetics. Research has not yet provided a definitive answer about which drugs and chemicals (if any) have absolutely no harmful effects on the developing fetus. Thus, women who are or might become pregnant are encouraged to check with their medical provider before using any chemical substance or medication (prescription or nonprescription). Exposure to previously discussed environmental hazards, such as high doses of radiation and X rays, particularly in the early stages of pregnancy, should also be limited.

MATERNAL INFECTIONS

Although the placenta effectively filters out many infectious organisms, it cannot prevent all disease-causing agents from reaching the unborn child. Some of these agents are known to cause fetal abnormalities (Table 3-3). Whether a fetus will be affected and, if

Table 3-2 Examples of Potentially Teratogenic Drugs

- analgesics (more than an occasional dose of aspirin or ibuprofen)
- antibiotics (particularly tetracyclines and streptomycin)
- anticonvulsants (such as Dilantin)
- anticoagulants (used to thin the blood, such as Coumadin)
- antidepressants
- antihistamines
- antihypertensives (used to treat high blood pressure)
- antineoplastic drugs (used to treat cancers and some forms of arthritis, such as Methotrexate)
- antiviral agents
- hormones (such as diethylstilbesterol [DES] and progesterin)
- large doses of vitamin A (in excess of 10,000 IU; includes some acne treatments such as Accutane and Retin-A)
- thyroid and antithyroid drugs
- diet pills
- nicotine
- cocaine, heroin, marijuana, methadone

Table 3-3 Examples of Potentially Teratogenic Maternal Conditions and Infections

- chickenpox
- cytomegalovirus (CMV)
- diabetes
- Fifth disease
- herpes
- HIV
- mumps
- Rubella (German measles)
- syphilis
- toxoplasmosis

Note: Information about any of these infectious illnesses can be found on the Centers for Disease Control's Web site at *www.cdc.gov*. Click *Health* and then click *Diseases*.

so, the resulting type of abnormality, depends on the particular illness and stage of pregnancy when the infection occurs. For example, a pregnant woman who develops rubella (German measles) during the first 4 to 8 weeks following conception is at high risk for giving birth to an infant who has heart problems or is deaf, blind, or both (an example of the extreme vulnerability of the fetus during its earliest weeks). *Note*: Rubella can be controlled if women who do not have natural immunity are immunized following a pregnancy or not less than 3 to 4 months prior to a pregnancy.

Fortunately, only a small percentage of babies exposed to infectious agents will experience abnormalities. It is still unknown why some babies are affected, whereas others are not. What is reasonably certain is that pregnant women who are well nourished, have good prenatal care, are generally healthy, and free of addictive substances have a higher probability of giving birth to a strong and healthy infant.

An Infant's Arrival: Labor and Delivery

For most women, childbirth is a natural process that follows months of anticipation and preparation. Several birthing options are available to families today, including birthing centers, hospitals, and home deliveries with physicians or certified nurse midwives in attendance. Although the fundamental labor and delivery process is similar for most mothers-to-be, the actual experience is often unique. Labor and delivery can occur prematurely, on time, or beyond one's expected due date, be long or short in duration, be considered relatively easy or difficult, and occur with or without complications.

The onset of labor is usually signaled by a number of changes. Approximately 2 weeks before labor begins, the mother might observe that she is carrying the baby lower in her abdomen. This occurs as the baby's head drops into the birth canal in preparation for delivery and is commonly referred to as *lightening*. The mother might also notice that her contractions are becoming stronger and more regular as they prepare the birth canal for delivery. When active labor begins, she might experience a small amount of bloody discharge as the plug of mucus that has protected the opening of the birth canal for 9 months becomes dislodged. Some mothers also have a leaking of amniotic fluid if the sac surrounding the fetus tears or breaks.

The normal birthing process is divided into three stages. The first and longest stage lasts approximately 14 to 17 hours for first-time mothers and 6 to 8 hours for subsequent births. During this stage, contractions slowly cause the diameter of the **cervix** to expand (dilate) in preparation for delivery. Stage two begins when the cervix is completely dilated and lasts until the baby is delivered, a period of approximately $\frac{1}{2}$ to $1\frac{1}{2}$ hours. Contractions become more intense and painful throughout this stage. When the baby is born, the umbilical cord is clamped, and the infant now functions independently. The third and final stage begins after the baby is born and ends when the placenta is delivered; this stage usually lasts only a few minutes.

The majority of births proceed normally and without complications. However, a small percentage of deliveries might require some form of medical intervention. In less than 5 percent of live births, the baby decides to descend feet first or bottom first (rather than head first) into the birth canal. This situation usually requires a **cesarean section** (C-section) to be performed (Robilio et al., 2007). A C-section can also be necessary when labor does not progress, the mother's birth canal is too small, the umbilical cord prolapses, or a medical problem such as fetal distress develops. Medical intervention might also be used to assist the baby out of the birth canal. Forceps (a salad tong–like device) are placed around the baby's head and used to pull the baby out gently during contractions. Temporary bruises can be left on the baby's face or head, but these will fade within several days. Vacuum-assisted births are replacing the use of forceps in many hospitals today. A large, plastic or rubber cap is fitted on the baby's head and suction is applied, creating a gentle traction to aid the baby in exiting the birth canal.

Throughout the birth process, the infant is monitored closely for signs of distress. Heart rate is checked by using a stethoscope or ultrasound device (Doppler) or by placing a tiny electrode on the baby's head. The newborn's condition is assessed at 1 minute and 5 minutes, using the Apgar scale (Figure 3-8). The infant receives a score between 0 and 2 in each of five areas: appearance, pulse, grimace, activity, and respirations; a score of eight or better is considered normal (Apgar, 1953). The Apgar scale provides a reliable measure of how well the infant is doing at the time but is not a predictor of future health problems.

Healthy mothers and babies are typically released from the hospital within 24 to 48 hours after the birth. Mothers who have had a C-section or health complications will usually remain in the hospital for several days longer. Infants born prematurely or of low birth weight will be hospitalized until they are healthy enough to go home.

Cultural differences can influence how a mother and her family perceive pregnancy and a child's birth (Karasz, Dempsey, & Fallek, 2007). Some groups view pregnancy and delivery as normal events that require little special attention or recognition. Others consider a child's birth an experience to be shared by extended family members

---

cervix—the lower portion of the uterus that opens into the vagina.

cesarean section—the delivery of a baby through an incision in the mother's abdomen and uterus.

Figure 3-8

Apgar scale for evaluating newborns.

Source: Adapted from V. Apgar, (1953).

	0	1	2
Appearance (skin color)	Bluish or pale	Pink, except extremities	Pink all over
Pulse	None	Fewer than 100 beats/minute	Greater than 100 beats/minute
Grimace (reflex response)	None	Makes some facial response.	Strong response: cries, coughs, or sneezes
Activity (muscle tone)	Limp	Weak flexion of extremities	Active movement
Respiration (breathing)	None	Slow and/or irregular	Regular; strong cry

VIDEO CONNECTIONS

Clip 6

Newborn Assessment: For nine months, the newborn has relied on its mother for all essential needs—nutrients, oxygen, warmth, and so on. At birth, he or she arrives into an unfamiliar world and must immediately take over many of these functions. Careful monitoring of the newborn's vital signs (heart rate, breathing) provides valuable information about how well he or she is making this transition.

Critical Thinking Questions:

1. How would you describe the newborn's appearance immediately following birth?
2. What is the Apgar scale and how is the test administered?
3. What information does the Apgar provide?
4. What does a low score indicate?

(Savage et al., 2007). Myths and ideas about everything from the mother's diet to how she responds to physical discomforts, sexuality, and daily living routines are also unique to various cultural groups. Although these views can differ from your own, it is important to show respect and support for the family's beliefs and values.

Maternal Depression

New mothers often undergo a range of mixed emotions following a baby's birth. Feelings of exhilaration, uncertainty, anxiety, and overwhelming fatigue might come and go at a moment's notice. A majority of new mothers experience these mood swings, commonly referred to as the *baby blues* (Figure 3-9), several days following delivery. Symptoms can include weepiness, sadness, anxiety, difficulty sleeping, lack of energy, appetite loss, irritability, or any or all of these (Wong et al., 2006). A combination of hormonal changes, lack of sleep, and added responsibilities are thought to trigger these feelings, which typically disappear within two weeks. Compassionate support from family members and friends, moderate exercise, adequate rest and a healthy diet can help ease this temporary discomfort. However, a doctor should be consulted if symptoms are severe or continue because this could be a sign of postpartum depression.

Fewer than 10 to 12 percent of new mothers will experience signs of postpartum depression (Dietz et al., 2007). The illness typically develops within 6 months of delivery and causes symptoms that are similar to the baby blues. However, postpartum depression often persists from several months to as long as 1 year and can include symptoms that are more serious, such as hallucinations, thoughts of causing harm to the baby, hopelessness, or suicide. These feelings can interfere with the quality of emotional attachment established between mother and baby (Taylor et al., 2005). Mothers who have a prior history of nonpregnancy-related depression tend to experience a higher rate of postpartum depression. Treatment can include antidepressant medication, counseling, supportive relationships, and attention to good health practices (e.g., diet, exercise, sleep, setting aside personal time).

Figure 3-9

Estimated incidence of maternal depression.

Source: U.S. Department of Health and Human Services, Health Resources and Services Administration, *Women's Health USA 2005*. Rockville, MD: U.S. Department of Health and Human Services, 2005.

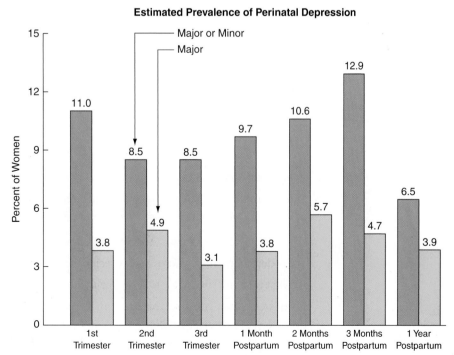

S U M M A R Y

A human pregnancy requires approximately 266 days (nine months) from conception until a baby is fully developed. The mother's general health, age, quality of diet, emotional state, and physical fitness influence healthy fetal development. Exposure to environmental factors (teratogens) such as certain infectious illnesses, alcohol, addictive drugs, smoking, and some medications (prescription and over-the-counter) can have a harmful effect. Mothers can take steps to improve their chances of having a healthy pregnancy and infant by obtaining routine prenatal care, maintaining good health, following a nutritious diet, gaining an appropriate amount of weight (not too much or too little), participating in routine exercise, and maintaining a positive state of mental health.

Most mothers experience a normal labor and delivery, although a C-section might be performed if complications develop. Babies who are born prematurely or at a low birth weight will remain in the hospital until they are healthy and have gained sufficient weight. Baby blues are fairly common among new mothers. Only a small percentage of mothers will experience serious signs of depression that require medical treatment.

KEY TERMS

amniocentesis
anencephaly
cervix
cesarean section
cleft lip/cleft palate
conception
CVS
embryo
genes

implantation
low birth weight (LBW)
placenta
premature infant
sonogram
spina bifida
temperament
teratogens
zygote

APPLY WHAT YOU KNOW

A. Apply What You Have Learned

Reread the brief developmental sketch about Anna and Miguel at the beginning of the chapter. How might you answer the following questions?

1. Which stage of pregnancy is Anna currently experiencing?

2. What developmental features are characteristic of a fetus at three months?

3. At what point is Anna likely to begin feeling the baby move?

4. If you were Anna's doctor, what recommendations would you make for improving her chances of having a healthy baby?

5. What practices should Anna avoid during pregnancy to improve her chances of having a healthy baby?

6. What negative effects might Anna's smoking have on her pregnancy?

7. Which nutrients are especially important for Anna to include in her daily diet?

B. Review Questions

1. Discuss three practices that promote a healthy pregnancy.

2. Describe three factors that appear to be hazardous to fetal development.

3. Identify one characteristic of fetal development that occurs during each month of development.

4. What role(s) does the placenta perform during pregnancy?

5. What characteristics would you expect to observe in a child who has Fetal Alcohol Syndrome (FAS)? Explain how this condition can be prevented.

HELPFUL WEBSITES

Visit the book companion website at *www.cengage.com/education/allen* for links to these websites and additional resources.

REFERENCES

American College of Obstetricians & Gynecologists. (2008). Nutrition during pregnancy. Accessed on April 10, 2008, from *http://www.acog.org/publications/patient_education/bp001.cfm*.

Apgar, V. (1953). Proposal for a new method of evaluation of the newborn infant. *Current Researches in Anesthesia & Analgesia, 32*(4), 260–267.

Badovinac, R., Werler, M., Williams, P., Kelsey, K., & Hayes, C. (2006). Folic acid-containing supplement consumption during pregnancy and risk for oral clefts: A meta-analysis. *Birth Defects Research Part A: Clinical and Molecular Teratology, 79*(1), 8–15.

Black, K. (2007). Stress, symptoms, self-monitoring confidence, well-being, and social support in the progression of preeclampsia/gestational hypertension. *Journal of Obstetric, Gynecologic & Neonatal Nursing, 36*(5), 419–429.

Borders, A., Grobman, W., Amsden, L. & Holl, J. (2007). Chronic stress and low birth weight neonates in a low-income population of women. *Obstetrics & Gynecology, 109*(2), 331–338.

Browne, M., Bell, E., Druschel, C., Gensburg, L., Mitchell, A., Lin, A., Romitti, P., & Correa, A. (2007). Maternal caffeine consumption and risk of cardiovascular malformations. *Birth Defects Research, Part A: Clinical & Molecular Teratology, 79*(7), 533–543.

Caughey, A., Stotland, M., Washington, E., & Escobar, G. (2007). Maternal and obstetric complications of pregnancy are associated with increasing gestational age at term. *American Journal of Obstetrics & Gynecology, 196*(2), 155.e1–155.e6.

Chen, X., Wen, S., Fleming, N., Demissie, K., Rhoads, G., & Walker, M. (2007). Teenage pregnancy and adverse birth outcomes: A large population based retrospective cohort study. *International Journal of Epidemiology, 36*(2), 368–373.

Chiriboga, C., Kuhn, L., & Wasserman, G. (2007). Prenatal cocaine exposures and dose-related cocaine effects on infant tone and behavior. *Toxicology and Teratology. 29*(3), 323–330.

Cleary-Goldman, J., Malone, F., Vidaver, J., Ball, R., Nyberg, D., Comstock, C., Saade, G., Eddleman, K., Klugman, S., Dugoff, L., Timor-Tritsch, I., Craigo, S., Carr, S., Wolfe, H., Bianchi, D., & D'Alton, M. (2005). Impact of maternal age on obstetric outcome. *Obstetrics & Gynecology, 105*(5), 983–990.

Conde-Agudelo, A., Rosas-Bermudez, A., & Kafury-Goeta, A. (2007). Effects of birth spacing on maternal health: A systematic review. *American Journal of Obestetrics & Gynecology, 196*(4), 297–308.

Cramer, M., Chen, L., Roberts, S., & Clute, D. (2007). Evaluating the social and economic impact of community-based prenatal care. *Public Health Nursing, 24*(4), 329–336.

Dietz, P., Williams, S., Callaghan, W., Bachman, D., Whitlock, E., & Hornbrook, M. (2007). Clinically identified maternal depression before, during, and after pregnancies ending in live births. *American Journal of Psychiatry, 164*(10), 1515–1520.

Dugoua, J., Perri, D., Seely, D., Mills, E., & Koren, G. (2008a). Safety and efficacy of blue cohosh (Caulophyllum thalictroides) during pregnancy and lactation. *Canadian Journal of Clinical Pharmacology, 15*(1), e66–73.

Dugoua, J., Seely, D., Perri, D., Koren, G., & Mills, E. (2008b). Safety and efficacy of chastree (Vitex agnuscastus) during pregnancy and lactation. *Canadian Journal of Clinical Pharmacology, 15*(1), e74–79.

Environmental Protection Agency (EPA). (2004). *What you need to know about mercury in fish and shellfish.* Retrieved on November 30, 2007, from *http://www.cfsan.fda.gov/~dms/admehg3.html.*

Henderson, H., & Wachs, T. (2007). Temperament theory and the study of cognition-emotion interactions across development. *Developmental Review, 27*(3), 396–427.

Hindmarsh, P., Geary, M., Rodeck, C., Kingdom, J., & Cole, T. (2007). Factors predicting ante- and postnatal growth. *Pediatric Research, 63*(1), 99–102.

Iveli, M., Morles, S., Rebolledo, A., Savietto, V., Salemme, S., Apeztegula, M., Cecotti, N., Drut, R., & Milesi, V. (2007). Effects of light ethanol consumption during pregnancy: Increased frequency of minor anomalies in the newborn and altered contractility of umbilical cord artery. *Pediatric Research, 61*(4), 456–461.

Johnson, A., Hatcher, B., El-Khorazaty, M., Milligan, R., Bhaskar, B., Rodan, M., Richards, L., Wingrove, B., & Laryea, H. (2007). Determinants of inadequate prenatal care utilization by African American women. *Journal of Health Care for the Poor & Underserved, 18*(3), 620–636.

Karasz, A., Dempsey, K., & Fallek, R. (2007). Cultural differences in the experience of everyday symptoms: A comparative study of South Asian and European American women. *Culture, Medicine & Psychiatry, 31*(4), 473–497.

Lawrence, C., Bonner, H., Newsom, R., & Kelly, S. (2008). Effects of alcohol exposure during development on play behavior and c-Fos expression in response to play behavior. *Behavior & Brain Research, 188*(1), 209–218.

Lu, M., Kotelchuck, M., Culhane, J., Hobel, C., Klerman, L., & Thorp, J. (2006). Preconception care between pregnancies: The content of internatal care. *Maternal & Child Health, 10* (5 Suppl), S107–122.

Luke, B., & Brown, M. (2007). Elevated risks of pregnancy complications and adverse outcomes with increasing maternal age. *Human Reproduction, 22*(5), 1264–1272.

Lumeng, J., Cabral, H., Gannon, K., Heeren, T., & Frank, D. (2007). Pre-natal exposures to cocaine and alcohol and physical growth patterns to age 8 years. *Neurotoxicology & Teratology, 29*(4), 446–457.

Macarthur, A., McBride, M., Spinelli, J., Tamaro, S., Gallagher, R., & Theriault, G. (2008). Risk of childhood leukemia associated with parental smoking and alcohol consumption prior to conception and during pregnancy: The cross-Canada childhood leukemia study. *Cancer Causes & Control, 19*(3), 283–295.

Martin, L., McNamara, M., Milot, A., Halle, T., & Hair, E. (2007). The effects of father involvement during pregnancy on receipt of prenatal care and maternal smoking. *Maternal & Child Health Journal, 11*(6), 595–602.

Moore, E., Ward, R., Wetherill, L., Rogers, J., Autti-Rämö, I., Fagerlund, A., Jacobson, S., Robinson, L., Hoyme, H., Mattson, S., & Foroud, T. (2007). Unique facial features distinguish fetal alcohol syndrome patients and controls in diverse ethnic populations. *Alcoholism, Clinical & Experimental Research, 31*(10), 1707–1013.

National Center for Health Statistics. (2007). *Prenatal care–2004.* Accessed on November 29, 2007, from *http://www.cdc.gov/nchs/fastats/prenatal.htm.*

Park, J., Vincent, D., & Hastings-Tolsma, M. (2007). Disparity in prenatal care among women of colour in the USA. *Midwifery, 23*(1), 28–37.

Penner, J., & Brown, A. (2007). Prenatal infectious and nutritional factors and risk of adult schizophrenia. *Expert Review of Neurotherapeutics, 7*(7), 797–805.

Pitkin, R. (2007). Folate and neural tube defects. *American Journal of Clinical Nutrition, 85*(1), 285S–288S.

Ricciotti, H. (2008). State of the art reviews: Nutrition and lifestyle for a healthy pregnancy. *American Journal of Lifestyle Medicine, 2*(2), 151–158.

Robilio, P., Boe, N., Danielsen, B., & Gilbert, W. (2007). Vaginal vs. cesarean delivery for preterm breech presentation of singleton infants in California: A population-based study. *Journal of Reproductive Medicine, 52*(6), 473–479.

Savage, C., Anthony, J., Lee, R., Kappesser, M., & Rose, B. (2007). The culture of pregnancy and infant care in African American women: An ethnographic study. *Journal of Transcultural Nursing, 18*(3), 215–223.

Schmitz, M., Denardin, D., Laufer, S., Pianca, T., Hutz, M., Faraone, S., & Rohde, L. (2007). Smoking during pregnancy and attention-deficit/hyperactivity disorder, predominantly inattentive type: A case-control study. *Journal of the American Academy of Child & Adolescent Psychiatry, 45*(11), 1338–1345.

Streissguth, A. (2007). Offspring effects of prenatal alcohol exposure from birth to 25 years: The Seattle Prospective Longitudinal Study. *Journal of Clinical Psychology in Medical Settings, 14*(2), 81–101.

Taylor, A., Atkins, R., Kumar, R., Adams, D., & Glover, V. (2005). A new mother-to-infant bonding scale: Links with early maternal mood. *Archives of Women's Mental Health, 8*(1), 45–51.

Tough, S., Siever, J., & Johnston, D. (2007). Retaining women in a prenatal randomized control trial in Canada: Implications for program planning. *BMC Public Health, 7*(147), 148–159.

University of Wisconsin-Madison. (March 12, 2007). Mercury contamination of fish warrants worldwide public warning. *ScienceDaily.* Accessed November 30, 2007, from *http://www.sciencedaily.com/releases/2007/03/070308084514.htm.*

U.S. Department of Health & Human Services (HHS). (2005). U.S. Surgeon General releases advisory on alcohol use in pregnancy. Accessed on April 10, 2008, from *http://www.surgeongeneral.gov/pressreleases/sg02222005.html.*

Weiss, S., St. John-Seed, M., & Harris-Muchell, C. (2007). The contribution of fetal drug exposure to temperament: Potential teratogenic effects on neuropsychiatric risk. *Journal of Child Psychology and Psychiatry, 48*(8), 773–784.

Wong, D., Perry, S., Hockenberry, M., Leonard, D., & Lowdermilk, D. (2006). *Maternal child nursing care* (3rd ed.). New York: C.V. Mosby.

Wyrobek, A., Eskenazi, B., Young, S., Arnheim, N., Tiemann-Boege, I., Jabs, E., Glaser, R., Pearson, F., & Evenson, D. (2006). Advancing age has differential effects on DNA damage, chromatin integrity, gene mutations, and aneuploidies in sperm. *Proceedings of the National Academies of Science of the United States of America*, 103(25), 9601–9606.

Xue, F., Holzman, C., Rahbar, M., Trosko, K., & Fischer, L. (2007). Maternal fish consumption, mercury levels, and risk of preterm delivery. *Environmental Health Perspectives*, 115(1), 42–47.

BOOK COMPANION WEBSITE

The book-specific website at *www.cengage.com/education/allen* offers students a variety of study tools and useful resources such as chapter overviews and notes, tutorial quizzes, web links, frequently asked questions, discussion questions, glossary/flashcards, internet exercises, references and more. To register or purchase access to the premium resources for this text including video clips tied to chapter content, go to *www.cengage.com/login*.

Infancy: Birth to Twelve Months

Objectives

After reading this chapter, you should be able to:

- Compare and contrast the physical characteristics of a typical four-month-old with those of a ten-month-old infant.

- Define the term *reflexive motor activity* and provide at least four examples.

- Explain why a four-week-old baby appears to walk when held in a standing position.

- React to the statement that "babies can't learn."

- Discuss ways in which babies communicate with adults.

- Describe five activities that would promote a four-week-old infant's cognitive development.

- Explain the phenomenon known as "stranger anxiety."

MEET JUAN

Anna and Miguel beamed as they watched their infant son Juan sleep. Anna is thankful that her pregnancy went smoothly and that Juan is healthy despite being born almost two weeks early. Their family and friends often tell them what a "good baby" Juan seems to be. He sleeps 3–4 hours between feedings, follows their every movement, is discovering his fingers and toes, and often falls asleep peacefully in his father's arms.

Juan's parents cannot believe their son will already be two months old next week. When placed on his stomach, he tries to pick up his head to study the brightly colored geometric pictures his mother has fastened to the sides of the crib. He is also beginning to reach and grasp the small stuffed toys his parents offer to him. Anna is fascinated by how much Juan seems to be learning each day. Their pediatrician is also pleased with Juan's rate of growth and development.

Anna's maternity leave will soon end. She finds it difficult to think about returning to her job at the bank and having to leave Juan. However, she finds some comfort in the fact that Miguel's mother, having raised four children of her own, has offered to care for Juan until they are able to locate space in a nearby child care center. Juan's parents have visited several neighborhood programs and placed his name on waiting lists, but none have openings for an infant at this time.

The Newborn (Birth to One Month)

The healthy newborn infant is truly amazing. Within moments of birth, he or she begins to adapt to an outside world that is radically different from the one experienced **in utero**. All body systems are in place and ready to function at birth. The newborn's body immediately assumes responsibility for breathing, eating, elimination, and regulation of body temperature. However, these systems are still quite immature, thus making the newborn completely dependent on adults for survival.

Motor development (movement) is both reflexive and protective. There is no voluntary control of the body during the early weeks. Although newborn babies sleep most of the time, they do not lack awareness. They are sensitive to their environment and have unique methods of responding to it. Crying is their primary method for communicating needs and emotions. Perceptual and cognitive abilities are present, but they are primitive and relatively difficult to distinguish from one another during the initial weeks following birth (Aslin & Fiser, 2005).

DEVELOPMENTAL PROFILES AND GROWTH PATTERNS

Growth and Physical Characteristics

The newborn's physical characteristics are distinct from those of a slightly older infant. At birth, the skin often appears wrinkled. Within the first few days, it will dry out and might begin to peel in some areas. The skin color of all babies is relatively light but will gradually darken to a shade characteristic of their genetic background. The head frequently assumes an unusual shape as the result of the birth

---

in utero—Latin term for "in the mother's uterus."

process, but it begins to take on a relatively normal shape within the first week. Hair color and amount vary. Additional characteristics include the following:

- Weight at birth averages 6.5–9 pounds (3.0–4.1 kg); females weigh approximately 7 pounds (3.2 kg), and males weigh approximately 7.5 pounds (3.4 kg).
- Five to 7 percent of birth weight is lost in the days immediately following birth.
- Weight increases an average of 5–6 ounces (0.14–0.17 kg) per week during the first month.
- Length at birth ranges between 18 and 21 inches (45.7–53.3 cm).
- Respiration rate is approximately 30–50 breaths per minute; breathing can be somewhat irregular in rhythm and rate.
- Chest appears small and cylindrical; it is nearly the same size as the head.
- Normal body temperature ranges from 96°F–99°F (35.6°C–37.2°C).
- Body temperature is irregular during the first few weeks due to immature body systems and a thin fat layer beneath the skin.
- Skin is sensitive, especially on the hands and mouth.
- Head is large in relation to body and accounts for nearly 1/4 of the total body length.
- Head circumference averages 12.5–14.5 inches (31.7–36.8 cm) at birth (Figure 4-1).
- "Soft" spots (**fontanels**) are located on the top (anterior) and back (posterior) of the head (Figure 4-2).
- Tongue appears large in proportion to mouth.
- Cries without tears.
- Eyes are extremely sensitive to light.
- Sees outlines and shapes; unable to focus on distant objects.

Figure 4-1

Measurement of head circumference.

(continued)

---

fontanels—small openings (sometimes called "soft spots") in the infant's skull bones; covered with soft tissue. Eventually, they grow closed.

Birth to 1 month

Figure 4-2

Location of fontanels.

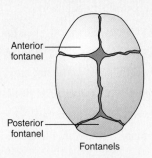

Anterior fontanel

Posterior fontanel

Fontanels

Motor Development

The newborn's motor skills are purely reflexive movements that are designed primarily for protection and survival. During the first month, the infant gains some control over several of these early reflexes. Gradually, many of these reflexes disappear as the infant's central nervous system matures and begins to take over control of purposeful behavior (Bartlett, 1997). The failure of reflexes to disappear according to schedule can be an early indicator of possible neurological problems (McPhillips & Jordan-Black, 2007; Herschkowitz, 2000). During the first month, the infant:

● Engages in motor activity that is primarily reflexive (Figure 4-3):

● Swallowing, sucking, gagging, coughing, yawning, blinking, and elimination reflexes are present at birth.

● Rooting reflex is triggered by gently touching the sensitive skin around the cheek and mouth; the infant turns toward the cheek being stroked.

Figure 4-3 Summary of reflexes.

Appears	swallow,* gag,* cough,* yawn,* blink suck rooting Moro (startle) grasp stepping plantar elimination tonic neck reflex (TNR)	Landau tear* (cries with tears)	parachute palmar grasp pincer grasp				
(Age)	(birth)	(1–4 mos)	(4–8 mos)	(8–12 mos)	(12–18 mos)	(18–24 mos)	(3–4 years)
Disappears		grasp suck (becomes voluntary) step root tonic neck reflex (TNR)	Moro (startle)	palmar grasp plantar reflex	Landau	parachute	elimination (becomes voluntary)

* Permanent; present throughout person's lifetime.

- Moro (startle) reflex is set off by a sudden loud noise or touch, such as bumping of the crib or quick lowering of the infant's position downward (as if dropping); both arms are thrown open and away from the body, then quickly brought back together over the chest.
- Grasping reflex occurs when the infant tightly curls its fingers around an object placed in its hand.
- Stepping reflex involves the infant moving the feet up and down in walking-like movements when held upright with feet touching a firm surface (Figure 4-4).
- Tonic neck reflex (TNR) occurs when the infant, in supine (face up) position, extends arm and leg on the same side toward which the head is turned; the opposite arm and leg are flexed (pulled in toward the body). This is sometimes called the "fencing position" (Figure 4-5).
- Plantar reflex is initiated when pressure is placed against the ball of the infant's foot, causing the toes to curl.

- Maintains "fetal" position (back flexed or rounded, extremities held close to the body, knees drawn up), especially when asleep.

- Holds hands in a fist; does not reach for objects.

- When held in a prone (face down) position, baby's head falls lower than the horizontal line of the body with hips flexed and arms and legs hanging down (Figure 4-6).

- Has good muscle tone in the upper body when supported under the arms.

- Turns head from side to side when placed in a prone position.

Figure 4-4

Stepping reflex.

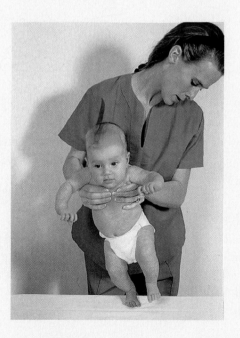

(continued)

Figure 4-5

Tonic neck reflex (TNR).

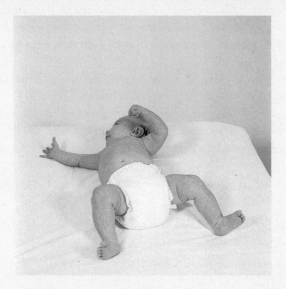

Figure 4-6

Prone suspension.

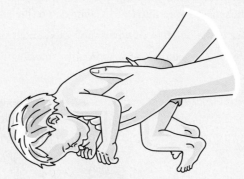

- **Pupils** dilate (enlarge) and constrict (become smaller) in response to light.
- Eyes do not always work together and may appear crossed at times.
- Attempts to track (follow) objects that are out of direct line of vision; unable to coordinate eye and hand movements.

Perceptual-Cognitive Development

The newborn's perceptual-cognitive skills are designed to capture and hold the attention of family and caregivers and to gain some sense of the environment. Hearing is the most well developed of the skills. Newborns can hear and respond to differences among certain sounds and are especially responsive to their mother's voice (Bergeson & Trehub, 2007). They often find sounds and movements, such as cooing,

---

pupil—the small, dark, central portion of the eye.

rocking, and jiggling, soothing. Newborns also are responsive to touch, with the skin around the mouth and hands being especially sensitive. Vision is present, although limited. However, newborns are especially attracted to highly contrasting (black-and-white) geometric designs. They are able to briefly focus both eyes on objects that are close and moving slowly (Simion, Regolin, & Bulf, 2008).

From the earliest days of life, newborns are absorbing information through all their senses, learning from what they see, hear, touch, taste, and smell. Thus, the newborn's cognitive behaviors can be characterized as purely reflexive. They take the form of sucking, startle responses, grimacing, flailing of arms and legs, and uncontrolled eye movements, all of which overlap with perceptual responses. During the first month, the infant:

- Blinks eyes in response to a fast-approaching object.
- Follows a slowly moving object through a complete 180-degree arc.
- Follows objects moved vertically if object is close to infant's face (10–15 inches [25.4–38.1 cm]).
- Continues looking about, even in the dark.
- Begins to study own hand when lying in TNR position.
- Hears as well (with the exception of quiet sounds) at birth as do most adults; hearing is more acute than vision.
- Prefers to listen to mother's voice rather than a stranger's; opens eyes and looks toward mother.
- Often synchronizes body movements to speech patterns of parent or caregiver.
- Distinguishes some tastes; shows preference for sweet liquids.
- Has a keen sense of smell present at birth; turns toward preferred (sweet) odors, away from strong or unpleasant odors (Pomeras, Schirrer, & Abadie, 2002).

Speech and Language Development

The beginnings of speech and language development can be identified in several of the newborn's reflexes. These include the bite-release action that occurs when the infant's gums are rubbed, the rooting reflex, and the sucking reflex. In addition, the new baby communicates directly and indirectly in a number of other ways.

- Crying and fussing are major forms of communication at this stage.
- Reacts to loud noises by blinking, moving, stopping a movement, shifting eyes about, or exhibiting a startle response.
- Shows a preference for certain sounds, such as music and human voices, by calming down or quieting.
- Turns head in an effort to locate voices and other sounds.
- Makes occasional sounds other than crying.

Social-Emotional Development

Newborns possess a variety of built-in social skills. They indicate needs and distress and respond to parents' or caregivers' reactions (Messinger & Fogel, 2007). The infant thrives

(continued)

*Birth to
1 month*

on feelings of security and soon displays a sense of attachment to primary caregivers. The newborn:

- Experiences a brief period of calm alertness immediately following birth; gazes at parents and listens to their voices.
- Sleeps 17 to 19 hours per day; is gradually awake and responsive for longer periods (Figure 4-7).
- Likes to be held close and cuddled when awake; opens eyes and looks toward mother.
- Shows qualities of individuality; each infant varies in ways of responding or not responding to similar situations.
- Begins to establish an emotional attachment, or a **bonding** relationship, with parents and caregivers; opens eyes; relaxes body tension.
- Develops a gradual sense of security or trust with parents and caregivers. Able to sense caregiver differences and responds accordingly. For example, an infant might become tense with an adult who is unfamiliar or uncomfortable with the infant.

Figure 4-7

Infants spend most of their time sleeping.

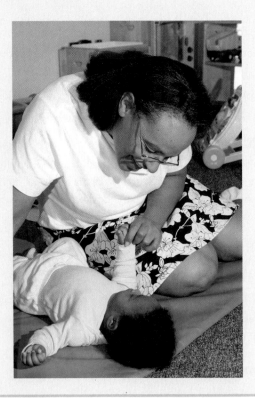

---

bonding—the establishment of a close, loving relationship between an infant and adult, usually the mother and father; sometimes called *attachment*.

VIDEO CONNECTIONS

Birth to
1 month

Clip 7

Reflex Development: Newborns are not capable of purposeful movement. However, this does not suggest that newborns are passive individuals. Reflexes serve important functions and gradually give way to rapid and increasingly complex motor development.

Critical Thinking Questions:

1. Which involuntary reflexes are considered to be critical for the infant's survival?
2. What does it indicate when one or more of the infant's reflexes are absent, do not fade at the correct time, or reappear later on?
3. What is meant by the term *involuntary*?
4. What effect does the status of an infant's reflex system have on cognitive development?

• DAILY ROUTINES •

Eating

- Takes six to ten feedings, totaling approximately 22 ounces (660 ml) per 24 hours at the beginning of this period; later, the number of feedings will decrease to five or six as the amount consumed increases.
- Drinks 2 to 4 ounces of breast milk or formula per feeding; takes 25 to 30 minutes to complete a feeding; may fall asleep toward the end.
- Expresses the need for food by crying.
- Benefits from being fed in an upright position; this practice reduces the risk of choking and of developing ear infections (Tully, 1998).

Toileting, Bathing, and Dressing

- Signals the need for a diaper change by crying. (If crying does not stop when diaper has been changed, another cause should be sought.)
- Enjoys bath; keeps eyes open, coos, and relaxes body tension when placed in warm water.
- Expresses displeasure when clothes are pulled over head (best to avoid over-the-head clothes).
- Prefers to be wrapped firmly (swaddled) in a blanket; coos, stops crying, and relaxes muscles; swaddling seems to foster a sense of security and comfort.
- Can have one to four bowel movements per day.

(continued)

• D A I L Y   R O U T I N E S • *(continued)*

Sleeping

- Begins to sleep four to six periods per 24 hours after the first few days following birth; one of these might be 5–7 hours in length.
- Cries sometimes before falling asleep (usually stops if held and rocked briefly).
- *Placing baby on his or her back only and on a firm mattress to sleep reduces the risk of sudden infant death syndrome (SIDS).* Also, remove all pillows, fluffy blankets and bumper pads, toys, and other soft items from crib or sleeping areas. Dress infant lightly to avoid overheating.

Play and Social Activities

- Prefers light and brightness; might fuss if turned away from the light.
- Stares at faces in close visual range (10–12 inches [25.4–30.5 cm]).
- Signals the need for social stimulation by crying; stops when picked up or put in infant seat close to voices and movement.
- Is content to lie on back much of the time.
- Needs to be forewarned (e.g., touched, talked to) before being picked up.
- Enjoys lots of touching and holding; however, can become fussy with over- stimulation.
- Enjoys en face (face-to-face) position (Farroni et al., 2005).

Learning Activities

Tips for families and teachers:

- Respond with gentle and dependable attention to baby's cries so he or she learns that help is always available. (Infants always cry for a reason; crying signals a need.)
- Make eye-to-eye contact when baby is in an alert state; make faces or stick out your tongue, activities that new babies often imitate. (Imitation is an important avenue for early learning.)
- Talk or sing to a baby in a normal voice during feeding, diapering, and bathing; vary voice tone and rhythm of speech.
- Show delight in baby's responsiveness: smile, laugh, comment. (Mutual responsiveness and social turn-taking are the bases for all teaching and learning in the months and years ahead.)

- Show baby simple pictures (young babies are attracted to black-and-white geometric designs and drawings of faces); gently move a stuffed animal or toy in baby's visual pathway approximately 10–15 inches (25–37.5 cm) from baby's face to encourage visual tracking; hang toys or mobile within baby's visual range (change often—novelty increases fascination).

- Take cues from baby; too much stimulation can be as distressing as too little attention; stop activities temporarily if baby begins to cry, becomes fussy, or loses interest.

Birth to 1 month

Developmental Alerts

Check with a health care provider or early-childhood specialist if, by one month of age, the infant *does not*:

- Show alarm or startle responses to loud noise.
- Suck and swallow with ease.
- Show gains in height, weight, and head circumference.
- Grasp with equal strength with both hands.
- Make eye-to-eye contact when awake and being held.
- Roll head from side to side when placed on stomach.
- Express needs and emotions with distinctive cries and patterns of vocalizations that can be distinguished from one another.
- Usually stop crying or become soothed (relaxed) when picked up and held.

Safety Concerns

Before the baby arrives, be sure to complete first aid and cardiopulmonary resuscitation (CPR) courses. Always be aware of new safety issues as the baby continues to grow and develop.

Burns

- Never heat baby bottles in a microwave oven; hot spots can form and burn the baby's mouth.
- Set temperature of hot water heater so that it is no higher than 120°F.
- Always check temperature of water before bathing baby.

(continued)

Safety Concerns *(continued)*

Choking

- Learn CPR.
- Always hold infant in an upright position while feeding; do not prop bottles.

Suffocation

- Provide a firm mattress that fits crib snugly to prevent infant from becoming wedged in open cracks.
- *Always put infants to sleep on their back;* this practice reduces the risk of sudden infant death syndrome (SIDS). Tuck bottom edges of a light blanket under bottom end of the mattress.
- Remove all soft items, such as fluffy blankets, bumper pads, stuffed animals, or pillows, from the baby's crib.
- Install smoke and carbon monoxide detectors near the baby's room.

Transportation

- Always use an approved, rear-facing carrier when transporting the baby in a vehicle; check for proper installation.

One to Four Months

During these early months, the wonders of infancy continue to unfold. Growth proceeds at a rapid pace. Body systems are fairly well stabilized, with temperature, breathing patterns, and heart rate becoming more regular. Motor skills improve as strength and voluntary muscle control increase. Longer periods of wakefulness encourage the infant's socioemotional development. Social responsiveness begins to appear as infants practice and enjoy using their eyes to explore the environment. As social awareness develops, the infant gradually establishes a sense of trust and emotional attachment to parents and caregivers (Hofer, 2006).

Although crying remains a primary way of communicating and of gaining adult attention, more complex communication skills are beginning to emerge. Infants soon find great pleasure in imitating the speech sounds and gestures of others (Dunham, Dunham, & Curwin, 1993). Cooing often begins around two months of age and represents an important step in the acquisition of language and give-and-take interaction with others.

Learning takes place continuously throughout the infant's waking hours as newly acquired skills are used for exploring and gathering information about a still new and unfamiliar environment. However, differences in cultural expectations and environmental conditions can influence the rate and acquisition of these skills. Critical brain development is fostered by providing the baby with numerous opportunities for learning (see Learning Activities). However, it is important to note once again that perceptual, cognitive, and motor development are closely interrelated and nearly impossible to differentiate during these early months.

DEVELOPMENTAL PROFILES AND GROWTH PATTERNS

1 to 4 months

Growth and Physical Characteristics

- Averages 20–27 inches (50.8–68.6 cm) in length; grows approximately one inch (2.54 cm) per month (measured with infant lying on back, from top of the head to bottom of heel, knees straight and foot flexed).
- Weighs an average of 8–16 pounds (3.6–7.3 kg); females weigh slightly less than males.
- Gains approximately 1/4–1/2 pound (0.11–0.22 kg) per week.
- Breathes at a rate of approximately 30–40 breaths per minute; rate increases significantly during periods of crying or activity.
- Normal body temperature ranges from 96.4°F–99.6°F (35.7°C–37.5°C).
- Head and chest circumference are nearly equal.
- Head circumference increases approximately 3/4 inch (1.9 cm) per month until two months, then increases 5/8 inch (1.6 cm) per month until four months. Increases are an important indication of continued brain growth.
- Continues to breathe using abdominal muscles.
- Posterior fontanel closes by the second month; anterior fontanel closes to approximately 1/2 inch (1.3 cm).
- Skin remains sensitive and easily irritated.
- Arms and legs are of equal length, size, and shape; easily flexed and extended.
- Legs may appear slightly bowed.
- Feet appear flat with no arch.
- Cries with tears.
- Begins moving eyes together in unison (binocular vision).
- Detects color (color vision is now present) (Mercuri et al., 2007).

Motor Development

- Reflexive motor behaviors are changing (Figure 4-3):
  - Tonic neck and stepping reflexes disappear.
  - Rooting and sucking reflexes are well developed.

(continued)

1 to 4 months

Figure 4-8

Landau reflex.

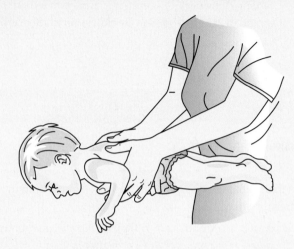

- Swallowing reflex and tongue movements are still immature; continues to drool; is not able to move food (other than milk) to the back of the mouth.
- Grasp reflex gradually disappears.
- Landau reflex appears near the middle of this period: when baby is held in a prone (face down) position, the head is held upright and legs are fully extended (Figure 4-8).

- Grabs onto objects using entire hand (palmar grasp); however, strength is insufficient to hold onto items at the beginning of this period.

- Holds hands in an open or semi-open position much of the time.

- Muscle tone and development are equal for boys and girls.

- Movements tend to be large and jerky, gradually becoming smoother and more purposeful as muscle strength and control improve.

- Raises head and upper body on arms when in a prone position (Figure 4-9).

Figure 4-9

Begins to raise up on arms.

- Turns head side to side when in a supine (face up) position; near the end of this period, can hold head up and in line with the body.

- Shows greater activity level in upper body parts: clasps hands above face, waves arms about, reaches for objects.

- Begins rolling from front to back by turning head to one side and allowing trunk to follow. Near the end of this period, infant can roll from front to back to side at will.

- Can be pulled to a sitting position, with considerable head lag and rounded back at the beginning of this period. Later, can be positioned to sit with minimal head support (Figure 4-10). By 4 months, most infants can sit with support, holding their head steady and keeping back fairly erect; enjoys sitting in an infant seat or being held on an adult's lap.

Perceptual-Cognitive Development

- Fixates on a moving object held at a distance of 12 inches (30.5 cm); smoother visual tracking of objects across 180-degree pathway, vertically and horizontally.

- Continues to gaze in direction of moving objects that have disappeared.

- Exhibits some sense of size, color, and shape recognition of objects in the immediate environment—for example, recognizes his or her own bottle even when bottle is turned about, thus presenting a different shape.

- Ignores (does not search for) a bottle that falls out of a crib or a toy hidden under a blanket: "out of sight, out of mind." (The infant has not yet developed what Piaget refers to as **object permanence**) (Piaget, 1954).

- Watches hands intently.

- Moves eyes from one object to another.

- Focuses on small object and reaches for it; usually follows own hand movements.

Figure 4-10

Can be pulled to a sitting position.

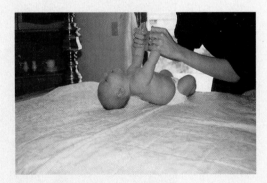

1 to 4 months

(continued)

---

object permanence—Piaget's sensorimotor stage when infants understand that an object exists even when it is not in sight.

- Alternates looking at an object, at one or both hands, and then back at the object.

- Imitates gestures that are modeled: bye-bye, patting head.

- Hits at object closest to right or left hand with some degree of accuracy.

- Looks in the direction of a sound source (sound localization).

- Connects sound and rhythms with movement by moving or jiggling in time to music, singing, or chanting.

- Distinguishes parent's face from stranger's face when other cues, such as voice, touch, or smell, are also available (Kelly et al., 2005).

- Attempts to keep toy in motion by repeating arm or leg movements that started the toy moving in the first place.

- Begins to mouth objects (Figure 4-11).

1 to 4 months

Speech and Language Development

- Reacts (stops whimpering, startles) to sounds, such as a voice, rattle, or doorbell. Later, will search for source by turning head and looking in the direction of sound.

- Coordinates vocalizing, looking, and body movements in face-to-face exchanges with parent or caregiver; can follow and lead in keeping communication going.

- Babbles or coos when spoken to or smiled at; even babies who are deaf will begin to babble (Koopmans-van Beinum, Clement, & Dikkenberg-Pot, 2001).

Figure 4-11

Begins mouthing objects.

- Coos, using single vowel sounds (*ah, eh, uh*); also imitates his or her own sounds and vowel sounds produced by others.
- Laughs out loud.

Social-Emotional Development

- Imitates, maintains, terminates, and avoids interactions—for example, infants can turn at will toward or away from a person or situation.
- Reacts differently to variations in adult voices; for example, might frown or appear anxious if voices are loud, angry, or unfamiliar.
- Enjoys being held and cuddled at times other than feeding and bedtime.
- Coos, gurgles, and squeals when awake.
- Smiles in response to a friendly face or voice; smiles occurring during sleep are thought to be reflexive (Messinger & Fogel, 2007).
- Entertains self for brief periods by playing with fingers, hands, and toes.
- Enjoys familiar routines such as being bathed and having diaper changed (Figure 4-12).
- Delights (squeals, laughs) in play that involves gentle tickling, laughing, and jiggling.
- Spends much less time crying.
- Recognizes and reaches out to familiar faces and objects, such as father or bottle; reacts by waving arms and squealing with excitement.
- Stops crying when parent or caregiver comes near.

1 to 4 months

Figure 4-12

Recognizes and responds to familiar routines.

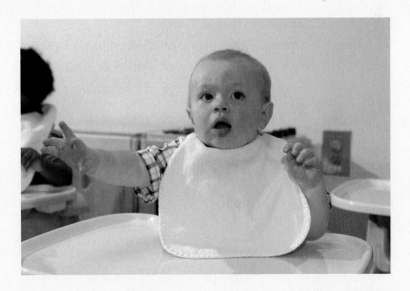

VIDEO CONNECTIONS

Clip 8

Language Development: Infants are equipped with the ability to communicate their needs from the moment of birth. Parents and caregivers must learn to distinguish subtle differences in an infant's cries and body language to determine what he or she is trying to express.

Critical Thinking Questions:

1. What is "motherese" and what purpose does it serve?
2. In what ways does the nonverbal infant communicate?
3. What clues does a one- to four-month-old infant give that suggests he or she has some receptive language ability?

• D A I L Y   R O U T I N E S •

Eating

- Takes five to eight feedings (5 to 6 ounces each) per day.
- Begins fussing before anticipated feeding times; does not always cry to signal the need to eat.
- Needs only a little assistance in getting nipple to mouth; may begin to help caregiver by using own hands to guide nipple.
- Sucks vigorously; might choke on occasion because of the vigor and enthusiasm of sucking.
- Becomes impatient if bottle or breast continues to be offered once hunger is satisfied.
- Requires only breast milk or formula to meet all nutrient needs; not ready to eat solid foods.

Toileting, Bathing, and Dressing

- Enjoys bath time on most occasions; kicks, laughs, and splashes.
- Has one or two bowel movements per day; might skip a day.
- Begins to establish a regular time or pattern for bowel movements.

Sleeping

- Falls asleep for the night soon after the evening feeding.
- Begins to sleep through the night; many babies do not sleep more than six hours at a stretch for several more months.
- Averages 14–17 hours of sleep per day; often awake for two or three periods during the daytime.

- Sometimes begins thumb sucking during this period.
- Begins to entertain self before falling asleep: "talks," plays with hands, jiggles crib.

Play and Social Activity

- Spends waking periods engaged in physical activity: kicking, turning head from side to side, clasping hands together, grasping objects.
- Vocalizes with delight; becomes more "talkative."
- Smiles and coos when being talked and sung to; might cry when the social interaction ends.
- Appears happy when awake and alone (for short periods of time).

1 to 4 months

Learning Activities

Tips for families and teachers:

- Imitate baby's vocalizations and faces (grunting, smacking, yawning, squinting, frowning). When baby begins to smile, smile back and sometimes remark, "You are smiling! Happy baby!"
- Sing songs and read to baby out of magazines, books, or whatever interests you; it is the sound of your voice and your closeness that matter.
- Play simplified peek-a-boo (hold cloth in front of your own face, drop it, and say "peek-a-boo"); repeat if baby shows interest.
- Gently stretch and bend baby's arms and legs while making up an accompanying song; later, start a gentle "bicycling" or arm-swaying activity.
- Touch baby's hand with a small toy* (soft rattles or other quiet noisemakers are especially good); encourage baby to grasp toy.
- Walk around with baby, touching and naming objects. Stand with baby in front of a mirror, touching and naming facial features: "Baby's mouth, Daddy's mouth. Baby's eye, Mommy's eye."
- Position an unbreakable mirror near the crib so baby can look and talk to himself or herself.
- Hang brightly colored or geometric pictures (black and white) or objects near baby's crib; change often to maintain baby's interest and attention.
- Fasten (*securely*) small bells to baby's booties; this helps baby localize sounds and learn at the same time that he or she has power and can make things happen simply by moving about.

  __Rule of Fist:__ Toys and other objects given to an infant should be no smaller than the baby's fist (1.5 inches; 3.8 cm) to prevent choking or swallowing.

Developmental Alerts

Check with a health care provider or early-childhood specialist if, by four months of age, the infant *does not*:

- Continue to show steady increases in height, weight, and head circumference.
- Smile in response to the smiles of others. (The social smile is a significant developmental milestone.)
- Gaze at and follow a moving object with eyes focusing together.
- Bring hands together over mid-chest.
- Turn head to locate sounds.
- Begin to raise head and upper body when placed on stomach.
- Reach for objects or familiar persons.

Safety Concerns

Continue to implement safety practices described for the previous stages. Always be aware of new safety issues as the baby continues to grow and develop.

Burns

- Do not bring hot beverages or appliances near baby.
- Check temperature of bottles (if warming formula or breast milk) before offering them to an infant.

Choking

- Check rattles and stuffed toys for small parts that could become loose. Purchase only toys larger than 1.5 inches (3.75 cm) in diameter.
- Remove all small items within baby's reach.

Falls

- Attend to baby at all times when on an elevated surface (e.g., changing table, sofa, counter, bed); baby might turn over or roll unexpectedly.
- Always place infant carriers on the floor (not on table or countertop).

Sharp Objects

- Keep pins and other sharp objects out of baby's reach.
- Check nursery furniture for sharp or protruding edges; always purchase furnishings and toys that comply with federal safety standards (see Helpful Websites).

Four to Eight Months

Between 4 and 8 months, infants are developing a wide range of skills and greater ability to use their bodies. Infants seem to be busy every waking moment, manipulating and mouthing toys and other objects. They "talk" all the time, making vowel and consonant sounds in ever greater variety and complexity (Sebastián-Gallés, 2007). They initiate social interactions and respond to all types of cues such as facial expressions, gestures, and the comings and goings of everyone in their world. Infants at this age are both self-occupied and sociable (Figure 4-13). They move easily from spontaneous, self-initiated activity to social activities initiated by others.

Figure 4-13

Is becoming more verbal and outgoing.

4 to 8 months

DEVELOPMENTAL PROFILES AND GROWTH PATTERNS

Growth and Physical Characteristics

- Gains approximately one pound (2.2 kg) per month in weight.
- Doubles original birth weight.
- Increases length by approximately 1/2 inch (1.3 cm) per month; average length is 27.5–29 inches (69.8–73.7 cm).
- Head and chest circumferences are nearly equal.
- Head circumference increases by an average of 3/8 inch (0.95 cm) per month until six to seven months of age; this rate then slows to approximately 3/16 inch (0.47 cm) per month. Head circumference should continue to increase steadily, indicating healthy, ongoing brain growth.
- Takes approximately 25–50 breaths per minute, depending on activity; rate and patterns vary from infant to infant; breathing is abdominal.

(continued)

- Begins to develop teeth, with upper and lower incisors coming in first.
- Gums can become red and swollen, accompanied by increased drooling, chewing, biting, and mouthing of objects.
- Legs often appear bowed; bowing gradually disappears as infant grows older.
- True eye color is established.

Motor Development

- Reflexive behaviors are changing (Figure 4-3).

  - Blinking reflex is well established.
  - Sucking reflex becomes voluntary.
  - Moro reflex disappears.
  - Parachute reflex appears toward the end of this stage: when held in a prone, horizontal position and lowered suddenly, infant throws out arms as a protective measure (Figure 4-14).
  - Swallowing reflex appears (a more complex form of swallowing that involves tongue movement against the roof of mouth); this allows the infant to move solid foods from front of mouth to the back for swallowing.

- Reaches for objects with both arms simultaneously; later reaches with one hand or the other.
- Transfers objects from one hand to the other; still grasps objects using entire hand (palmar grasp).
- Handles, shakes, and pounds objects; puts everything in mouth.
- Helps to hold onto own bottle during feedings.

4 to 8 months

Figure 4-14

Parachute reflex.

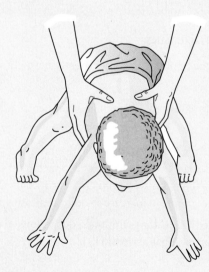

Figure 4-15

Sits alone with support.

- Sits alone without support, holding head erect, back straightened, and arms propped forward for support (Figure 4-15).
- Pulls self into a crawling position by rising up on arms and drawing knees up beneath the body; rocks back and forth but generally does not move forward.
- Rolls over from front to back and back to front.
- Begins scooting backward, sometimes accidentally, when placed on stomach; soon will learn to crawl forward.
- Enjoys being placed in standing position, especially on someone's lap; jumps in place.
- Begins to pick up objects using finger and thumb (pincer grip) near the end of this period (Figure 4-16).

Perceptual-Cognitive Development

- Turns toward and locates familiar voices and sounds; this behavior can be used for informal testing of an infant's hearing.
- Focuses eyes on small objects and reaches for them.
- Uses hand, mouth, and eyes in coordination to explore own body, toys, and surroundings.
- Imitates actions, such as pat-a-cake, waving bye-bye, and playing peek-a-boo.
- Shows evidence of **depth perception**; tenses, pulls back, and becomes fearful of falling from high places such as changing tables and stairs.

Figure 4-16

Pincer grip.

Pincer grip

(continued)

4 to 8 months

---

depth perception—ability to determine the relative distance of objects from the observer.

(continued) DEVELOPMENTAL PROFILES AND GROWTH PATTERNS

- Looks over side of crib or high chair for objects dropped; delights in repeatedly throwing objects overboard for adult to retrieve.

- Searches for toy or food that has been partially hidden under cloth or behind screen; beginning to understand that objects continue to exist even when they cannot be seen. (Piaget refers to this as object permanence.)

- Handles and explores objects in a variety of ways: visually, turning them around, feeling all surfaces, banging, and shaking.

- Picks up inverted object (for instance, recognizes a cup even when it is positioned differently).

- Ignores second toy or drops toy in one hand when presented with a new toy; unable to deal with more than one toy at a time.

- Reaches accurately with either hand.

- Plays actively with small toys such as rattle or block.

- Bangs objects together playfully; bangs spoon or toy on table.

- Continues to put everything into mouth.

- Establishes full attachment to mother or primary caregiver: seeks out and prefers to be held by this adult, which coincides with a growing understanding of object permanence.

4 to 8 months

VIDEO CONNECTIONS

Clip 9

Module 1: 0–2 years; Section 3: Infants and Toddlers, Cognitive and Language Development (Attachment)

Attachment: A special emotional bond is formed between parent and infant through a process of give-and-take interactions. A sense of trust and security develops as infants and their parents begin to synchronize their response patterns. Studies have shown that this attachment is essential for the infant's future emotional development.

Critical Thinking Questions:

1. What are some of the things parents do to foster the attachment process?
2. What is a reciprocal relationship and what purpose does it serve?
3. Why do infants develop "stranger anxiety?"
4. What can parents do to help infants get through this phase? What can teachers do to help the child and his or her family?

Speech and Language Development

- Responds appropriately to own name and simple requests such as "come," "eat," "wave bye-bye" (Figure 4-17).
- Imitates some nonspeech sounds such as cough, tongue click, and lip smacking.
- Produces a full range of vowels and some consonants: *r, s, z, th,* and *w.*
- Responds to variations in the tone of voice of others—anger, playfulness, sadness.
- Expresses emotions, such as pleasure, satisfaction, and anger, by making different sounds.
- "Talks" to toys.
- Babbles by repeating same syllable in a series: *ba, ba, ba.*
- Reacts differently to noises, such as a vacuum cleaner, phone ringing, or dog barking; might cry, whimper, or look for reassurance from parent or caregiver.

Social-Emotional Development

- Delights in observing surroundings; continuously watches people and activities.
- Begins to develop an awareness of self as a separate individual from others.
- Becomes more outgoing and social in nature: smiles, coos, and reaches out.
- Distinguishes among and responds differently to strangers, teachers, parents, and siblings.
- Responds differently and appropriately to facial expressions: frowns, smiles.
- Imitates facial expressions, actions, and sounds.

4 to 8 months

Figure 4-17

Recognizes and responds to own name.

(continued)

(continued) DEVELOPMENTAL PROFILES AND GROWTH PATTERNS

- Remains friendly toward strangers at the beginning of this stage; later, is reluctant to be approached by or left with strangers; exhibits **stranger anxiety**.
- Enjoys being held and cuddled; indicates desire to be picked up by raising arms and vocalizing.
- Establishes a trust relationship with family members and teachers if physical and emotional needs are met consistently; by six months, begins to show preference for primary caregiver.
- Laughs out loud.
- Becomes upset if toy or other objects are taken away.
- Seeks attention by using body movements, verbalizations, or both.

• DAILY ROUTINES •

Eating

- Adjusts feeding times to the family's schedule; usually takes three or four feedings per day, each 6 to 8 ounces, depending on sleep schedule.
- *Caution:* Infants should not be allowed to drink formula or juice from a bottle for extended periods of time. Extensive damage can occur when teeth are in prolonged contact with these fluids, resulting in a condition known as baby bottle tooth decay (BBTD) (Tiberia et al., 2007). A small amount of water offered after feedings rinses the teeth and helps to reduce the risk of BBTD.
- Shows interest in feeding activities; reaches for cup and spoon while being fed.
- Able to wait a half hour or more after awakening for first morning feeding.
- Has less need for sucking.
- By six months, begins to accept a small amount of pureed foods, such as cereal and vegetables, when placed well back on tongue (if placed on tip, infant will push food back out).
- Closes mouth firmly or turns head away when hunger is satisfied.

Toileting, Bathing, and Dressing

- Prefers being free of clothes.
- Splashes vigorously with both hands and sometimes feet during bath time.
- Moves hands constantly; nothing within reach is safe from being spilled, placed in the mouth, or dashed to the floor.
- Pulls off own socks; plays with strings, buttons, and Velcro closures on clothing.

4 to 8 months

stranger anxiety—a cross-cultural phenomenon in which infants begin to show distress or fear when approached by persons other than their primary caregivers.

• D A I L Y   R O U T I N E S •

- Has one bowel movement per day as a general rule, often at about the same time.
- Urinates often and in large quantity; female infants tend to have longer intervals between wetting.

Sleeping

- Awakens early in the morning; usually falls asleep soon after evening meal.
- Begins to give up need for a late-night feeding.
- Sleeps 11–13 hours through the night.
- Takes two or three naps per day. (However, there is great variability among infants in terms of frequency and length of naps.)

Play and Social Activity

- Enjoys lying on back; arches back, kicks, stretches legs upward, grasps feet and brings them to mouth.
- Looks at own hands with interest and delight; may squeal or gaze at them intently.
- Plays with soft, squeaky toys and rattles; puts them in mouth and bites and chews on them.
- "Talks" happily to self: gurgles, growls, makes high squealing sounds.
- Differentiates between people: lively with those who are familiar, might ignore or become anxious with others.
- Likes rhythmic activities: being bounced, jiggled, swayed about gently.

4 to 8 months

Learning Activities

Tips for families and teachers:

- Gradually elaborate on earlier activities: imitate baby's sounds, facial expressions, and body movements; name body parts; look in the mirror together and make faces; read, talk, and sing to the baby throughout the day.
- Use the baby's name during all kinds of activities so that baby begins to recognize it: "*Kyle* is smiling," "*Carla's* eyes are wide open." "*Tyrel* looks sleepy."
- Provide toys, rattles, and household items that make noise as baby shakes or waves them about (a set of measuring spoons or plastic keys, shaker cans, squeak toys; remember the **Rule of Fist**).
- Place objects slightly out of reach to encourage baby's movement and eye–hand coordination.

(continued)

Learning Activities *(continued)*

- Read aloud and often to baby, even the evening newspaper or your favorite magazine. Babies will not understand what you are saying, but they will begin to learn about word sounds, voice inflections, facial expressions, and that reading is an enjoyable experience (Im, Parlakian, & Osborn, 2007).

- Play, dance, and move around with baby to music on the radio or CD; vary the tempo and movement: gentle jiggling, dancing, turning in circles; dance in front of the mirror, describing movements to the baby.

- Sing all types of songs to baby—silly songs, lullabies, popular tunes; encourage the baby to "sing" along and imitate your movements.

- Allow plenty of time for bath time. This activity provides an important opportunity for learning in all developmental areas as well as an overall enjoyment of the experience.

- Play "This little piggy," "Where's baby's (nose, eye, hand . . .)," and other simple games invented on the spot such as taking turns at shaking rattles, gently rubbing foreheads, or clapping hands.

4 to 8 months

Developmental Alerts

Check with a health care provider or early childhood specialist if, by eight months of age, the infant *does not*:

- Show an even, steady increase in weight, height, and head size (too slow and too rapid growth are both causes for concern).
- Explore his or her own hands and objects placed in his or her hands.
- Hold and shake a rattle.
- Smile, babble, and laugh out loud.
- Search for hidden objects.
- Begin to pick up objects using a pincer grip.
- Have an interest in playing games such as pat-a-cake and peek-a-boo.
- Show interest in or respond to new or unusual sounds.
- Reach for and grasp objects.
- Sit alone.
- Begin to eat some solid (pureed) foods.

Safety Concerns

Continue to implement safety practices described for the previous stages. Always be aware of new safety issues as the baby continues to grow and develop.

Burns

- Keep electrical cords out of reach and electrical outlets covered; inspect the condition of electrical cords and replace or remove them if worn or frayed.
- Take precautions to protect baby from accidentally touching hot objects such as oven or fireplace doors, space heaters, candles, curling irons, burning cigarettes, or hot beverage cups.

Falls

- Use approved safety gates to protect baby from tumbling down stairs; gates are also useful for keeping baby confined to an area for supervision.
- When using a highchair, stroller, or grocery cart, always fasten the restraining straps.
- Always raise crib sides to their maximum height and lock when baby is in bed.

Poisons

- Use safety latches on cabinet doors and drawers where potentially poisonous substances (e.g., medications, cleaning supplies, cosmetics, garden chemicals) might be stored.

Strangulation

- Never fasten teethers or pacifiers on a cord or around baby's neck. Remove crib gyms and mobiles after baby reaches five months or begins pushing up on hands and knees.
- Avoid any clothing with drawstrings.

8 to 12 months

Eight to Twelve Months

Between eight and twelve months of age, the infant is gearing up for two major developmental events—walking and talking. These milestones usually begin about the time of the first birthday, although a child's cultural background may influence the rate and nature of these early skills (Kelly et al., 2006). The infant is increasingly able to manipulate small objects and spends a great deal of time practicing by picking up and releasing toys or whatever else is at hand. Infants at this age are also becoming extremely sociable (Berk, 2006).

Figure 4-18

Enjoys adult attention.

They find ways to be the center of attention and to win approval and applause from family and friends (Figure 4-18). When applause is forthcoming, the infant joins in with delight. The ability to imitate improves and serves two purposes: to extend social interactions and to help the child learn many new skills and behaviors in the months of rapid development that lie ahead.

DEVELOPMENTAL PROFILES AND GROWTH PATTERNS

8 to 12 months

Growth and Physical Characteristics

- Gains in height are slower than during the previous months, averaging $\frac{1}{2}$ inch (1.3 cm) per month. Infants reach approximately 1½ times their birth length by the first birthday.
- Weight increases by approximately one pound (0.5 kg) per month; birth weight nearly triples by one year of age: infants weigh an average of 21 pounds (9.6 kg).
- Respiration rates vary with activity: typically, 20–45 breaths per minute.
- Body temperature ranges from 96.4°F–99.6°F (35.7°C–37.5°C); environmental conditions, weather, activity, and clothing still affect variations in temperature.
- Circumferences of head and chest remain equal.
- Uses abdominal muscles for breathing.
- Anterior fontanel begins to close.
- Approximately four upper and four lower incisors and two lower molars erupt.
- Arms and hands are more developed than feet and legs (cephalocaudal development); hands appear large in proportion to other body parts.

- Legs might continue to appear bowed.
- Feet appear flat because the arch has not yet fully developed.
- Visual acuity is approximately 20/100.
- Both eyes work in unison (true binocular coordination).
- Can see distant objects (15–20 feet away) and points at them.

Motor Development

- Reaches with one hand leading to grasp an offered object or toy.
- Manipulates objects, transferring them from one hand to the other (Bourgeois et al., 2005).
- Explores new objects by poking with one finger.
- Uses deliberate pincer grip to pick up small objects, toys, and finger foods.
- Stacks objects; also places objects inside one another.
- Releases objects or toys by dropping or throwing; cannot intentionally put an object down.
- Begins pulling self to a standing position.
- Begins to stand alone, leaning on furniture for support; moves or "cruises" around obstacles by side-stepping (Figure 4-19).
- Maintains good balance when sitting; can shift positions without falling.
- Creeps on hands and knees; crawls up and down stairs (Berger, Theuring, & Adolph, 2007).
- Walks with adult support, holding onto adult's hand; can begin to walk alone.

Figure 4-19

Supports self by leaning on objects.

8 to 12 months

(continued)

(continued) DEVELOPMENTAL PROFILES AND GROWTH PATTERNS

VIDEO CONNECTIONS

Clip 10

Motor Development: Motor development proceeds rapidly during the first year. Infants' motor abilities advance quickly from a reflexive stage to one that permits them to move about, explore, and manipulate their environment.

Critical Thinking Questions:
1. Which fine motor skills are most eight- to twelve-month-old infants able to perform?
2. What is a pincer grasp?
3. How does a pincer grasp differ from an ulnar or palmar grasp?
4. What purpose do improved motor skills and coordination serve?
5. How might cultural differences influence an infant's motor development?

Perceptual-Cognitive Development

- Watches people, objects, and activities in the immediate environment.
- Shows awareness of distant objects (15–20 feet away) by pointing at them.
- Responds to hearing tests (voice localization); however, loses interest quickly and, therefore, can be more difficult to test informally.
- Beginning to understand the meaning of some words (receptive language).
- Follows simple instructions such as "wave bye-bye," "clap hands."
- Reaches for toys that are visible but out of reach.
- Puts everything into mouth.
- Continues to drop first item when other toys or items are offered.
- Recognizes the reversal of an object: cup upside down is still a cup.
- Imitates activities: hitting two blocks together, playing pat-a-cake.
- Drops toys intentionally and repeatedly; looks in direction of fallen object.
- Shows appropriate use of everyday items: pretends to drink from cup, put on a necklace, hug doll, brush hair, make stuffed animal "walk."
- Shows some sense of spatial relationships: puts block in cup and takes it out when requested to do so.
- Begins to show an understanding of causality—for example, hands mechanical toy back to adult to have it rewound.

8 to 12 months

- Shows some awareness of the functional relationship of objects; puts spoon in mouth, uses brush to smooth hair, turns pages of a book (Barrett, Davis, & Needham, 2007).
- Searches for completely hidden toy or object by the end of this period.

Speech and Language Development

- Babbles or jabbers deliberately to initiate social interaction; might shout to attract attention, listen, and then shout again.
- Shakes head for "no" and might nod for "yes."
- Responds by looking for voice when name is called.
- Babbles in sentence-like sequences, "ma ma ma ma," "ba ba ba"; followed later by jargon (syllables and sounds common to many languages uttered with language-like inflection).
- Waves bye-bye; claps hands when asked.
- Says "da-da" and "ma-ma."
- Imitates sounds that are similar to those the baby has already learned to make; will also imitate motor noises, tongue clicking, lip smacking, and coughing.
- Enjoys rhymes and simple songs; vocalizes and dances to music.
- Hands toy or object to an adult when appropriate gestures accompany the request.

Social-Emotional Development

- Exhibits a definite fear of strangers; clings to or hides behind parent or caregiver (stranger anxiety); often resists separating from familiar adult (separation anxiety) (Figure 4-20).
- Wants an adult to be in constant sight; might cry and search room when one is not immediately visible.

Figure 4-20

Displays fear of adults other than primary caregivers ("stranger anxiety").

8 to 12 months

(continued)

- Enjoys being near and included in daily activities of family members and teachers; is becoming more sociable and outgoing.
- Enjoys novel experiences and opportunities to examine new objects.
- Shows need to be picked up and held by extending arms upward, crying, or clinging to adult's legs.
- Begins to exhibit assertiveness by resisting caregiver's requests; might kick, scream, toss toys, or throw self on the floor.
- Offers toys and objects to others.
- Often becomes attached to a favorite toy or blanket; cries when it is missing.
- Looks up and smiles at person who is speaking upon hearing his or her name.
- Repeats behaviors that get attention; jabbers continuously.
- Carries out simple directions and requests; understands the meaning of "no," "yes," "come here," and other common phrases.

• D A I L Y   R O U T I N E S •

Eating

- Eats three meals per day plus mid-morning or mid-afternoon snacks such as juice, fruit, crackers, and cereal.
- Begins to refuse bottle.
- Enjoys eating and usually has a good appetite.
- Learns to drink from a cup; wants to hold it alone; will even tilt head backward to get the last drop.
- Begins to eat finger foods; might remove food from mouth, look at it, and put it back in.
- Develops certain likes and dislikes for foods.
- Continuously active; infant's hands might be so busy that a toy is needed for each hand to prevent a cup or dish from being turned over or food grabbed and tossed.

Toileting, Bathing, and Dressing

- Enjoys bath time; splashes and plays with washcloth, soap, and water toys.
- Loves to let water drip from a sponge or washcloth, pour water from cup to cup.
- Shows great interest in pulling off hats, taking off shoes and socks.
- Fusses when diaper needs changing; might pull off soiled or wet diaper.
- Cooperates to some degree in being dressed; helps put arms in armholes, might even extend legs to have pants put on.

8 to 12 months

- Has one or two bowel movements per day.
- Remains dry after nap on occasion.

Sleeping

- Goes to bed willingly but might not fall asleep immediately; plays or walks around in crib before eventually falling asleep on top of the covers.
- Sleeps until early morning.
- Plays alone and quietly for 15–30 minutes after awakening; then begins to make demanding noises, signaling the need to be up and about.
- Plays actively in the crib when awake; crib sides must be up and securely fastened.
- Takes one afternoon nap most days; length varies from infant to infant.

Play and Social Activities

- Enjoys large motor activities: pulling to stand, cruising, standing alone, creeping.
- Some babies are walking at this point.
- Enjoys putting things on head: basket, bowl, cup; finds this very funny and expects people to notice and laugh.
- Puts objects in and out of each other: pans that nest, toys in and out of a box.
- Enjoys hiding behind chairs to play "Where's baby?"
- Throws things on floor and expects them to be returned.
- Shows interest in opening and closing doors and cupboards.
- Gives an object to an adult on request; expects to have it returned immediately.
- Responds to "no-no" by stopping; alternatively, the infant might smile, laugh, and continue inappropriate behavior, thus making a game out of it.

8 to 12 months

Learning Activities

Tips for families and teachers:

- Continue to elaborate on previously suggested activities; sing, read, talk, play simple games, and encourage the baby's efforts.
- Always pick up on the baby's lead whenever the baby initiates a new response or invents a new version of a familiar game (the roots of creativity).
- Provide safe floor space close to parent or caregiver; learning to sit, crawl, stand, and explore are a baby's major tasks during these months.

(continued)

Learning Activities *(continued)*

- Read and tell short stories about everyday happenings in the baby's life; also read from sturdy, brightly colored picture books, allowing the baby to help hold the book and turn the pages. Point to pictures and label the object to help babies begin to make associations; "Soft brown kitten," "Happy puppy," "Big red pail."

- Talk about ongoing activities, naming and emphasizing key words: "Here is the *soap*," "You are *squeezing* the sponge," "Let's *wash hands* before you eat."

- Give baby simple instructions: "Pat Mommy's head," "Pat baby's head." Allow adequate time for response; if the baby seems interested but does not respond, demonstrate the response.

- Accept the baby's newly invented game of dropping things off of a highchair or out of the crib; act surprised, laugh, return dropped object, and do not scold. This is baby's way of learning about many things: cause and effect, gravity, and adults' patience.

- Provide containers that the baby can fill with small toys or other objects and then empty out. (**Rule of Fist** still applies.)

- Give the baby push and pull toys, toys with wheels, and large balls to roll. (Helping to unpack canned goods and rolling them across the kitchen floor is an all-time favorite game.)

Developmental Alerts

Check with a health care provider or early childhood specialist if, by 12 months of age, the infant *does not*:

- Blink when fast-moving objects approach the eyes.
- Begin to develop teeth.
- Imitate simple sounds.
- Follow simple verbal requests: "come," "bye-bye."
- Pull self to a standing position.
- Transfer objects from hand to hand.
- Show anxiety toward strangers by crying or refusing to be held.
- Interact playfully with parents, caregivers, and siblings.
- Feed self; hold own bottle or cup; pick up and eat finger foods.
- Creep or crawl on hands and knees.

8 to 12 months

Safety Concerns

Continue to implement safety practices described for the previous stages. Always be aware of new safety issues as the baby continues to grow and develop.

Choking

- Cut finger foods into small bites (1/4 inch [0.63 cm] or smaller). Avoid sticky foods (e.g., raisins, caramels, peanut butter) and hard foods (e.g., raw carrots, hard candies, nuts).
- Keep small objects such as buttons, dry cat food, coins, and pen tops out of baby's reach; keep garbage cans closed tightly. *Any item that fits through a toilet paper tube is too small for young children.*

Drowning

- Remove unsupervised sources of water, including bath water, fountains, pet dishes, and wading pools. Place safety devices on toilet lids.
- Enclose pools with fences and latched gates; install alarms on windows and doors. Never leave a young child unsupervised in a pool or bathtub, even to answer the telephone.

Falls

- Always strap infants into highchairs, grocery carts, and strollers and on changing tables. Never allow them to stand up in or on these objects (unless you are holding onto the infant).
- Keep crib sides up and locked.
- Pad sharp corners and edges of furniture and cabinet doors.
- Place safety gates across stairs.

Strangulation

- Purchase clothing, such as jackets, with elastic instead of pull strings in the hoods.
- Fasten cords on all blinds and curtains up high and out of children's reach.

Suffocation

- Keep plastic bags and wrappings out of baby's reach; knot them and discard immediately.
- Remove lids from airtight containers such as plastic storage tubs and toy chests.

SUMMARY

The span between birth and a child's first birthday is marked by dramatic changes in all developmental areas. Gains in height and weight occur at a rate greater than at any other time during the life span. Good nutrition plays a key role in assuring healthy growth; malnutrition can severely limit a child's growth potential. Evolving changes in physical development, coupled with rapidly improving motor skills, transform the infant from a nonambulatory, reflexive state to one over which the child begins to master some purposeful control. This period also marks one of the most important stages of brain development in terms of size (actual number of brain cells) and the establishment of nerve connections—both of which are essential for the acquisition of speech and language as well as perceptual-cognitive, motor, and personal-social abilities. Many factors influence this learning process, including genetics, culture, environment, and the expectations of individuals with whom the infant interacts.

KEY TERMS

bonding
depth perception
fontanels
in utero

object permanence
pupil
stranger anxiety

APPLY WHAT YOU KNOW

A. Apply What You Have Learned

Reread the brief developmental sketch about Juan and his parents, Anna and Miguel, at the beginning of the chapter. How might you answer the following questions?

1. Based on what you learned in this chapter, would you consider Juan's development to be progressing typically for his age? Explain.

2. Should you expect Juan to still be waking up for nighttime feedings at this age? Explain.

3. What activities can Anna and Miguel begin doing now to encourage Juan's long-term language development?

4. What changes can Juan's parents expect in his motor development by the time he turns seven months old?

5. If space in a child care program does not become available until Juan reaches seven or eight months of age, would you expect him to experience stranger anxiety? Explain.

6. How would you respond to Juan's parents if they expressed concern about his disinterest in pulling himself to a standing position or taking any steps by his first birthday?

B. Review Questions

1. Explain why a ten-month-old infant might begin fussing and refusing to be left with a familiar babysitter.

2. Identify and discuss three informal methods for determining whether a newborn's hearing is functional.

3. Identify three newborn reflexes that typically disappear by one year of age. Why should you be concerned if they do not fade?

4. What are some things that families and teachers can do with infants to promote early literacy skills?

5. Identify three perceptual-cognitive skills that appear during late infancy (8–12 months) and provide a behavioral example that illustrates each.

HELPFUL WEBSITES

Visit the book companion website at *www.cengage.com/education/allen* for links to these websites and additional resources.

REFERENCES

Aslin, R., & Fiser, J. (2005). Methodological challenges for understanding cognitive development in infants. *Trends in Cognitive Development, 9*(3), 92–98.

Bartlett, D. (1997). Primitive reflexes and early motor development. *Journal of Developmental Behavioral Pediatrics, 18*(3), 151–157.

Barrett, T., Davis, E., & Needham, A. (2007). Learning about tools in infancy. *Developmental Psychology, 43*(2), 352–368.

Berk, L. E. (2006). *Child development.* New York: Allyn & Bacon.

Berger, S., Theuring, C., & Adolph, K. (2007). How and when infants learn to climb stairs. *Infant Behavior & Development, 30*(1), 36–49.

Bergeson, T., & Trehub, S. (2007). Signature tunes in mothers' speech to infants. *Infant Behavior & Development, 30*(4), 648–654.

Bourgeois, K., Khawar, A., Neal, S. A., & Lockman, J. (2005). Infant manual exploration of objects, surfaces, and their interrelations. *Infancy, 8*(3), 233–252.

Dunham, P., Dunham, F., & Curwin, A. (1993). Lexical development during middle infancy: A mutually driven infant-caregiver process. *Developmental Psychology, 28*, 827–831.

Farroni, T., Johnson, M., Menon, E., Zulian, L., Faraguna, D., & Csibra, G. (2005). Newborn's preference for face-relevant stimuli: Effects of contrast polarity. *Proceedings of the National Academy of Sciences, 102*(47), 17,245–17,250.

Herschkowitz, N. (2000). Neurological bases of behavioral development in infancy. *Brain Development, 22*(7), 411–416.

Hofer, M. (2006). Psychobiological roots of early attachment. *Current Directions in Psychological Science, 15*(2), 84–88.

Im, J., Parlakian, R., & Osborn, S. (2007). Rocking and rolling: Supporting infants, toddlers and their families. Stories – their powerful role in language and literacy. *Young Children, 62*(1), 52–53.

Kelly, D., Quinn, P., Slater, A., Lee, K., Gibson, A., Smith, M., Ge, L., & Pascalis, O. (2005). Three-month-olds, but not newborns prefer own-race faces. *Developmental Science, 8*(6), F31–36.

Kelly, Y., Sacker, A., Schoon, I., & Nazroo, J. (2006). Ethnic differences in achievement of developmental milestones by 9 months of age: The Millennium Cohort Study. *Developmental Medicine & Child Neurology, 48*(10), 825–830.

Koopmans-van Beinum, F., Clement, C., & Dikkenberg-Pot, I. (2001). Babbling and the lack of auditory speech perception: A matter of coordination? *Developmental Science, 4*(1), 61–70.

McPhillips M., & Jordan-Black, J. (2007). Primary reflex persistence in children with reading difficulties (dyslexia): A cross-sectional study. *Neuropsychologia, 45*(4), 748–754.

Mercuri, E., Baranello, G., Romeo, D., Cesarini, L., & Ricci, D. (2007). The development of vision. *Early Human Development, 83*(12), 795–800.

Messinger, D., & Fogel, A. (2007). The interactive development of social smiling. *Advances in Child Development & Behavior, 35*, 327–366.

Piaget, J. (1954). *The construction of reality in the child.* New York: Basic Books.

Pomeras, C., Schirrer, J., & Abadie, V. (2002). Analysis of the olfactory capacity of healthy children before language acquisition. *Journal of Developmental Behavior & Pediatrics, 23*(4), 203–207.

Sebastián-Gallés, N. (2007). Biased to learn language. *Developmental Science, 10*(6), 713–718.

Simion, F., Regolin, L., & Bulf, H. (2008). A predisposition for biological motion in the newborn baby. *Proceedings from the National Academy of Sciences, 105*(2), 809–813.

Tiberia, M., Milnes, A., Feigal, R., Morley, K., Richardson, D., Croft, W., & Cheung, W. (2007). Risk factors for early childhood caries in Canadian preschool children seeking care. *Pediatric Dentistry, 29*(3), 201–208.

Tully, S. B. (1998). Otitis media and infant feeding position. *Advanced Nurse Practitioner, 6*(4), 44–48.

BOOK COMPANION WEBSITE

The book-specific website at *www.cengage.com/education/allen* offers students a variety of study tools and useful resources such as chapter overviews and notes, tutorial quizzes, web links, frequently asked questions, discussion questions, glossary/flashcards, internet exercises, references and more. To register or purchase access to the premium resources for this text including video clips tied to chapter content, go to *www.cengage.com/login*.

Toddlerhood: Twelve to Twenty-four Months

Objectives

After reading this chapter, you should be able to:

- Describe the motor abilities of a typical one-year-old and two-year-old.

- Discuss how the speech and language skills of a two-year-old differ from those of a one-year-old.

- Explain why toddlers are often described as picky eaters or as having a poor appetite.

- Define the concept of egocentricity and give an example.

- Provide two illustrations of the two-year-old's improved understanding of size and spatial relationships.

• MEET ANNA AND JUAN

Juan's parents divorced five months ago, when he was just eighteen months old. Now he and his mother, Anna, are living in a small apartment near his grandmother's house. As a single parent, Anna often feels overwhelmed by the burdens of working evenings at a local restaurant and caring for her two-year-old. Juan spends his mornings playing alone in his bedroom or watching television while his mother sleeps. When he gets bored playing with the few toys in his room, he often heads into the kitchen and begins pulling things from the drawers and cabinets. His activity usually awakens his mother and results in a scolding and occasional spanking. Books, magazines, and newspapers are notably absent in their apartment. Juan's mother has little interest in reading and prefers to get her news from the television. Occasionally, Anna takes Juan to a neighborhood park to play, but most of the equipment is in poor condition and designed for older children. He usually ends up playing alone in the sandbox with Styrofoam cups, plastic spoons, and sticks he finds lying around, while his mother chats with her friends.

Juan adores his father, Miguel, and spends every other weekend at his house. However, when he returns home, Anna finds Juan unmanageable and disobedient. She blames Miguel for their son's behavior problems, and they often end up arguing in front of Juan. His grandmother is concerned about the effect his parents' divorce might be having on Juan's development. He utters only two or three words that anyone can understand and shows little interest in the books his grandmother borrows from her neighbor. Increasingly, he resorts to aggression, hitting, yelling, and throwing objects whenever he becomes frustrated. He refuses to help dress himself when asked, is defiant when told to get ready for bed, and often runs the other way when his mother calls.

Twelve to Twenty-Four Months

Toddlers are dynamos, full of unlimited energy, enthusiasm, and curiosity. Although their rate of growth slows considerably during this stage, important developmental changes are taking place. The toddler begins this period with the limited motor, social, language, and cognitive abilities of an infant and ends it with the relatively sophisticated skills of a young child.

Improving motor skills enable toddlers to move about on their own, to explore, and to test their surroundings. Rapid development of speech and language contributes to more complex thinking and learning abilities. Defiance and negative responses become more commonplace near the end of this stage as toddlers gradually begin to assert their independence. Although adults might find this behavior troublesome at times, Erikson (Erikson, 1959) described it as an important step in helping children achieve a sense of **autonomy** and degree of personal control over their environment. However, this early independence is not always encouraged in all cultures (Klein & Chen, 2001).

---

autonomy—a sense of self as separate from others.

The One-Year-Old

The ability to stand upright and toddle from place to place enables one-year-olds to understand their surroundings better. They become talkers and doers, stopping only for much-needed meals and bedtimes. Their curiosity mounts, their skills become increasingly advanced, and their energy level seems never-ending. One-year-olds believe that everything and everyone exists for their sole benefit (Piaget & Inhelder, 1967). Eventually, this **egocentricity**, or self-centeredness, gives way to a greater respect for others. However, for now, the one-year-olds are satisfied to declare everything "mine." They prefer to play alone (solitary play), imitating the actions of other children rather than joining in.

DEVELOPMENTAL PROFILES AND GROWTH PATTERNS

Growth and Physical Characteristics

- Grows at a considerably slower rate during this period.
- Height increases approximately 2–3 inches (5.0–7.6 cm) per year; toddlers reach an average height of 32–35 inches (81.3–88.9 cm).
- Weighs approximately 21–27 pounds (9.6–12.3 kg); gains 1/4–1/2 pound (0.13–0.25 kg) per month; weight is now approximately 3 times the child's birth weight.
- Breathes at a rate of 22–30 respirations per minute; rate varies with emotional state and activity.
- Heart rate (pulse) is approximately 80–110 beats per minute.
- Head size increases slowly and grows approximately 1/2 inch (1.3 cm) every six months; anterior fontanel is nearly closed at eighteen months as the bones of the skull thicken.
- Chest circumference is larger than head circumference.
- Teeth begin to erupt rapidly; six to ten new teeth will appear during this period.
- Legs might still appear bowed.
- Body shape changes; toddlers take on more adult-like appearance but still appear top-heavy; abdomen protrudes, back is swayed.
- Visual acuity is approximately 20/60.

Motor Development

- Crawls skillfully and quickly.
- Stands alone with feet spread apart, legs stiffened, and arms extended for support.
- Gets to feet unaided.

(continued)

egocentricity—believing that everything and everyone is there for your purpose.

(continued) **DEVELOPMENTAL PROFILES AND GROWTH PATTERNS**

- Walks unassisted near the end of this period (most children); might still be unsteady and fall often; not always able to maneuver around obstacles such as furniture or toys.

- Uses furniture to lower self to floor; collapses backward into a sitting position or falls forward on hands and then sits.

- Releases an object voluntarily.

- Enjoys pushing or pulling toys while walking (Figure 5-1).

- Picks up objects and throws them repeatedly; direction becomes more deliberate.

- Attempts to run; has difficulty stopping and usually just drops to the floor.

- Crawls up stairs on all fours; goes down stairs backward in the same position.

- Sits in a small chair.

- Carries toys from place to place.

- Enjoys crayons and markers for scribbling; uses whole-arm movement when drawing.

- Helps feed self; enjoys holding spoon (often upside down) and drinking from a glass or cup; not always accurate at getting utensils into mouth; frequent spills should be expected.

- Helps turn pages of a book during story time.

- Stacks two to four objects with reasonable accuracy.

Figure 5-1

Likes toys that can be pushed and pulled.

VIDEO CONNECTIONS

Clip 11

Speech and Language Development: One-year-olds are learning that language is a functional tool, useful for making requests, informing adults about their needs, and letting others know where they stand! Perhaps even more significant is their level of understanding, which far exceeds their ability to use spoken language.

Critical Thinking Questions:

Focus your attention on the last half of the observation module.

1. Which perceptual-cognitive skills is the female toddler displaying? Explain.

2. Were you able to understand what the toddler was saying? Could her mother understand? Explain why this is often the case.

3. Would you consider her speech and language skills to be typical for a one-year-old?

4. In what ways did her mother reinforce the child's language efforts?

5. Which behaviors suggest that the toddler is in a stage of autonomy?

Perceptual-Cognitive Development

- Enjoys object-hiding activities:

    - Early in this period, the child always searches in the same location for a hidden object (if the child has watched the hiding of an object). Later, the child will search in several locations (Mash et al., 2006).

- Passes toy to other hand when offered a second object (referred to as *crossing the midline*—an important neurological development).

- Manages three to four objects by setting an object aside (on lap or floor) when presented with a new toy.

- Puts toys in mouth less often.

- Enjoys looking at picture books (Figure 5-2).

- Demonstrates an understanding of functional relationships (objects that belong together):

    - Puts spoon in bowl and then uses spoon, pretending to eat.
    - Pounds wooden pegs with toy hammer.
    - Tries to make a doll stand up and walk.

- Shows or offers another person a toy to look at.

- Names many everyday objects.

- Shows increasing understanding of spatial and form discrimination (puts all large pegs in a pegboard; places three geometric shapes in large formboard or puzzle).

(continued)

Figure 5-2

Enjoys looking at picture books.

- Places several small items (blocks, clothespins, cereal pieces) in a container or bottle and delights in dumping them out.
- Tries to make mechanical objects work after watching someone else do so.
- Uses some facial expressions, but they are not always accurate representations.

Speech and Language Development

- Produces considerable jargon (puts words and sounds together into speech-like [inflected] patterns).
- Uses one word to convey an entire thought (**holophrastic speech**); the meaning depends on the inflection ("me" might be used to request more cookies or desire to feed self). Later, the toddler produces two-word phrases to express a complete thought (**telegraphic speech**) ("more cookie," "Daddy bye-bye").
- Follows simple directions ("Give Daddy the cup").
- Points to familiar persons, animals, and toys when asked.
- Understands and identifies three body parts if someone names them (receptive language) ("Show me your nose [toe, ear]").
- Indicates a few desired objects and activities by name ("bye-bye," "cookie," "story"); verbal request is often accompanied by an insistent gesture.

holophrastic speech—using a single word to express a complete thought.
telegraphic speech—uttering two-word phrases to convey a complete thought.

Figure 5-3

Responds to simple questions.

- Responds to simple questions with "yes" or "no" and appropriate head movement (Figure 5-3).
- Produces speech that is 25 to 50 percent **intelligible** during this period.
- Locates familiar objects upon request (if child knows location of objects).
- Acquires and uses five to fifty words (expressive language); typically, these are words that refer to the names of animals, food, and toys.
- Uses gestures, such as pointing or pulling, to direct adult attention.
- Enjoys rhymes and songs; tries to join in; dances and sings along.
- Seems aware of reciprocal (back and forth) aspects of conversational exchanges; engages in some turn-taking in other forms of vocal exchanges, such as making and imitating sounds.

Social-Emotional Development

- Remains friendly toward others; usually less wary of strangers.
- Helps pick up and put away toys (Figure 5-4).
- Plays alone for short periods.
- Enjoys being held and read to.
- Observes and imitates adult actions in play (Meltzoff, 2007).
- Enjoys adult attention; likes to know that an adult is near; gives hugs and kisses.
- Recognizes self in mirror.
- Enjoys the companionship of other children but does not play cooperatively.
- Begins to assert independence; often refuses to cooperate with daily routines that once were enjoyable; resists getting dressed, putting on shoes, eating, taking a bath; wants to try doing things without help.

(continued)

intelligible—language that can be understood by others.

(continued) DEVELOPMENTAL PROFILES AND GROWTH PATTERNS

Figure 5-4

Helps to pick up toys.

- Resorts to tantrums occasionally when things go wrong or if overly tired, hungry, or frustrated (Wakschlag et al., 2007).
- Shows exceeding curiosity about people and surroundings (approaches and talks to strangers, wanders away when left unattended, searches through cabinets).

• DAILY ROUTINES •

Eating

- Has smaller appetite; lunch is often the preferred meal (Marotz, 2009).
- Goes on occasional food jags (willingness to eat only a few foods); sometimes described as a picky or fussy eater; neither requires nor wants a large amount of food.
- Holds food in mouth without swallowing it on occasion; this usually indicates that the child does not need or want more to eat.
- Uses spoon with some degree of skill (if hungry and interested in eating).
- Shows good control of cup (lifts it up, drinks from it, sets it down, holds it with one hand).
- Helps to feed self; some toddlers of this age can feed themselves independently, others still need help.

Toileting, Bathing, and Dressing

- Tries to wash self; plays with washcloth and soap.
- Helps with dressing (puts arms in sleeves, lifts feet to have socks put on). Likes to dress and undress self (takes off own shoes and socks); often puts shirt on upside down and backward or both feet in one pant leg.

- Lets adult know when diaper or pants are soiled or wet.
- Begins to gain some control of bowels and bladder (intervals between wetting/soiling becoming longer, resulting in fewer accidents). Complete control often not achieved until around age 3 (often longer for boys).

Sleeping

- Sleeps 10–12 hours through the night. Might fall asleep at dinner if nap has been missed.
- Experiences occasional difficulty falling asleep; overflow of energy shown in bouncing on the bed, calling for parent, demanding a drink or trip to the bathroom, singing, making and remaking bed—all of which seem to be ways of "winding down." A short, consistent bedtime routine and quiet story often promote relaxation and help the toddler prepare for sleep.
- Makes many requests at bedtime for stuffed toys, a book or two, a special blanket.

Play and Social Activity

- Develops a strong sense of property rights; "mine" is heard frequently. Sharing is difficult; often hoards toys and other items.
- Enjoys helping but often gets into trouble when left alone (smears toothpaste, tries on lipgloss, empties dresser drawers, unrolls toilet paper).
- Enjoys being read to; especially likes stories with repetition, such as *Is Your Mama a Llama, One Duck Stuck, Five Little Monkeys, Bang! Bang! Toot! Toot!*, and Dr. Seuss books; likes to point to and talk about pictures.
- Likes to go on walks; stops frequently to look at things (rocks, bits of paper, insects); squats to examine and pick up objects; much dawdling with no real interest in getting to any place in particular.
- Plays alone (solitary play) most of the time, although beginning to show some interest in other children; engages in lots of watching. Participates in some occasional **parallel play** (play alongside but not with another child). Might offer play items to another child, but there is little cooperative (purposeful) play (exception can be children who have spent considerable time in group care) (Brownell, Ramani, & Zerwas, 2006).
- Seems to feel more secure and better able to settle down at bedtime if the door is left slightly ajar with light turned on in another room.
- Continues to nap; however, naps that are too long or too late can interfere with bedtime.
- Wakes up slowly from nap; cannot be hurried or rushed into any activity.

---

parallel play—playing alongside or near another person but not involved in their activity.

Learning Activities

Tips for families and teachers:

- Respond to the toddler's jabbering and voice inflections, both in kind (playfully) and with simple words and questions; maintain conversational turn-taking.

- Encourage the toddler to point to familiar objects in picture books, catalogues, and magazines; name the objects and encourage (do not insist) the toddler to imitate.

- Hide a toy or other familiar object in an obvious place and encourage the toddler to find it (give clues as needed).

- Provide blocks, stacking rings, shape-sorting boxes, and nesting cups; such toys promote problem-solving and eye–hand coordination.

- Allow frequent water play; the sink is always a favorite when an adult is working in the kitchen. (*Caution:* An absorbent towel or throw rug will catch spills and drips, thus reducing the chances of slipping or falling.)

- Put favorite toys in different parts of the room so the toddler must get to them by crawling, cruising, or walking (thus practicing motor skills).

- Provide toys that can be pushed or pulled; a stable plastic or wooden riding toy to steer and propel with the feet; arrange safe, low places for climbing over, under, and on top of.

Developmental Alerts

Check with a health care provider or early-childhood specialist if, by 24 months of age, the child *does not*:

- Attempt to talk or repeat words.

- Understand some new words.

- Respond to simple questions with "yes" or "no."

- Walk alone (or with very little help).

- Exhibit a variety of emotions: anger, delight, fear, surprise.

- Show interest in pictures.

- Recognize self in a mirror (smile at, point to, or state own name).

- Make eye contact when responding to questions or making a request (unless this is a cultural taboo).

- Attempt self-feeding (hold own cup to mouth and drink).

Safety Concerns

Continue to implement safety practices described for the previous stages. Always be aware of new safety issues as the child continues to grow and develop.

Burns (Thermal and Electrical)

- Cover all electrical outlets with plastic caps.
- Protect toddlers from touching hot oven doors, space heaters, hot water pipes, fireplace doors, outdoor grills, toasters, and other hot surfaces.
- Keep cords from irons, hair curlers, and other hot electrical appliances up and out of reach.
- Apply sunscreen to prevent sunburns. Have toddler wear a hat and long sleeves during long sun exposure.

Choking

- Remove objects and toys that have small pieces (less than 1½ inch [3.75 cm] in diameter) such as coins, watch or calculator batteries, marbles, pen tops, beads, buttons, gum and hard candies, paper clips, latex balloons, and plastic bags.
- Cut foods into small pieces; insist that children eat sitting down; avoid serving foods such as popcorn, pretzels, hot dogs (unless cut crosswise and in very small pieces), raw carrots, whole grapes, nuts, and hard candies.

Water Hazards

- Eliminate sources of accessible water such as an unsupervised swimming or wading pool, mop bucket, fish tank, outdoor water feature; purchase and use locking devices on toilet seats; *children can drown in less than 2 inches (5 cm) of water.*
- Install a fence, gates, locks, and alarm system to protect toddlers from wandering into unsupervised backyard pools or hot tubs.

Falls

- Place safety gates across stairwells; secure them properly to door frame. Gates can also be used to keep toddlers in rooms where they can be closely supervised.
- Keep doors to outside, garage, bathrooms, and stairwells locked.
- Pad sharp corners of tables and chairs.
- Eliminate tripping hazards (e.g., electrical cords, rugs, wet spills, highly waxed floors); clear pathways of furniture and toys.

(continued)

Safety Concerns *(continued)*

Poisons

- Store medications (including vitamins, cough syrups, ointments, and other nonprescription drugs), automotive and garden chemicals, and cleaning supplies in a locked cabinet. (High shelves are not always safe from children who can climb.)

- Check for and remove poisonous plants from indoor and outdoor environments. (Contact a local county extension agent for information.)

Strangulation

- Avoid clothing with drawstrings around the head or neck.

- Make sure strings on pull toys are no longer than 14 inches (35 cm) in length; supervise their use closely. Remove any toys or clothing with strings from toddler's bed before sleeping.

- Fasten cords from curtains or blinds so they are high and inaccessible to children.

The Two-Year-Old

This year can be terrific as well as a challenge—for the child, family, and teachers. Exasperated adults often describe a two-year-old as impossible (or demanding, unreasonable, contrary). However, the two-year-old's fierce determination, tantrums, and inability to accept limits are part of normal development and are seldom under his or her control (Gillespie & Seibel, 2006) (Figure 5-5). The two-year-old faces demands that can sometimes be overwhelming: new skills and behaviors to be learned and remembered, needs and feelings that are difficult to express, learned responses to be perfected, and puzzling adult expectations with which to comply. However, toddlers are also gaining an emerging sense of self-confidence as their developmental skills and awareness improve. This can result in moment-to-moment struggles as they try to resolve conflicting desires for independence (autonomy) or dependence (Erikson, 1959). Is it any wonder that two-year-olds are frustrated, have difficulty making choices, and say no even to things they really want?

Although this year of transition can be somewhat trying for all, many good things also happen. Two-year-olds are noted for their frequent and spontaneous outbursts of laughter and affection. New skills are learned quickly as a result of determined interest in self-discovery and independence (Chen & French, 2008; Dix et al., 2007). Gradually, the two-year-old begins to function more ably and amiably as newly acquired skills and earlier learning are consolidated.

Figure 5-5

Toddlers often exhibit
a strong determination.

DEVELOPMENTAL PROFILES AND GROWTH PATTERNS

Growth and Physical Characteristics

- Gains an average of 2–2.5 pounds (0.9–1.1 kg) per year; weighs approximately 26–32 pounds (11.8–14.5 kg) or about 4 times the weight at birth.
- Grows approximately 3–5 inches (7.6–12.7 cm) per year; average height is 34–38 inches (86.3–96.5 cm) tall.
- Assumes a more erect posture; abdomen still large and protruding and back swayed because abdominal muscles are not yet fully developed.
- Respirations are slow and regular (approximately 20–35 breaths per minute).
- Body temperature continues to fluctuate with activity, emotional state, and environment.
- Brain reaches about 80 percent of its adult size.
- Eruption of teeth is nearly complete; second molars appear, for a total of twenty deciduous, or baby, teeth.

Motor Development

- Walks with a more erect, heel-to-toe pattern; able to maneuver around obstacles in pathway.
- Runs with greater confidence; has fewer falls.
- Squats for long periods while playing.
- Climbs stairs unassisted (but not with alternating feet) holding onto the railing for support.
- Balances on one foot (for a few moments), jumps up and down but might fall.
- Begins to achieve toilet training during this year (depending on the child's level of physical and neurological development), although accidents should still be expected; the child will indicate readiness for toilet training.

(continued)

2-year-olds

- Throws large ball underhand without losing balance.
- Holds cup or glass (be sure it is unbreakable) in one hand.
- Unbuttons large buttons; unzips large zippers.
- Opens doors by turning doorknobs.
- Grasps large crayon with fist; scribbles enthusiastically on a large piece of paper (Figure 5-6).
- Climbs up on chair, turns around, and sits down.
- Enjoys pouring and filling activities—sand, water, Styrofoam peanuts.
- Stacks four to six objects on top of one another.
- Uses feet to propel wheeled riding toys.

Perceptual-Cognitive Development

- Follows simple requests and directions.
- Exhibits eye–hand movements that are better coordinated; can put objects together, take them apart; fit large pegs into pegboard (Ornkloo & von Hofsten, 2007).
- Begins to use objects for purposes other than intended (might push a block around as a boat, turn a box into a drum).
- Completes simple classification tasks based on one dimension (separates toy dinosaurs from toy cars); this is an important development for learning math skills later.
- Stares for long moments; seems fascinated by, or engrossed in, figuring out a situation (where the tennis ball has rolled, where the dog has gone, what has caused a particular noise).
- Engages in self-selected activities for longer periods (sits quietly, remains focused) (Figure 5-7).
- Shows discovery of cause and effect (squeezing the cat makes her scratch or run away, turning the door handle makes it open).
- Knows where familiar persons should be; notes their absence; finds a hidden object by looking in the last hiding place first.
- Names objects in picture books; might pretend to pick something off the page and taste or smell it.
- Recognizes and expresses pain and its location.

Figure 5-6

Holds crayon in fist
and scribbles.

Figure 5-7

Remains focused on
activities for longer
periods.

- Enjoys being read to if allowed to participate by pointing, making relevant noises, and turning pages.

- Realizes that language is effective for getting others to respond to needs and preferences. Makes simple requests ("More cookies?"); refuses adult wishes ("No!") (Huttenlocher et al., 2007).

- Uses 50 to 300 words; vocabulary continuously increasing.

- Has broken the **linguistic code**; that is, much of a two-year-old's talk has meaning to him or her but not always to adults (Vygotsky's "self-talk").

- Understands significantly more language than is able to communicate verbally; most two-year-olds' **receptive language** is more developed than their **expressive language** (Berk, 2006).

- Utters three- and four-word statements; uses conventional word order to form more complete sentences.

- Refers to self as "me" or sometimes "I" rather than by name ("Me go bye-bye"); has no trouble verbalizing "mine."

- Expresses negative statements by tacking on a negative word such as "no" or "not" ("Not more milk").

- Asks repeatedly, "What's that?"

- Uses some plurals but not always correctly ("See the gooses"); often over-generalizes grammatical rules. Talks about objects and events not immediately present. (This is both a cognitive and a linguistic advance.)

- Experiences occasional stammering and other common **dysfluencies**.

- Produces speech that is as much as 65 to 70 percent intelligible.

(continued)

linguistic code—verbal expression that has meaning to the child.
receptive language—understanding words that are heard.
expressive language—words used to verbalize thoughts and feelings.
dysfluency—repetition of whole words or phrases uttered without frustration and often at the beginning of a statement, such as, "Let's go, let's go get some cookies."

Social-Emotional Development

- Shows signs of empathy and caring (comforts another child who is hurt or frightened); sometimes is overly affectionate in offering hugs and kisses to children.

- Continues to use physical aggression if frustrated or angry; this response is more exaggerated for some children than for others; physical aggression usually diminishes as verbal skills improve (Lewis & Ramsay, 2004).

- Expresses frustration through temper tantrums; frequency of tantrums often peaks during this year; cannot be reasoned with while tantrum is in progress.

- Finds it difficult to wait or take turns; often impatient.

- Enjoys "helping" with household chores; imitates everyday activities (might try to toilet a stuffed animal, or feed or bathe a doll).

- Orders family members and teachers around; is bossy; makes demands and expects immediate compliance from adults.

- Watches and imitates the play of other children but seldom joins in; content to play alone (Figure 5-8).

- Offers toys to other children but is usually possessive of playthings; still tends to hoard toys.

- Finds it difficult to make choices; wants it both ways.

- Shows much defiance; shouting "no" becomes almost automatic.

- Wants everything just so; is quite ritualistic; expects routines to be carried out exactly as before and belongings to be placed where they belong.

Figure 5-8

Content to play alone, but observes and may imitate other children's actions.

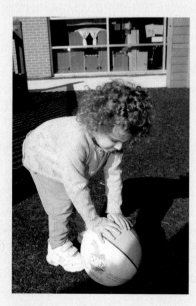

Clip 12

Cognitive Development: Children younger than 2 learn about their world primarily through their senses—touch, sight, sound, smell, and taste. Hand toddlers a new toy, and they might look it over, shake it, pound it on the table, and then pop it into to their mouths (assuming that it is small enough). Thus, safety remains a priority, and it is up to adults to maintain environments that protect toddlers from unintentional harm.

Critical Thinking Questions:

1. Would you describe the two-year-old's predominant form of play as non-social activity or associative play, based on information presented in the video? Explain.

2. Do you think parents should organize play groups for their two-year-olds and expect them to benefit from the experience?

3. What toys would support the two-year-old's sensorimotor mode of learning?

2-year-olds

• DAILY ROUTINES •

Eating

- Has fair appetite; interest in food fluctuates with periods of growth; lunch is often the preferred meal.

- Sometimes described as a picky or fussy eater; often has strong likes and dislikes (which should be respected); might go on food jags (eating only certain foods such as peanut butter and jelly sandwiches, macaroni and cheese) (Satter, 2000).

- Likes simple, recognizable foods; dislikes mixtures; wants foods served in familiar ways.

- Needs between-meal snacks, which should be of good nutritive value (fresh fruits or vegetables, cheese/whole-grain crackers), with junk foods limited.

- Feeds self with increasing skill but might be "too tired" or disinterested at times.

- Has good control of cup or glass, although frequent spills are likely to happen.

- Learns table manners through verbal instruction and by imitating those of adults and older children.

Toileting, Bathing, and Dressing

- Enjoys bath if allowed ample playtime (*must never be left alone*); tries to wash self; might object to being washed and squirm when being dried off.

- Dislikes, even resists, having hair washed.

- Tries to help when being dressed; needs simple, manageable clothing; can usually undress self without much effort (Figure 5-9).

(continued)

2-year-olds

Figure 5-9

Attempts to dress self but still needs help.

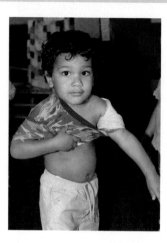

- Shows signs of readiness for bowel training (some children might have already mastered bowel control); uses appropriate words, upset when pants are soiled, runs to bathroom.

- Stays dry for longer periods of time (one sign of readiness for toilet training); other signs include interest in watching others use toilet, holding a doll or stuffed animal over toilet, clutching self, willingness to sit on potty for a few moments, expressing discomfort about being wet or soiled.

Sleeping

- Sleeps between 9–12 hours at nighttime.

- Still requires afternoon nap; needs time to wake up slowly.

- Resists going to bed; however, usually complies if given ample warning and can depend on a familiar bedtime routine (story, talk time, special toy) (Spagnola & Fiese, 2007).

- Takes awhile to fall asleep, especially if overly tired; might sing, talk to self, bounce on bed, call for parents, make and remake the bed (again, ways of winding down).

Play and Social Activity

- Enjoys dressing up and imitating family activities (wearing father's hat makes the child a "daddy"; putting on high-heeled shoes make the child a "mommy").

- Likes to be around other children but does not always play well with them (observes intently, imitating other children's actions [parallel play] but is unlikely to join in).

- Displays extreme negativism toward parents and caregivers at times—an early step toward establishing independence; shouts "no" or runs when asked to pick up toys, get ready for bed, or come to the dinner table.

- Pretends to have an imaginary friend as a constant companion.

- Explores everything in the environment, including other children; might shove or push other children as if to test their reaction.

Learning Activities

Tips for families and teachers:

- Play games, such as large lotto and picture dominoes, that are based on matching colors, animals, facial expressions, and everyday objects.
- Offer manipulative materials to foster problem-solving and eye–hand coordination: large beads for stringing; brightly colored cubes; puzzle boxes; and large, plastic, interlocking bricks.
- Provide toy replicas of farm and zoo animals, families, cars, trucks, and planes for sorting and imaginative play.
- Read to the child regularly; provide colorful picture books for naming objects and describing everyday events; use simple, illustrated storybooks (one line per page) so the child can learn to "tell" the story.
- Share nursery rhymes, simple finger plays, and action songs; respond to, imitate, and make up simple games based on the child's spontaneous rhyming or chanting.
- Set out (and keep a close eye on) washable paints, markers, chalk, large crayons, and large paper for artistic expression.
- Help with make-believe activities; for example, save empty cereal and cracker boxes, paper grocery bags, and plastic juice containers with intact labels for playing store.
- Provide wagons; large trucks and cars that can be loaded, pushed, or sat upon; doll carriage or stroller; a rocking boat; bean bags and rings for tossing.

2-year-olds

Developmental Alerts

Check with a health care provider or early-childhood specialist if, by the third birthday, the child *does not:*

- Eat a fairly well-rounded diet, even though amounts are limited.
- Walk confidently with few stumbles or falls; climb steps with help.
- Avoid bumping into objects.
- Carry out simple, two-step directions: "Come to Daddy and bring your book"; express desires; ask questions.
- Point to and name familiar objects; use two- or three-word sentences.
- Enjoy being read to; help to hold the book, name and point to objects.
- Show interest in playing with other children (watching, perhaps imitating).
- Indicate a beginning interest in toilet training (runs to bathroom, pulls pants down, uses appropriate words).
- Sort familiar objects according to a single characteristic such as type, color, shape, or size.
- Make eye contact when making a request or responding to questions (unless this is a cultural taboo).

Safety Concerns

Continue to implement safety practices described for the previous stages. Always be aware of new safety issues as the child continues to grow and develop.

Burns

- Set temperature of hot water heater no higher than 120°F.
- Purchase and use protective devices on bathtub and sink faucets.
- Keep hot liquids (e.g., coffee cups, kettles) out of reach.

Choking

- Continue to cut food into small pieces; insist that children eat sitting down; avoid popcorn, hot dogs (unless cut crosswise in small pieces), raw carrots, whole grapes, nuts, and hard candies.

Water

- Supervise any source of accessible water (e.g., wading pool, fish tank, garden pond or fountain, bathtub). *Children can drown in less than 2 inches (5 cm) of water. Never leave children unattended.*

Play Environment

- Securely fasten bookcases, filing cabinets, dressers, and shelves to the wall to prevent them from tipping over.
- Place toys on lower shelves so they are accessible.
- Keep doors to the outside and stairwells locked.
- Cover electrical outlets and remove unnecessary electrical cords.

Poisons

- Store all medicines (including vitamins and other nonprescription drugs), automotive and garden chemicals, and cleaning supplies in a locked cabinet. (High shelves are not safe from children who can climb.)
- Check for and remove poisonous plants from indoor and outdoor environments. (Contact a local county extension agent for information.)

Strangulation

- Avoid dress-up clothing that could become entangled around a child's neck (e.g., neck ties, drawstrings).

2-year-olds

S U M M A R Y

Toddlers continue to undergo important physical changes, although their rate of growth begins to slow. Improving motor skills tend to outpace toddlers' cognitive development—their understanding of cause and effect, judgment of size and distance, and functionality—placing them at high risk of unintentional injury. Although vocabulary (expressive language) might be limited, toddlers' understanding of language (receptive language) is generally more advanced. Dramatic increases in the number of words and their usage occur between the first and second birthdays. Toddlers enjoy being read to, singing, repeating simple words, and imitating adult behavior. Curiosity frequently gets them into trouble as they experiment with everyday objects, explore every nook and cranny, and attempt to take things apart. Efforts to achieve autonomy often result in bouts of defiance and temper tantrums. Despite all their challenging characteristics, toddlers are endearing bundles of potential!

KEY TERMS

autonomy
dysfluency
egocentricity
expressive language
holophrastic speech

intelligible
linguistic code
parallel play
receptive language
telegraphic speech

APPLY WHAT YOU KNOW

A. Apply What You Have Learned

Reread the brief developmental sketch about Juan and his family at the beginning of the chapter. How might you answer the following questions?

1. Should Juan's grandmother be concerned about his language development?

2. What factors in Juan's home environment might be limiting his language development?

3. What suggestions could you offer to Anna for encouraging Juan's language development, taking into consideration the family's financial situation?

4. If you were asked to evaluate Juan's behavior, would you consider his displays of anger and aggression to be typical or atypical of a toddler? Explain.

5. From a developmental perspective, explain why Juan continues to get into his mother's kitchen cabinets and dresser drawers despite repeated warnings not to do so.

6. Because Anna sleeps in the morning while Juan is playing, what special precautions should she take in their apartment to ensure his safety?

B. Review Questions

1. Identify two motor skills that one-year-olds and two-year-olds typically acquire.

2. Describe two developmentally appropriate activities that would promote a two-year-old's self-help skills; motor skills; language development.

3. Why are toddlers more likely to experience tantrums? In what ways would you expect to see a one-year-old to begin asserting his or her independence?

4. Why are toddlers at high risk for unintentional injury? What steps must adults take to reduce this risk?

5. What is holophrastic speech? Provide two or three examples to illustrate this form of speech. At what age would this form of speech be considered typical?

6. What are some things families and teachers can do to help two-year-olds settle down for sleep?

7. Describe three activities designed to help two-year-olds learn about the concept of size.

HELPFUL WEBSITES

Visit the book companion website at *www.cengage.com/education/allen* for links to these websites and additional resources.

REFERENCES

Berk, L. E. (2006). *Child development.* (7th ed.). New York: Allyn & Bacon.

Brownell, C., Ramani, G., & Zerwas, S. (2006). Becoming a social partner with peers: Cooperation and social understanding in one- and two-year-olds. *Child Development, 77*(4), 803–821.

Chen, X., & French, D. (2008). Children's social competence in cultural context. *Annual Review of Psychology, 59*(1), 591–616.

Dix, T., Stewart, A., Gershoff, E., & Day, W. (2007). Autonomy and children's reactions to being controlled: Evidence that both compliance and defiance may be positive markers in early development. *Child Development, 78*(4), 1204–1221.

Erikson, E. (1959). Identity and the life cycle. *Psychological Issues, 1,* 1–171.

Gillespie, L., & Seibel, N. (2006). Self-regulation: A cornerstone of early childhood development. *Young Children, 61*(4), 34–39.

Huttenlocher, J., Vasilyeva, M., Waterfall, H., Vevea, J., & Hedges, L. (2007). The varieties of speech to young children. *Developmental Psychology, 43*(5), 1062–1083.

Klein, M., & Chen, D. (2001). *Working with children from diverse backgrounds.* Albany, NY: Delmar.

Lewis, M., & Ramsay, D. (2004). Development of self-regulation, personal pronoun use, and pretend play during the 2nd year. *Child Development, 75*(6), 1821–1831.

Marotz, L. (2009). *Health, safety, and nutrition for the young child.* (7th ed.). Clifton Park, NY: Thomson Delmar Learning.

Mash, C., Novak, E., Berthier, N., & Keen, R. (2006). What do two-year-olds understand about hidden-object events? *Developmental Psychology, 42*(2), 263–271.

Meltzoff, A. (2007). "Like me": A foundation for social cognition. *Developmental Science, 10*(1), 126–134.

Ornkloo, H., & von Hofsten, C. (2007). Fitting objects into holes: On the development of spatial cognition skills. *Developmental Psychology, 43*(2), 404–416.

Piaget, J., & Inhelder, B. (1967). *The child's conception of space.* New York: Norton.

Satter, E. (2000). *Child of mine: Feeding with love and good sense.* Palo Alto, CA: Bull Publishing.

Spagnola, M., & Fiese, B. (2007). Family routines and rituals: A context for development in the lives of young children. *Infants & Young Children, 20*(4), 284–299.

Wakschlag, L., Briggs-Gowan, M., Carter, A., Hill, C., Danis, B., Keenan, K., McCarthy, K., & Leventhal, B. (2007). A developmental framework for distinguishing disruptive behavior from normative misbehavior in preschool children. *Journal of Child Psychology and Psychiatry, 48*(10), 976–987.

BOOK COMPANION WEBSITE

The book-specific website at *www.cengage.com/education/allen* offers students a variety of study tools and useful resources such as chapter overviews and notes, tutorial quizzes, web links, frequently asked questions, discussion questions, glossary/flashcards, internet exercises, references and more. To register or purchase access to the premium resources for this text including video clips tied to chapter content, go to *www.cengage.com/login*.

Early Childhood: Three-, Four-, and Five-Year-Olds

MEET FOUR-YEAR-OLD JUAN AND HIS MOTHER, ANNA

Anna's interest in resuming her education was sparked after she attended a recruiting program sponsored by the local community college. When Anna discovered there was space for Juan at the child care center on campus, she was even more determined. Anna knows that Juan's language and social development are delayed and believes he will benefit from having more opportunities to interact with children his own age.

Each morning, Anna drops Juan off at the child care center while she attends classes and works in the school cafeteria. However, Juan has been slow to adjust to his new school. He often prefers to play alone, seldom stays involved in any activity for more than a few minutes, and insists on carrying his blanket wherever he goes.

Despite her busy schedule, Anna sets aside time in the evenings to play with Juan. They talk about things he has

Objectives

After reading this chapter, you should be able to:

- Contrast the major developmental characteristics of typical three-, four-, and five-year-olds with those of toddlers.

- Describe the food preferences, eating habits, and calorie needs of typical three-year-olds, four-year-olds, and five-year-olds.

- Discuss the preschooler's need for adult attention and then trace the ways these needs change with increasing independence.

- Compare and contrast the average three-year-old's language skills with those of an average five-year-old.

- Describe at least five things that adults can do to promote cognitive development and support emergent literacy with three-year-olds, four-year-olds, and five-year-olds.

done in school that day and sometimes work together on building or art projects. Before Juan heads to bed, they always sit quietly and read several story books together. Anna is becoming increasingly confident in her ability to encourage Juan's development ever since attending a parent education class at the college. She now realizes how simple, everyday things she does with her son help him learn. Anna thinks she would enjoy working with young children and is seriously considering becoming an early education teacher.

Three-, Four-, and Five-Year Olds

Three-, four-, and five-year-olds are typically full of energy, eagerness, and curiosity (Figure 6-1). They seem to be constantly on the move as they engross themselves totally in whatever captures their interest at the moment. During these years, motor skills are being perfected. Creativity and imagination are evident in everything children do, from dramatic play to their artwork and storytelling. Vocabulary and intellectual skills are expanding rapidly, enabling children to express ideas, solve problems, and plan ahead. Some children might be learning to speak more than one language if their parents are also bilingual. Others might begin to acquire a second language when they enroll in an early childhood program (if the program is not conducted in their native tongue) (Paradis, 2007). Little is known about the processes involved in acquiring a second language. However, the experience has an understandable effect on many aspects of children's development (Bialystok, 2007; Páez, Tabors, & López, 2007).

Figure 6-1

Children are exceptionally curious and inquisitive at this age.

Preschool children strongly believe in their own opinions but, at the same time, they are beginning to understand that others have needs and feelings too. They are also developing some degree of control over their own behavior (Denham et al., 2003). They strive for independence yet need reassurance that an adult is available to give assistance, to comfort, mediate, or to rescue if need be.

The Three-Year-Old

3-year-olds

Three-year-olds tend to be more peaceful, relaxed, and cooperative. Conflicts with adults that grew out of the two-year-old's struggle for independence are now fewer and less intense. In fact, many three-year-olds are willing to abide by adults' directions most of the time. They are able to delay their own gratification longer; that is, they have less need to have what they want "right now" (Liebermann, Giesbrecht, & Müller 2007). They take obvious delight in themselves and life in general and show an irrepressible urge to find out all about everything in the world around them.

DEVELOPMENTAL PROFILES AND GROWTH PATTERNS

Growth and Physical Characteristics

- Growth is steady, although slower than during the first two years.
- Height increases 2–3 inches (5–7.6 cm) per year; average height is 38–40 inches (96.5–101.6 cm), nearly double the child's birth length.
- Adult height can be predicted from measurements of height at three years of age; males are approximately 53 percent of their adult height; females are 57 percent of their adult height.
- Gains an average of 3–5 pounds (1.4–2.3 kg) per year; weight averages 30–38 pounds (13.6–17.2 kg).
- Heart rate (pulse) averages 90–110 beats per minute.
- Respiratory rate is 20–30, depending on activity level; child continues to breathe abdominally.
- Temperature averages 96°F–99.4°F (35.5°C–37.4°C); affected by exertion, illness, and stress.
- Legs grow more rapidly in length than do arms, giving the three-year-old a taller, thinner, adult-like appearance.
- Circumference of head and chest is equal; head size is in better proportion to the body.
- Neck appears to lengthen as "baby fat" disappears.
- Posture is more erect; abdomen no longer protrudes.
- Has a full set of baby teeth (20 teeth).
- Needs to consume approximately 1,500 calories daily.
- Visual acuity is approximately 20/40, using the Snellen E chart.

(continued)

3-year-olds

Motor Development

- Walks up and down stairs unassisted, using alternating feet; might jump from bottom step, landing on both feet.
- Balances momentarily on one foot.
- Kicks a large ball.
- Feeds self; needs minimal assistance.
- Jumps in place.
- Pedals a small tricycle or riding toy.
- Catches a large bounced ball with both arms extended.
- Enjoys swinging on a swing (not too high or too fast); laughs and asks to be pushed.
- Shows improved control of crayons or markers; uses vertical, horizontal, and circular strokes.
- Holds crayon or marker between first two fingers and thumb (**tripod grasp**), not in a fist as earlier (Figure 6-2).
- Turns pages of a book one at a time.
- Enjoys building with blocks.
- Builds a tower of eight or more blocks.
- Plays with clay; pounds, rolls, and squeezes it with enthusiasm.
- Begins to show **hand dominance**.
- Carries a container of liquid, such as a cup of milk or bowl of water, without much spilling; pours liquid from pitcher into another container.
- Manipulates large buttons and zippers on clothing.
- Washes and dries hands; brushes own teeth but not thoroughly.
- Achieves complete bladder control, for the most part, during this time.

Figure 6-2

Uses tripod grasp
to hold marker.

---

tripod grasp—hand position whereby an object, such as a pencil, is held between the thumb and first and second fingers.

hand dominance—preference for using one hand over the other; most individuals are said to be either right-handed or left-handed.

VIDEO CONNECTIONS

Clip 13

Motor Development: Three-year-olds have mastered most basic gross motor skills and now will begin to concentrate their efforts on improving strength, accuracy, and coordination.

Critical Thinking Questions:

1. What other physical characteristics (in addition to height and weight gains) are typical of the three-year-old?

2. Describe several indoor and outdoor activities that would help three-year-olds improve the precision of their gross motor skills.

3. What motor skills would you expect a typically developing three-year-old to be capable of performing?

4. How might culture contribute to differences in children's gross motor skill development?

3-year-olds

Perceptual-Cognitive Development

- Listens attentively to age-appropriate stories.
- Makes relevant comments during stories, especially those that relate to home and family events.
- Spends considerable time looking at books; may pretend to read to others by explaining the pictures.
- Requests stories with riddles, guessing, and suspense.
- Points with a fair degree of accuracy to correct pictures when given sound-alike words (*keys-cheese; fish-dish; sand-band; cat-bat*).
- Plays realistically
    - Feeds doll, puts it down for a nap, covers it up to stay warm (Figure 6-3).
    - Hooks truck and trailer together, loads truck, drives away making motor noises.
- Experiments with things to see how they work; takes objects apart and reassembles them into new "inventions" (Kamii, Miyakawa, & Kato, 2007).
- Places eight to ten pegs in a pegboard or six round and six square blocks in a formboard.
- Attempts to draw; imperfectly copies circles, squares, and some letters.
- Identifies triangle, circle, square; can point to requested shape.
- Sorts objects logically on the basis of one dimension, such as color, shape, or size; usually chooses color or size as basis for classification (all red beads in one pile, green beads in another) (Deak, Ray, & Pick, 2002).

(continued)

3-year-olds

Figure 6-3

Engages in realistic make-believe play.

- Shows understanding of basic size-shape comparisons much of the time; will indicate which is bigger when shown a tennis ball and a golf ball; also understands "smaller of the two" (Nguyen & Murphy, 2003).
- Names and matches, at minimum, primary colors (red, yellow, blue).
- Arranges cubes in a horizontal line; also positions cubes to form a bridge.
- Counts objects out loud (Figure 6-4).
- Points to picture that has "more" (cars, planes, or kittens).
- Shows some understanding of duration of time by using phrases such as "all the time," "all day," "for two days"; some confusion remains: "I didn't take a nap tomorrow."

Figure 6-4

Counts objects out loud.

Speech and Language Development

- Talks about objects, events, and people not present: "Jerry has a pool in his yard."
- Talks about the actions of others: "Daddy's mowing the grass."
- Adds information to what has just been said: "Yeah, and then he grabbed it back."
- Answers simple questions appropriately.
- Asks many questions, particularly about location and identity of objects and people.
- Uses an increasing number of speech forms that keep conversation going: "What did he do next?" "Where are we going now?" (Papafragou et al., 2007).
- Calls attention to self, objects, or events in the environment: "Watch my helicopter fly."
- Promotes the behavior of others: "Let's jump in the water. You go first."
- Joins in social interaction rituals: "Hi," "Bye," "Please," "Let's go."
- Comments about objects and ongoing events: "There's a house"; "The tractor's pushing a boat."
- Vocabulary has increased; now uses 300 to 1,000 words.
- Recites nursery rhymes, sings songs.
- Uses understandable speech most of the time.
- Produces expanded noun phrases: "big, brown dog."
- Produces verbs with "ing" endings; uses "-s" to indicate more than one; often puts "-s" on already pluralized forms (geeses, mices, deers).
- Indicates negatives by inserting "no" or "not" before a simple noun or verb phrase ("Not baby").
- Answers "What are you doing?" "What is this?" and "Where?" questions dealing with familiar objects and events.

Social-Emotional Development

- Seems to understand taking turns but is not always willing to do so.
- Laughs frequently; is friendly and eager to please.
- Has occasional nightmares and fears about the dark, monsters, or fire.
- Joins in simple games and group activities, sometimes hesitantly.
- Talks to self often.
- Identifies self as a "boy" or "girl" (Ruble et al, 2007).
- Uses objects symbolically in play (block of wood might be a truck, a ramp, a bat) (Figure 6-5).
- Observes other children playing; might join in for a short time; often plays parallel to other children.
- Defends toys and possessions; is becoming aggressive at times, grabbing a toy, hitting another child, hiding toys.
- Engages in make-believe play alone and with other children (Ma & Lillard, 2006).

3-year-olds

(continued)

(continued) **DEVELOPMENTAL PROFILES AND GROWTH PATTERNS**

- Shows affection toward children who are younger or children who get hurt.
- Sits and listens to stories up to 10 minutes at a time; does not bother other children who are listening to the story; becomes upset if disturbed or interrupted.
- Might continue to have a special blanket, stuffed animal, or toy for comfort.

Figure 6-5

Uses toys to represent real objects.

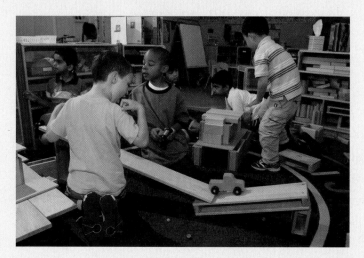

• D A I L Y R O U T I N E S •

Eating

- Prefers small servings; appetite is fair. Dislikes many cooked vegetables; eats almost everything else; should not be forced to eat (Parlakian & Lerner, 2007).
- Feeds self independently if hungry. Uses spoon in semi-adult fashion; might spear food with fork (Figure 6-6).
- Eats slowly at times; plays around with food when not hungry.
- Pours milk and juice with fewer spills; serves individual portions from a serving dish with some prompting from an adult: "Fill it up to the line"; "Take only two spoonfuls."
- Drinks a great deal of milk. (Be sure child does not fill up on milk to the exclusion of other much-needed foods.)

Toileting, Bathing, and Dressing

- Helps wash self in bathtub but is not always thorough; often resists getting out of tub.
- Brushes own teeth, but adults should continue to monitor child's technique.

• D A I L Y   R O U T I N E S •

Figure 6-6

Handles utensils with relative skill.

3-year-olds

- Takes care of own toilet needs during the daytime. (Boys, especially, might continue to have daytime accidents resulting in wet pants.)
- Some children sleep through the night without wetting the bed; others are in transition—they might stay dry at night for days or weeks, then go back to night-wetting for a period.
- Manages undressing better than dressing, although is capable of putting on some articles of clothing.
- Manipulates zippers, large buttons, and snaps with improving ability.

Sleeping

- Sleeps 10–12 hours most nights; often wakes up early in the morning.
- Begins to give up afternoon naps; however, continues to benefit from a midday quiet time.
- Prepares for bed independently most of the time; has given up many earlier bedtime rituals but still needs a bedtime story or song and tucking-in.
- Has dreams that might cause the child to awaken.
- Sometimes wanders at night; quiet firmness might be needed in returning child to his or her own bed.

Play and Social Activity

- Wants to be included in everything; the "me too" age.
- Joins in spontaneous group play for short periods; very social; beginning to play cooperatively more often.

(continued)

• D A I L Y   R O U T I N E S • *(continued)*

- Argues or quarrels with other children occasionally; adults should allow children to settle their own disagreements unless physical harm is threatened.
- Dresses up and participates in dramatic play reflecting everyday activities. Some children still exhibit strong **gender** and role stereotypes: "Boys can't be nurses"; "Only girls can be dancers."
- Responds well to options rather than to commands: "Do you want to put your pajamas on before or after the story?"
- Finds sharing still difficult but seems to understand the concept.

3-year-olds

Learning Activities

Tips for families and teachers:

- Allow children to create new uses for safe household items and discards: blanket over a table to create a cave or tent; spoons for pretend cooking; discarded mail for playing post office; hose with trickle of water for washing tricycle or wagon; plastic milk carton for a floating boat; paint brush and water for painting.
- Provide somewhat more complex manipulative materials: parquetry blocks; pegboards with multicolored pegs; various items to count, sort, and match; construction sets with medium-size, interlocking pieces.
- Offer art and craft materials that encourage experimentation: crayons, washable markers, chalk, playdough, round-tipped scissors, papers, glue, paints, and large brushes (supervision is required).
- Keep on hand a plentiful supply of books about animals, families, everyday events, alphabet and counting activities, poems and rhymes; continue daily reading sessions.
- Make regular trips to the library; allow plenty of time for children to make their own book selections. Include some nonfiction books on topics that interest children, such as animals, the ocean, and the planets.
- Spend time together outdoors: kick, hit, or throw balls; catch bugs; or play tag.
- Provide wheeled riding toys, wheelbarrow and garden tools, doll strollers, shopping carts, and so on that build eye–hand–foot dexterity through steering and maneuvering.
- Go for walks with children, *at the child's pace*; allow ample time for children to explore, examine, and collect rocks, bugs, leaves, seed pods; name and talk about things along the way.

gender—reference to being either male or female.

Developmental Alerts

Check with a health care provider or early-childhood specialist if, by the fourth birthday, the child *does not*:

- Have intelligible speech most of the time; have children's hearing checked if there is any reason for concern.
- Understand and follow simple commands and directions.
- State own name and age.
- Play near or with other children.
- Use three-word to four-word sentences.
- Ask questions and maintain eye contact.
- Stay with an activity for 3–4 minutes; play alone several minutes at a time.
- Jump in place without falling.
- Balance on one foot, at least briefly.
- Help with dressing self.
- Engage in pretend play, using common objects for different purposes.

3-year-olds

Safety Concerns

Continue to implement safety practices described for the previous stages. Always be aware of new safety issues as the child continues to grow and develop.

Burns

- Keep hot items out of children's reach.
- Place lighted candles, matches, and cigarette lighters where they are inaccessible.
- Monitor children carefully when grills, fireplaces, candles, or fireworks are lit.

Choking

- Avoid foods likely to cause choking, such as popcorn, nuts, raw carrots, hard candies, and grapes.
- Cut food into small pieces and insist that children sit quietly when eating.
- Supervise children closely when they are eating items with sticks, such as a lollipop or Popsicle.

(continued)

Safety Concerns *(continued)*

Drowning

- Continue to supervise children closely when around any source of water.
- Always empty wading pools.
- Fence in permanent pools; use pool alarm; keep gates closed and riding toys away from pool area.
- Know CPR!

Falls

- Provide sturdy, flat-soled shoes to prevent twisted ankles and tripping. Shoes with hard or slippery soles, sandals and slip-ons increase the risk of tripping or falling.

Poisons

- Avoid use of pesticides and chemicals on grass where children play; residues can get on hands and in sandboxes.
- Store hazardous substances, such as cleaning supplies, lawn chemicals, and medications, in locked cabinets.

Traffic

- Insist on holding the child's hand when walking in parking lots or crossing streets.
- Always buckle child securely into an appropriate car seat.

4-year-olds

The Four-Year-Old

Tireless bundles of energy, brimming over ideas, overflowing with chatter and activity—these are the characteristics typical of most four-year-olds. Bouts of stubbornness and arguments between child and adults can be frequent. Children often test limits, practice self-confidence, and firm up a growing need for independence. Many are loud, boisterous, even belligerent; they try adults' patience with silly talk and silly jokes, constant chatter, and endless questions. At the same time, they have many lovable qualities. They are enthusiastic, eager to be helpful, imaginative, and able to plan ahead to some extent: "When we get home, I'll make you a picture."

DEVELOPMENTAL PROFILES AND GROWTH PATTERNS

Growth and Physical Characteristics

- Gains approximately 4–5 pounds (1.8–2.3 kg) per year; weighs an average of 32–40 pounds (14.5–18.2 kg).
- Grows 2–2.5 inches (5.0–6.4 cm) in height per year; is approximately 40–45 inches (101.6–114 cm) tall.
- Heart rate (pulse) averages 90–110 beats per minute.
- Respiratory rate ranges from 20–30, varying with activity and emotional state.
- Body temperature ranges from 98°F–99.4°F (36.6°C–37.4°C).
- Head circumference is usually not measured after age three.
- Requires approximately 1,700 calories daily.
- Hearing acuity can be assessed by child's correct usage of sounds and language as well as by the child's appropriate responses to questions and instructions.
- Visual acuity is approximately 20/30 as measured on the Snellen E chart.

Motor Development

- Walks a straight line (tape or chalk line on the floor).
- Hops on one foot.
- Pedals and steers a wheeled toy with confidence; turns corners, avoids obstacles and oncoming "traffic."
- Climbs ladders, trees, playground equipment.
- Jumps over objects 5 or 6 inches (12.5 to 15 cm) high; lands with both feet together.
- Runs, starts, stops, and moves around obstacles with ease.
- Throws a ball overhand; distance and aim improving.
- Builds a tower with ten or more blocks.
- Forms shapes and objects out of clay: cookies, snakes, simple animals.
- Reproduces some shapes and letters (Figure 6-7).
- Holds a crayon or marker by using a tripod grasp.
- Paints and draws with purpose; might have an idea in mind but often has trouble implementing it, so calls the creation something else.

4-year-olds

Figure 6-7

Reproduces some shapes and letters.

(continued)

- Becomes more accurate at hitting nails and pegs with hammer.
- Threads small wooden beads on a string.

Perceptual-Cognitive Development

- Stacks at least five graduated cubes from largest to smallest; builds a pyramid of six blocks.
- Indicates whether paired words sound the same or different (*sheet–feet, ball–wall*).
- Names eighteen to twenty uppercase letters near the end of this year; some children might be able to print several letters and write their own name; might recognize some printed words (especially those that have a special meaning for the child).
- A few children will begin to read simple words in books such as alphabet books with only a few words per page and many pictures (Lonigan, Burgess, & Anthony, 2000).
- Selects and enjoys stories about how things grow and operate.
- Delights in wordplay, creating silly language.
- Understands the concepts of "tallest," "biggest," "same," and "more"; selects the picture that has the "most houses" or the "biggest dogs."
- Rote counts to 20 or more.
- Understands the sequence of daily events: "When we get up in the morning, we get dressed, have breakfast, brush our teeth, and go to school."
- Sorts, classifies, and patterns objects with various attributes (smallest to biggest; color and shape; things that float or sink).
- Recognizes and identifies missing puzzle parts (of person, car, animal) when looking at the picture.

Speech and Language Development

- Uses the prepositions *on, in,* and *under*.
- Uses possessives consistently (*hers, theirs, baby's*).
- Answers "Whose?" "Who?" "Why?" and "How many?" (Figure 6-8).
- Produces elaborate sentence structures: "The cat ran under the house before I could see what color it was" (Ramscar & Gitcho, 2007).

4-year-olds

Figure 6-8

Answers questions with authority.

- Uses almost entirely intelligible speech.

- Begins to use the past tense of verbs correctly: "Mommy closed the door," "Daddy went to work."

- Refers to activities, events, objects, and people that are not present.

- Changes tone of voice and sentence structure to adapt to listener's level of understanding: To baby brother, "Milk gone?" To mother, "Did the baby drink all of his milk?"

- States first and last name, gender, siblings' names, and sometimes home telephone number (Treiman et al., 2007).

- Answers appropriately when asked what to do if tired, cold, or hungry.

- Recites and sings simple songs and rhymes.

VIDEO CONNECTIONS

Clip 14

Language Development: Four-year-olds chatter endlessly. They have much to say and, in the process, are learning how to use language for thinking, problem-solving, and communicating their ideas to others. Cultural patterns influence how children develop and use written and spoken language.

Critical Thinking Questions:

1. What grammatical irregularities did you note in the little girl's description of recent bowling and putt-putt golf experiences (near the end of this video clip)?

2. Is her grammatical usage typical for a four-year-old?

3. How does the four-year-old use language to solve problems?

4. What differences would you anticipate in the language development skills of a four-year-old who is bilingual?

4-year-olds

Social-Emotional Development

- Is outgoing and friendly; overly enthusiastic at times.

- Changes moods rapidly and unpredictably; might laugh one minute, cry the next; often throws a tantrum over minor frustrations (a block structure that will not balance); sulks over being left out or denied a request (Fox & Lentini, 2006).

(continued)

- Holds conversations and shares strong emotions with imaginary playmates or companions; having an invisible friend is fairly common (Vygotsky's self-talk).
- Boasts, exaggerates, and bends the truth with made-up stories or claims of boldness; tests the limits with "bathroom" talk (Wright et al., 2008).
- Cooperates with others; participates in group activities.
- Shows pride in accomplishments; seeks frequent adult approval.
- Tattles on other children; often appears selfish; not always able to take turns or to understand taking turns under some conditions.
- Insists on trying to do things independently but can become so frustrated as to verge on tantrums when problems arise (paint that drips, paper airplane that will not fold correctly).
- Participates in role-playing and make-believe activities.
- Relies (most of the time) on verbal rather than physical aggression; might yell angrily rather than hit to make a point; threatens: "You can't come to my birthday party."
- Uses name-calling and taunting as ways of excluding other children: "You're such a baby."
- Establishes close relationships with playmates; beginning to have "best" friends (Figure 6-9).

4-year-olds

Figure 6-9

Begins to have a "best" friend.

• DAILY ROUTINES •

Eating

- Appetite fluctuates; hungry and eager to eat at one meal, disinterested in eating at the next.
- Might develop dislikes of certain foods and refuse them to the point of tears if pushed (such pressure can cause serious adult–child conflict).
- Able to use all eating utensils; quite skilled at spreading jelly or butter or cutting soft foods such as bread with a plastic or dinnerware knife.
- Eating and talking get in each other's way; talking usually takes precedence over eating.
- Shows interest in helping with meal preparations (dumping premeasured ingredients, washing vegetables, setting the table).

Toileting, Bathing, and Dressing

- Takes care of his or her own toileting needs; often demands privacy in the bathroom.
- Performs bathing and toothbrushing tasks with improved skill and attention; still needs some adult assistance and routine (subtle) inspection.
- Dresses self; can lace own shoes, button buttons, buckle belts. Becomes frustrated if problems arise in getting dressed while stubbornly refusing much-needed adult help.
- Can help sort and fold his or her own clean clothes, put clothes away, hang up towels, straighten and dust room; easily distracted, however.

Sleeping

- Averages 10–12 hours of sleep at night; might still take an afternoon nap.
- Bedtime usually not a problem if cues, rather than orders, signal the time (when the story is finished, when the clock hands are in a certain position).
- Some children fear the dark, but a light left on in the hallway is usually all that is needed.
- Getting up to use the toilet might require helping the child settle down for sleep again.

Play and Social Activities

- Playmates are important; plays cooperatively some of the time; can be bossy.
- Takes turns; shares (most of the time); wants to be with children every waking moment.
- Needs (and seeks out) adult approval and attention; might comment, "Look what I did."
- Understands and needs limits (but not too constraining); will abide by rules most of the time.
- Brags about possessions; shows off; boasts about family members.

4-year-olds

Learning Activities

Tips for families and teachers:

- Join in simple board and card games (picture lotto, Candyland) that depend on chance, not strategy; emphasis should be on playing, not winning. (Learning to be a good sport does not come until much later.)
- Provide puzzles with five to twenty pieces (number depends on the child), counting and alphabet games, matching games such as more detailed lotto.
- Offer a variety of simple scientific and mathematics materials: ruler, compass, magnifying glass, small scales, plastic eye droppers; encourage activities such as collecting leaves, growing worms, sprouting seeds.
- Appreciate (and sometimes join in) the child's spontaneous rhyming, chanting, silly name-calling, jokes, and riddles.
- Continue daily read-aloud times; encourage children to supply words or phrases, to guess *what comes next*, to retell the story (or parts of it) by telling what happened first, what happened last; introduce the idea of looking things up in a simple picture dictionary or encyclopedia. Go to the library regularly, allowing the child ample time to choose books.
- Participate in 30 to 60 minutes of vigorous physical activity with your child each day: go for a walk, play in the park, ride bikes, provide balls for kicking, throwing, and hitting; enroll in tumbling or dance classes, play in the sprinkler or "swim" in a plastic pool (*always requires an adult present*).

Developmental Alerts

Check with a health care provider or early-childhood specialist if, by the fifth birthday, the child *does not*:

- State his or her own name in full.
- Identify simple shapes: circle, square, triangle.
- Catch a large ball when bounced (have child's vision checked).
- Speak and be understood by strangers (have child's hearing checked).
- Have good control of posture and movement.
- Hop on one foot.
- Show interest in and respond to surroundings; ask questions, stop to look at and pick up small objects.
- Respond to statements without constantly asking to have them repeated.
- Dress self with minimal adult assistance; manage buttons, zippers.
- Take care of his or her own toilet needs; have good bowel and bladder control with infrequent accidents.

Safety Concerns

Continue to implement safety practices described for the previous stages. Always be aware of new safety issues as the child continues to grow and develop.

Burns

- Teach children the dangers of fire.
- Make sure smoke and carbon monoxide detectors are operational. Use cooking opportunities to help children learn appropriate safety practices.

Dangerous Objects

- Keep all chemicals, cleaning supplies, personal care products, medications, guns, and dangerous tools in locked storage; curiosity peaks during this stage.

Falls

- Always insist that children wear a bike helmet and pads when biking, skating, or skateboarding.
- Rethink the use of trampolines; many children sustain serious injuries, including head and spinal cord injuries (AAP, 1999).

Personal Safety

- Teach children their full name, telephone number, what to do if they become lost, and how to dial 911. Increased independence can cause children to wander too far from parents and teachers.

Toys

- When purchasing toys, evaluate their safety (e.g., rounded edges, not easily broken, no protruding wires, no electrical connections, nontoxic and nonflammable materials).
- Avoid toys with small parts if there are younger children in the home or child care setting.

Suffocation

- Remove doors from any unused freezer or refrigerator before disposing of the appliance.
- Select toy boxes with removable lids or use open containers to prevent children from being trapped by a fallen top. Remove lids from large plastic storage bins.

4-year-olds

The Five-Year-Old

More in control of themselves, both physically and emotionally, most five-year-olds are in a period of relative calm and are becoming increasingly self-confident and reliable. Their world is expanding beyond home, family, and schools or child care centers. Friendships and group activities are of major importance (Gleason & Hohmann, 2006).

Five-year-olds devote much of their time and attention to the practice and mastery of skills in all developmental areas (Figure 6-10). However, this quest for mastery, coupled with a high energy level and robust self-confidence, can lead to mishaps. Eagerness to do and explore often interferes with the ability to foresee danger or potentially disastrous consequences (Granié, 2007). Therefore, the child's safety and the prevention of unintentional injuries must be a major priority for families and caregivers (Marotz, 2009). At the same time, adults must not be overly protective and should handle their concerns in ways that do not interfere with the child's sense of curiosity, competence, and self-esteem.

Figure 6-10

Practice leads to mastery.

DEVELOPMENTAL PROFILES AND GROWTH PATTERNS

5-year-olds

Growth and Physical Characteristics

- Gains 4–5 pounds (1.8–2.3 kg) per year; weighs an average of 38–45 pounds (17.3–20.5 kg).
- Grows an average of 2–2.5 inches (5.1–6.4 cm) per year; is approximately 42–46 inches (106.7–116.8 cm) tall.
- Heart rate (pulse) is approximately 90–110 beats per minute.
- Respiratory rate ranges from 20–30, depending on activity and emotional status.
- Body temperature is stabilized at 98°F–99.4°F.
- Head size is approximately that of an adult's.
- Begins to lose baby (deciduous) teeth (Figure 6-11).
- Body is adult-like in proportion.
- Requires approximately 1,800 calories daily.

Figure 6-11

Begins losing "baby" teeth.

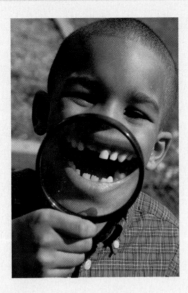

- Visual acuity is approximately 20/20 on the Snellen E chart.
- Visual tracking and **binocular vision** are well developed.

Motor Development

- Walks backward, toe to heel.
- Walks unassisted up and down stairs, alternating feet.
- Learns to turn somersaults (should be taught the right way to avoid injury).
- Touches toes without flexing knees.
- Walks a balance beam.
- Learns to skip using alternative feet.
- Catches a ball thrown from 3 feet away.
- Rides a tricycle or wheeled toy with speed and skillful steering; some children learn to ride bicycles, usually with training wheels.
- Jumps or hops forward ten times in a row without falling.
- Balances on either foot with good control for 10 seconds.
- Builds three-dimensional structures with small cubes by copying from a picture or model.
- Reproduces many shapes and letters (square, triangle, *A, I, O, U, C, H, L, T*).
- Demonstrates fair control of a pencil or marker; begins to color within the lines.

5-year-olds

(continued)

binocular vision—both eyes working together, sending a single image to the brain.

Figure 6-12

Hand dominance is often established by now.

- Cuts on the line with scissors (but not perfectly).
- Establishes hand dominance for the most part (Figure 6-12).

Perceptual-Cognitive Development

- Forms rectangle from two triangular pieces.
- Builds steps with set of small blocks.
- Understands and demonstrates concept of *same* shape, *same* size.
- Sorts objects on the basis of two dimensions, such as color and form.
- Sorts a variety of objects so that all things in the group have a single common feature (classification skill: all are food items or boats or animals) (Deak, Ray, & Pick, 2002).
- Understands the concepts of smallest and shortest; places objects in order from shortest to tallest, smallest to largest.
- Identifies objects with specified serial position: first, second, last.
- Rote counts to 20 and above; many children can count to 100 (Mix, Huttenlocher, & Levine, 1996).
- Recognizes numerals from 1 to 10.
- Understands the concepts of more/less than: "Which bowl has less water?"
- Understands the terms *dark*, *light*, and *early*: "I got up early, before anyone else. It was still dark."
- Relates clock time to daily schedule: "Time to go to bed when the little hand points to 8."
- Some children can tell time on the hour: five o'clock, two o'clock.

- Knows what a calendar is for.
- Recognizes and identifies penny, nickel, and dime; beginning to count and show interest in saving money.
- Knows alphabet; many children can name uppercase and lowercase letters and some letter sounds.
- Understands the concept of half; can say how many pieces an object has when it has been cut in half.
- Asks innumerable questions: Why? What? Where? When?
- Eager to learn new things.

Speech and Language Development

- Has vocabulary of 1,500 words or more.
- Tells a familiar story while looking at pictures in a book.
- Uses functional definitions (a ball is to bounce; a bed is to sleep in; a book is to read).
- Identifies and names four to eight colors.
- Recognizes the humor in simple jokes; makes up jokes and riddles.
- Produces sentences with five to seven words; much longer sentences are not unusual.
- States own birthday, name of city or town, and parents' names.
- Answers telephone appropriately; calls an adult to the telephone or takes a brief message.
- Produces speech that is almost entirely intelligible.
- Uses *would* and *could* appropriately.
- Uses past tense of irregular verbs consistently (*went, caught, swam*).
- Uses past-tense inflection (-ed) appropriately to mark regular verbs (*jumped, rained, washed*).

VIDEO CONNECTIONS

Clip 15

Social Skills and Play: Five-year-olds are imaginative, engaging, and social by nature. They usually get along well with other children, preferring to play with one or two friends at a time. However, they can also become bossy when things do not go their way.

Critical Thinking Questions:

1. What social skills must a child have to engage successfully in cooperative or constructive play?
2. What can teachers do to encourage children's development of positive social skills?
3. What do the terms *friend* and *friendships* mean from a five-year-old's perspective?

5-year-olds

(continued)

Social-Emotional Development

- Enjoys friendships; often has one or two special playmates (Denham et al., 2003) (Figure 6-13).

- Shares toys, takes turns, plays cooperatively (with occasional lapses); is often quite generous (Lane et al., 2007).

- Participates in group play and shared activities with other children; suggests imaginative and elaborate play ideas.

- Is usually affectionate and caring, especially toward younger or injured children and animals.

- Follows directions and carries out assignments most of the time; generally does what parent or teacher requests.

- Continues to need adult comfort and reassurance but might be less open in seeking and accepting comfort.

- Has better self-control; experiences fewer dramatic swings of emotions.

- Likes to tell jokes, entertain, and make people laugh.

- Takes pride in accomplishments; boasts at times and seeks adult acknowledgment and approval.

5-year-olds

Figure 6-13

Is sociable and enjoys spending time with friends.

• D A I L Y   R O U T I N E S •

Eating

- Has a good appetite but not at every meal.
- Likes familiar foods; prefers most vegetables raw rather than cooked.
- Often adopts food dislikes of family members, teachers, peers, or all three.
- "Makes" breakfast (pours cereal, gets out milk and juice) and lunch (spreads peanut butter and jam on bread).

Toileting, Bathing, and Dressing

- Takes full responsibility for his or her own toileting needs; might put off going to the bathroom until an accident occurs or is barely avoided.
- Bathes fairly independently but might need some help getting started.
- Dresses self completely; learning to tie shoes, sometimes aware when clothing is on wrong side out or backward.
- Careless with clothes at times; leaves them scattered about and forgets where they were left; needs many reminders to pick them up.
- Uses tissue for blowing nose but often does a careless or incomplete job; forgets to throw tissue away; needs reminder to wash hands.

Sleeping

- Manages all routines associated with getting ready for bed independently; can help with younger brother's or sister's bedtime routine.
- Averages 10 or 11 hours of sleep per night. Some five-year-olds might still nap.
- Dreams and nightmares are common.
- Delays going to sleep if the day has been especially exciting or if long-anticipated events are scheduled for the next day.

Play and Social Activities

- Carries out family chores and routines; is usually helpful and cooperative.
- Knows the "right" way to do something and often has the "right" answers to questions; seems somewhat opinionated and rigid in beliefs at times.
- Remains attached to home and family; willing to have an adventure but wants the adventure to begin and end at home; fearful that parents might leave or not come back.
- Plays well with other children most times, but three might be a crowd: two five-year-olds will often exclude the third.
- Shows affection and is protective toward younger siblings; might feel overburdened at times if younger child demands too much attention.

5-year-olds

Learning Activities

Tips for families and teachers:

- Provide inexpensive materials (computer paper, old magazines, wallpaper books, paint samples, scraps of fabric) for cutting, pasting, painting, coloring, folding; make a cardboard box loom for weaving; offer easy sewing activities and smaller beads for stringing; gather wood scraps, glue, and tools for simple carpentry.

- Continue to collect props and dress-up clothes that allow more detailed acting out of family and worker roles; visit and talk about community activities—house building, post office and mail deliveries, farmers' market; encourage play with puppets; assist in creating a stage. (A cutout carton works well.)

- Use a variety of books to help the child learn about the many joys and functions of books in everyday life; continue to read aloud regularly and frequently.

- Encourage the growing interest in paper-and-pencil games and number-, letter-, and word-recognition games that the child often invents but might need adult help in carrying out.

- Plan cooking experiences that allow the child to wash and chop vegetables; roll out cookies; measure, mix, and stir.

- Help set up improvised target games that promote eye–hand coordination (bean bag toss, bowling, ring toss, horseshoes, low hoop and basketball); ensure opportunities for vigorous play (wheeled toys; jungle gyms and parallel bars; digging, raking, sweeping, and hauling).

Developmental Alerts

Check with a health care provider or early-childhood specialist if, by the sixth birthday, the child *does not*:

- Alternate feet when walking up and down stairs.
- Speak in a moderate voice—not too loud, too soft, too high, or too low.
- Follow simple three-step directions in stated order: "Please go to the cupboard, get a cup, and bring it to me."
- Use four to five words in acceptable sentence structure.
- Cut on a line with scissors.
- Sit still and listen to an entire short story (5 to 7 minutes).
- Maintain eye contact when spoken to (unless this is a cultural taboo).
- Play well with other children; listen, take turns, offer assistance.
- Perform most self-grooming tasks independently (brush teeth, wash hands and face).

Safety Concerns

Continue to implement safety practices described for the previous stages. Always be aware of new safety issues as the child continues to grow and develop.

Falls

- Monitor parks and play areas for potential hazards such as broken glass, defective equipment, sharp objects, deep holes, inadequate cushioning material under play equipment, or animals.

Toys

- Refrain from purchasing toys that involve projectiles or require electricity; battery-operated toys are safer.

Traffic

- Teach street safety, especially to children who walk to and from school; review safe practices often.
- Teach children to run away and seek adult help if approached by a stranger. Tell them to yell, "You're not my mommy" or "You're not my daddy."
- Make sure that recommended car seats or restraints are appropriate for child's increasing weight and height.

Personal Safety

- *Never* leave children in a vehicle unattended for any length of time; temperatures (heat or cold) inside of a closed vehicle can quickly become deadly. Unattended children might also be targeted by potential kidnappers.
- Teach children a code word that can be used by persons authorized to pick them up from school.
- Teach children how to swim and make them aware of water safety rules.

Poisoning

- Use only nontoxic art supplies; check product labels carefully (see *www.cpsc.gov* for product information).
- Remind children not to put nonfood items (such as pills) into their mouth until they check with an adult.

5-year-olds

S U M M A R Y

Preschoolers—three-, four-, and five-year-olds—are on the move every waking moment and eager to learn about everything. They need a great deal of support and approval from adults, although this need becomes less obvious as they move out of the preschool and into the primary school years. Families and teachers play a major role in providing guidance and the types of learning opportunities that enable pre-schoolers to practice, refine, and extend the vast number of skills that define healthy development. At the same time, adults must set limits that protect children from unforeseen consequences of their exuberance and determination to grow up and do things for themselves. Each age-related section of the chapter closes with specific guidelines for adults and describes what to expect from each age, how to support development in each area, and how to identify a potential developmental problem.

KEY TERMS

binocular vision
gender

hand dominance
tripod grasp

APPLY WHAT YOU KNOW

A. Apply What You Have Learned

Reread the brief developmental sketch about Anna and Juan at the beginning of the chapter. How might you answer the following questions?

1. Assuming that Juan's motor development is progressing typically, what skills would you expect to observe?

2. Would you consider Juan's personal-social development appropriate for his age? Explain.

3. What social behaviors would be typical for a four-year-old?

4. How would you respond to Anna's question if she asked, "How much responsibility can I expect Juan to assume for his own personal care at his age?"

5. In addition to reading bedtime stories, what other types of activities might Anna engage in with Juan to further his language development?

6. Is it developmentally appropriate to expect Juan to identify and name six colors, count to 100, understand simple fractions (e.g., 1/2, 1/4), and begin to tell time? Explain.

B. Review Questions

1. Describe three motor skills that appear between two and five years of age.

2. Identify a personal-social skill that would be typical of a child at each of the following ages: three-year-olds, four-year-olds, five-year olds.

3. Describe three major speech and language skills that appear between three and five years of age (in order).

4. What self-help skills would you expect a typically developing four-year-old to be capable of performing?

5. Should a teacher be concerned about a four-year-old who exhibits frequent mood swings or often tattles? Why or why not?

6. Describe how a teacher might use a cooking activity to promote five-year-olds' perceptual-cognitive development.

HELPFUL WEBSITES

Visit the book companion website at *www.cengage.com/education/allen* for links to these websites and additional resources.

REFERENCES

American Academy of Pediatrics (AAP). (1999). Trampolines at home, school and recreational centers. *Pediatrics, 103*(5), 1053–1056.

Bialystok, E. (2007). Language acquisition and bilingualism: Consequences for a multilingual society. *Applied Psycholinguistics, 28*(3), 393–397.

Deak, G., Ray, S., & Pick, A. (2002). Matching and naming objects by shape or function: Age and context effects in preschool children. *Developmental Psychology, 18*(4), 503–518.

Denham, S., Blair, K., Demulder, E., Levitas, J., Sawyer, K., Major, S., & Queenan, P. (2003). Preschool emotional competence: Pathway to social competence? *Child Development, 74*(1), 238–244.

Fox, L., & Lentini, R. (2006). "You got it!" Teaching social and emotional skills. *Beyond the Journal.* Accessed on November 14, 2007, at *http://www.journal.naeyc.org/btj/200611pdf/BTJFoxLentini.pdf.*

Gleason, T., & Hohmann, L. (2006). Concepts of real and imaginary friendships in early childhood. *Social Development, 15*(1), 128–144.

Granié, M. (2007). Gender differences in preschool children's declared and behavioral compliance with pedestrian rules. *Journal of Family Psychology, 21*(3), 479–489.

Kamii, C., Miyakawa, Y., & Kato, T. (2007). Trying to make a lever work at ages 1 to 4: The development of "functions" (logico-mathematical thinking). *Early Education & Development, 18*(1), 145–161.

Lane, L., Stanton-Chapman, T., Jamison, K., & Phillips, A. (2007). Teacher and parent expectations of preschoolers' behavior: Social skills necessary for success. *Topics in Early Childhood Special Education, 27*(2), 86–97.

Liebermann, D., Giesbrecht, G., & Müller, U. (2007). Cognitive and emotional aspects of self-regulation in preschoolers. *Cognitive Development, 22*(4), 511–529.

Lonigan, C., Burgess, S., & Anthony, J. (2000). Development of emergent literacy and early reading skills in preschool children: Evidence from a latent-variable longitudinal study. *Developmental Psychology, 36*(5), 596–613.

Ma, L., & Lillard, A. (2006). Where is the real cheese? Young children's ability to discriminate between real and pretend acts. *Child Development, 77*(6), 1762–1777.

Marotz, L. (2009). *Health, safety, and nutrition for the young child.* Clifton Park, NY: Thomson Delmar Learning.

Mix, K., Huttenlocher, J., & Levine, S. (2002). Matching and naming objects by shape or function: Age and context effects in preschool children. *Developmental Psychology, 38*(4), 503–518.

Nguyen, S., & Murphy, G. (2003). An apple is more than just a fruit: Cross-classification in children's concepts. *Child Development, 74*(6), 1783–1806.

Páez, M., Tabors, P., & López, L. (2007). Dual language and literacy development of Spanish-speaking preschool children. *Journal of Applied Developmental Psychology, 28*(2), 85–102.

Papafragou, A., Li, P., Choi, Y., & Han, C. (2007). Evidentiality in language and cognition. *Cognition, 103*(2), 253–299.

Paradis, J. (2007). Second language acquisition in childhood. In E. Hoff & M. Shatz (Eds.), *Blackwell handbook of language development.* (pp. 387–405). Malden, MA: Wiley-Blackwell.

Parlakian, R., & Lerner, C. (2007). Promoting healthy eating habits right from the start. *Beyond the Journal.* Accessed on April 18, 2008, from *http://journal.naeyc.org/btj/200705/pdf/RockingandRolling.pdf.*

Ramscar, M., & Gitcho, N. (2007). Developmental change and the nature of learning in childhood. *Trends in Cognitive Science, 11*(7), 274–279.

Ruble, D., Taylor, L., Cyphers, L., Greulich, F., Lurye, L., & Shrout, P. (2007). The role of gender constancy in early gender development. *Child Development, 78*(4), 1121–1136.

Treiman, R., Cohen, J., Mulqueeny, K., Kessler, B., Schechtman, S. (2007). Young children's knowledge about printed names. *Child Development, 78*(5), 1458–1471.

Wright, C., Bacigalupa, C., Black, T., & Burton, M. (2008). Windows into children's thinking: A guide to storytelling and dramatization. *Early Childhood Education Journal, 35*(4), 363–369.

BOOK COMPANION WEBSITE

The book-specific website at *www.cengage.com/education/allen* offers students a variety of study tools and useful resources such as chapter overviews and notes, tutorial quizzes, web links, frequently asked questions, discussion questions, glossary/flashcards, internet exercises, references and more. To register or purchase access to the premium resources for this text including video clips tied to chapter content, go to *www.cengage.com/login.*

Early Childhood: Six-, Seven-, and Eight-Year-Olds

Objectives

After reading this chapter, you should be able to:

- Describe several sensory experiences that would be developmentally appropriate for six-, seven-, and eight-year-olds.

- Explain why behavior problems and emotional outbursts might reappear during this stage.

- Compare and contrast the speech and language skills of six- and eight-year-olds.

- Explain and demonstrate Piaget's concept of conservation.

- Identify and describe signs of reading readiness.

- Discuss the role of friendships in children's development.

MEET JUAN AND HIS FRIEND SERGIO

For weeks, Juan has repeatedly asked his mother when school will begin. Soon to turn seven, he is eagerly anticipating the start of first grade, riding on a school bus, and eating lunch in the cafeteria. Juan met his new teacher, Mr. Rosales, last week during the open house and is excited about having a "man teacher." His mother, Anna, thinks Juan will benefit from having a male role model since his father has stopped their weekend visits.

Juan is also happy that his best friend, Sergio, will be in the same class. Unlike Juan, who is an only child, Sergio is the youngest of five brothers and three sisters. His parents work long hours and show little interest in his school activities or homework. They view their primary role as caretakers and believe the teachers are responsible for helping their son learn. Sergio struggles to write his name, has difficulty sorting objects by category, and is unable to recognize and order numbers consistently. His kindergarten teacher was reluctant to advance him to the first grade, but Mr. Rosales assured her that he would devote extra time and attention to helping Sergio. Mr. Rosales is aware that Sergio's family speaks little English at home and has limited resources.

Juan thinks it is "pretty neat" that he will go to school all day like his mother, who plans to finish her associate's degree in early childhood education this spring. She is proud of her son's progress in school and works with him at home so that he continues to do well. Juan's advanced reading and writing skills are apparent in the imaginative stories he composes on the computer when he and his mother visit their local library. When he is finished, Juan often seeks out the librarian so that he can read his story to her. Juan is also learning to tell time and repeatedly wants his mother to ask him the time.

Six-, Seven-, and Eight-Year-Olds

The period following the preschool years is especially remarkable. Children are in a stage of developmental integration, organizing and combining various developmental skills to accomplish increasingly complex tasks. At this age, boys and girls alike are becoming increasingly competent at taking care of their own personal needs—washing, dressing, toileting, eating, getting up, and getting ready for school. They observe family rules about mealtimes, television, chores, and needs for privacy. They can be trusted to run errands and carry out simple responsibilities at home and school. In other words, these children are in control of themselves and their immediate world. Above all, six-, seven-, and eight-year-olds are ready and eager to go to school, even though they might be somewhat apprehensive when the time actually arrives. Going to school creates anxieties about things such as arriving on time, remembering to bring back assigned homework, having a new teacher, taking tests, and walking home alone or going to an after-school program (Askew & Field, 2007; Akande et al., 1999).

Learning to read is the most complex perceptual task the child encounters following the preschool years (Charlesworth, 2007; Piaget, 1926). Recognizing visual letter symbols and associating them with their spoken sound is an important component of **emerging literacy**. It also means that children must learn to combine letters to form words and to put these words together to form intelligible thoughts that can be read or spoken (Nolan, 2007). Complex as the task is, most children become more adept at reading between six and eight years of age; for some, the skill is soon taken for granted.

Sensory activities continue to be essential for children's learning (Figure 7-1). Developmental kindergartens and primary classes recognize this as fundamental practice (Magnuson, Ruhm, & Waldfogel, 2007). They provide sensory experiences that encourage children to manipulate a variety of materials—blocks; puzzles; paints, glue, paper, and found materials; sand, water, and dirt; musical instruments; and measurement devices. They also include project-based opportunities such as cooking, gardening, carpentry, and dramatic play that reinforce learning across all developmental areas. The National Association for the Education of Young Children (NAEYC) strongly endorses a **hands-on learning** approach with six-, seven-, and eight-year-olds as well as with younger children. This philosophy is clearly stated in NAEYC's *Developmentally Appropriate Practice in Early Childhood Programs Serving Children Birth through Age 8* (NAEYC, 1997). Particularly noteworthy are the subsections entitled "Principles of Child Development and Learning that Inform Developmentally Appropriate Practice (DAP)" and "Guidelines for Decisions about Developmentally Appropriate Practice" that outline the rationale for individualizing children's educational opportunities. Above all, this position statement acknowledges that each child is a unique individual whose developmental abilities, family and cultural heritage, needs, and learning style differ from those of other children. Other early-childhood professional organizations, including family child care and school-age programs, have also adopted similar recommendations.

Play continues to be one of the most important activities for fostering cognitive development in the early grades (Drew et al., 2008; Honig, 2007; Singer, Golinkoff, & Hirsh-Pasek, 2006). It is also a major route to enhancing social development and all

Figure 7-1

Children continue to learn best through sensory experiences.

---

emerging literacy—early experiences, such as being read and talked to, naming objects, and identifying letters, that prepare a child for later reading, writing, and language development.

sensory—refers to the five senses: hearing, seeing, touching, smelling, and tasting.

hands-on learning—a curriculum approach that involves children as active participants, encouraging them to manipulate, investigate, experiment, and solve problems.

other developmental skills. For the most part, six-, seven-, and eight-year-olds play well with other children, especially if the group is not too large. There is keen interest in making friends, being a friend, and having friends. At the same time, there also can be quarreling, bossing, and excluding: "If you play with Lynette, then you're not *my* friend." Some children show considerable aggression, but it often tends to be verbal, aimed at hurting feelings rather than at causing physical harm.

Friends are usually playmates that the child has ready access to in the neighborhood and at school. Friends often are defined as someone who is "fun," "pretty," "strong," "nice," or "awesome." Friendships at this age are easily established and readily abandoned; few are stable or long-lasting (Guralnick et al., 2006; Yugar & Shapiro, 2001).

Throughout the primary school years, many children seem almost driven by the need to do everything right, yet they enjoy being challenged and completing tasks. They like to build models, do craft projects, play board games, and participate in organized activities. Most children enjoy these early school years. They become comfortable with themselves, their families, and their teachers.

6-year-olds

VIDEO CONNECTIONS

Clip 16

Cognitive Development: Advances in cognitive abilities, including improving memory capacity, information processing, and abstract thinking, begin to open new opportunities for complex learning.

Critical Thinking Questions:

1. Describe Vygotsky's Zone of Proximal Development.
2. What is the teacher's role in this form of learning?
3. Do you consider this instructional approach to be developmentally appropriate or inappropriate for six-year-olds? Explain.
4. What is scaffolding?
5. How did the teacher respond to children's incorrect answers?

The Six-Year-Old

Exciting adventures begin to open up to six-year-olds as their coordination improves and their size and strength increase. New challenges are often met with a mixture of enthusiasm and frustration. Six-year-olds typically have difficulty making choices and,

Figure 7-2

Six-year-olds are curi-
ous and eager to learn.

6-year-olds

at times, are overwhelmed by unfamiliar situations. At the same time, changes in their cognitive abilities enable them to see rules as useful for understanding everyday events and the behavior of others.

For many children, this period also marks the beginning of formal, subject-oriented schooling. It should be noted that formal academic activities at this age are considered developmentally inappropriate by many early childhood educators (Hyson, 2003; NAEYC, 2002; Nel, 2000). Behavior problems and signs of stress or tension such as tics, nail-biting, hair-twisting, or bed-wetting might flair up. Generally, these pass as children become familiar with new expectations and the responsibilities associated with going to school. Despite the turmoil and trying times (for adults as well), most six-year-olds experience an abundance of good times marked by a lively curiosity, an eagerness to learn, an endearing sense of humor, and exuberant outbursts of affection and good will (Figure 7-2).

DEVELOPMENTAL PROFILES AND GROWTH PATTERNS

Growth and Physical Characteristics

- Growth occurs slowly but steadily.
- Height increases 2–3 inches (5–7.5 cm) each year: girls are an average of 42–46 inches (105–115 cm) tall; boys are an average of 44–47 inches (110–117.5 cm).
- Weight increases 5–7 pounds (2.3–3.2 kg) per year: girls weigh approximately 38–47 pounds (19.1–22.3 kg); boys weigh approximately 42–49 pounds (17.3–21.4 kg).
- Weight gains reflect significant increases in muscle mass.
- Heart rate (80 beats per minute) and respiratory rates (18–28 breaths per minute) are similar to those of adults; rates vary with activity.
- Body takes on a lanky appearance as long bones of the arms and legs begin a phase of rapid growth.

(continued)

(continued) DEVELOPMENTAL PROFILES AND GROWTH PATTERNS

- Loses baby **(deciduous) teeth**; permanent (secondary) teeth erupt, beginning with the two upper front teeth; girls tend to lose teeth at an earlier age than do boys.
- Visual acuity should be approximately 20/20; children testing 20/40 or less should have a professional evaluation (Tingley, 2007).
- Farsightedness is not uncommon and might be outgrown (Dobson, Harvey, & Miller, 2007).
- Develops more adult-like facial features and overall physical appearance.
- Requires approximately 1,600 to 1,700 calories per day.

Motor Development

- Has increased muscle strength; typically, boys are stronger than girls of similar size.
- Gains greater control over large and fine motor skills; movements are becoming more precise and deliberate, although some clumsiness persists.
- Enjoys vigorous physical activity (running, jumping, climbing, and throwing).
- Moves constantly, even when trying to sit still.
- Has increased dexterity and eye–hand coordination along with improved motor functioning, which facilitates learning to ride a bicycle (without training wheels), swim, swing a bat, or kick a ball.
- Enjoys art projects (likes to paint, model with clay, "make things," draw and color, put things together, and work with wood).
- Writes numbers and letters with varying degrees of precision and interest; might reverse or confuse certain letters (*b/d*, *p/g*, *g/q*, *t/f*) (Figure 7-3).

Figure 7-3

Ability to write numbers and letters improves.

deciduous teeth—initial set of teeth that eventually fall out; often referred to as *baby teeth*.

- Traces around hand and other objects.
- Folds and cuts paper into simple shapes.
- Ties own shoes (still a struggle for some children).

Perceptual-Cognitive Development

- Shows increased attention span; works at tasks for longer periods of time, although concentrated effort is not always consistent.
- Understands concepts such as simple time markers (today, tomorrow, yesterday) or uncomplicated concepts of motion (cars go faster than bicycles).
- Identifies seasons and major holidays and the activities associated with each.
- Enjoys the challenge of puzzles, counting and sorting activities, paper-and-pencil mazes, and games that involve counting or matching letters and words with pictures.
- Recognizes some words by sight; attempts to sound out words (some children might be reading well by this time).
- Identifies familiar coins (pennies, nickels, dimes, and quarters).
- Names and correctly holds up right and left hands fairly consistently.
- Clings to certain beliefs involving magic or fantasy (the Tooth Fairy swapping a coin for a tooth; the Easter Bunny bringing eggs).
- Has limited understanding about death and dying (believes it can be reversed or that he or she caused it to happen; often expresses fear that parents might die, especially his or her mother) (Slaughter, 2007; Christian, 1997).

Speech and Language Development

- Talks nonstop; might be described as a chatterbox.
- Carries on adult-like conversations; asks many questions.
- Learns as many as five to ten new words each day; vocabulary consists of approximately 10,000 to 14,000 words.
- Uses appropriate verb tenses, word order, and sentence structure.
- Uses language rather than tantrums or physical aggression to express displeasure: "That's mine! Give it back, or I'm telling."
- Talks self through steps required in simple problem-solving situations (although the logic might be unclear to adults).
- Imitates slang and profanity; finds "bathroom" talk extremely funny.
- Delights in telling jokes and riddles; often, the humor is far from subtle (Figure 7-4).

(continued)

6-year-olds

6-year-olds

Figure 7-4

Finds humor in almost everything.

- Enjoys being read to and making up stories.
- Is capable of learning more than one language; does so spontaneously in a bilingual or multilingual family (Hoff, 2006).

Social-Emotional Development

- Experiences sudden mood swings: can be "best friends" one minute, "worst of enemies" the next; loving one day, uncooperative and irritable the next; especially unpredictable toward mother or primary caregiver.
- Becomes less dependent on parents as friendship circle expands; still needs closeness and nurturing, yet has urges to break away and "grow up" (Piaget, 1929).
- Needs and seeks adult approval, reassurance, and praise; anxious to please; might complain excessively about minor hurts or illnesses to gain attention.
- Continues to be self-centered (egocentric); still sees events almost entirely from own perspective (views everything and everyone as there for child's own benefit).
- Easily disappointed and frustrated by self-perceived failure.
- Has difficulty composing and soothing self; dislikes being corrected or losing at games; might sulk, cry, refuse to play, or reinvent rules to suit own purposes.
- Is enthusiastic and inquisitive about surroundings and everyday events.
- Shows little or no understanding of ethical behavior or moral standards; often fibs, cheats, or takes items belonging to others.

- Knows when he or she has been "bad"; values of "good" and "bad" are based on school and family expectations and rules.
- Can be increasingly fearful of thunderstorms, the dark, unidentified noises, dogs, and other animals (Weems & Costa, 2005).

• D A I L Y   R O U T I N E S •

Eating

- Has a good appetite most of the time; often takes larger helpings than is able to finish. Might skip an occasional meal; usually makes up for it later.
- Has strong food preferences and definite dislikes; willingness to try new foods is unpredictable.
- Uses table manners that often do not meet adult standards; might revert to eating with fingers; puts too much food into mouth at one time; continues to spill milk or drop food in lap.
- Has difficulty using table knife for cutting and fork for anything but spearing food.
- Finds it difficult to sit through an entire meal; wiggles and squirms, gets off (or "falls" off) chair, drops utensils.

Toileting, Bathing, and Dressing

- Balks at having to take a bath; finds many excuses for delaying or avoiding a bath entirely.
- Manages toileting routines without much help; sometimes is in a hurry or waits too long so that "accidents" happen.
- Reverts occasionally to accidental soiling or wetting of pants during new experiences, such as in the first weeks of school or when under stress.
- Sleeps through most nights without having to get up to use the bathroom. *Note:* Some children, especially boys, might not maintain a dry bed for another year or so.
- Performs self-care routines such as handwashing, bathing, and toothbrushing in a hurry; not always careful or thorough; still needs frequent supervision and demonstrations to make sure routines are carried out properly.
- Expresses interest in selecting own clothes; still needs some guidance in determining occasion and seasonal appropriateness.
- Drops clothing on floor or bed, loses shoes around the house, and flings jacket down; often forgets where it is (Figure 7-5).

(continued)

Figure 7-5

Often forgetful when it comes to caring for clothes.

Sleeping

- Needs 9–11 hours of uninterrupted sleep.
- Sleeps through the night; some children continue to have nightmares and sleep disturbances (AAFP, 2005).
- Sometimes requests a night-light, special blanket, or favorite stuffed toy (might want all three).
- Finds numerous ways to avoid bedtime; when finally in bed, falls asleep quickly.
- Finds ways to amuse self with books, toys, television, or coloring if awake before the rest of the family.

Play and Social Activities

- Has strong sense of self, evident in terms of preferences and dislikes; uncompromising about wants and needs. (Often these do not coincide with adult plans or desires.)
- Is possessive about toys and books, parents and friends but is able to share on some occasions.
- Forms close, friendly relationship with one or two other children (often slightly older); play involves working together toward specific goals.
- Becomes intolerant of being told what to do; reverts to tantrums on occasion.
- Seeks teacher's attention, praise, and reassurance; now views teacher (rather than parent) as the ultimate source of "truth."

Learning Activities

Tips for families and teachers:

- Provide materials for coloring, cutting, pasting, and painting.

- Offer paper-and-pencil games (dot-to-dot, number-to-number, word search, hidden objects; copying and tracing activities).

- Provide (and frequently join in) simple card games (Hearts, Uno®, Flinch) and board games (Scrabble Junior, Candyland, checkers), especially those in which competitiveness is minimal.

- Keep a plentiful supply of books and magazines on hand for children to read and look at as well as for adults to read to children; encourage children to make up and tell their own stories. Make weekly trips to the library.

- Share children's interest in collecting objects; help them group, label, and display objects.

- Provide an assortment of dress-up clothes for boys and girls; use children's interests and familiar community workers as a guide for role-playing.

- Encourage simple cooking, carpentry, and construction activities with blocks, cars, trucks, planes, and zoo and farm animals. (Avoid battery-driven and other mechanical toys—when the novelty has worn off, they offer little involvement, hence limited learning.)

- Encourage at least 60 minutes of vigorous physical activity daily (bicycling; inline skating; swimming; gardening; throwing, catching, batting balls, walking).

- Involve children in cooking activities; use these opportunities to build language, math, science, and problem-solving skills.

6-year-olds

Developmental Alerts

Check with a health care provider or early-childhood specialist if, by the seventh birthday, the child *does not*:

- Show signs of ongoing growth (increasing height and weight); continuing motor development such as running, jumping, and balancing.

- Show some interest in reading and trying to reproduce letters, especially his or her own name.

- Follow simple, multiple-step directions: "Finish your book, put it on the shelf, and then get your coat on."

(continued)

Developmental Alerts   (continued)

- Follow through with instructions and complete simple tasks (putting dishes in the sink, picking up clothes, or finishing a puzzle). *Note:* All children forget. Task incompletion is not a problem unless a child *repeatedly* leaves tasks unfinished.

- Begin to develop alternatives to excessive use of inappropriate behavior to get his or her way.

- Develop a steady decrease in tension-type behavior that might have developed with the start of school or participation in an organized activity (repeated grimacing or facial tics, eye twitching, grinding of teeth, nail biting, regressive soiling or wetting, frequent stomachaches, or refusing to go to school).

Safety Concerns

Continue to implement safety practices described for the previous stages. Always be aware of new safety issues as the child continues to grow and develop.

Burns

- Keep matches and lighters in locked storage.

Falls

- Make sure clothing fits properly; skirts and pants that are too long can cause a child to trip or become entangled in play equipment. Remind children to keep shoes tied or Velcro straps fastened.

- Require children to wear helmets and other appropriate protective gear whenever they ride bikes, skateboards, or scooters.

Tools/Equipment

- Store machinery and sharp instruments in a safe place, out of children's reach.

- Teach children proper use of scissors, knives, hammers, and kitchen equipment.

Traffic

- Review safety rules to follow in and around motor vehicles, when crossing streets, or riding a bicycle. Teach children to dismount and walk their bike across streets.

- Discuss appropriate behavior on buses if your child rides one to school.

- Insist that children always wear a seatbelt when riding in motor vehicles.

Water

- Enroll children in swimming lessons and teach them proper safety rules to follow around pools. Have proper rescue equipment accessible.
- *Never leave children unattended near water.*

The Seven-Year-Old

Seven-year-olds are becoming more aware of themselves as individuals. They work hard at being responsible, being "good," and doing it "right" (Figure 7-6). They tend to take themselves seriously—too seriously at times. When they fail to live up to their own self-imposed expectations, they might sulk or become frustrated or withdrawn. It is as if children at seven are trying to think things through and integrate what they already know with the flood of new experiences coming their way (Rogoff, 1997). Worrying about what might or might not come to pass is also typical; for example, anticipating yet dreading second grade can create anxiety. Maybe the work will be too hard; maybe the teacher won't be nice; or maybe the other kids won't be friendly.

At the same time, children of this age have many positive traits. They are more reasonable and willing to share and cooperate. They are becoming better listeners and better at understanding and following through on what they are told. They are able to stay on task for longer periods of time and strive mightily to do everything perfectly (which only increases their worry load). Because of these complicated feelings, parents and teachers need to accept the mood swings. It seems the moods reflect the child's overwhelming efforts to cope with the conflicts inherent in being a seven-year-old (Ladd & Burgess, 2001).

7-year-olds

Figure 7-6

Seven-year-olds take pride in doing everything right.

Growth and Physical Characteristics

- Weight increase tends to be relatively small; a gain of 6 pounds (2.7 kg) per year is typical. Seven-year-olds weigh approximately 50–55 pounds (22.7–25 kg).
- Height increases an average of 2.5 inches (6.25 cm) per year. Girls are approximately 44–44.5 inches (110–116.3 cm) tall; boys are approximately 46–49.5 inches (115–124 cm) tall.
- Muscle mass is fairly equal for boys and girls.
- Physical growth continues slowly and steadily; a few girls might overtake some boys in height.
- Posture is more erect; arms and legs continue to lengthen, giving children a longer, leaner appearance.
- Energy level comes and goes, fluctuating between spurts of high energy and intervals of temporary fatigue.
- Still experiences a number of colds and other minor illnesses; however, these occur less frequently than at age six.
- Eyeballs continue to change shape and size; vision should be checked periodically to ensure good vision.
- Hair often grows darker in color.
- Permanent teeth continue to replace baby teeth.

Motor Development

- Exhibits large and fine motor control that is more finely tuned: balances on either foot; runs up and down stairs with alternating feet; throws and catches smaller balls; practices batting balls; manipulates a computer mouse, knitting needles, or paintbrush with greater precision (Figure 7-7).
- Tends to be cautious in undertaking more challenging physical activities such as climbing up or jumping down from high places.
- Practices a new motor skill over and over until mastered and then drops it to work on something else.
- Finds floor more comfortable than furniture when reading, playing games, or watching television; legs are often in constant motion.
- Uses knife and fork appropriately but inconsistently.
- Holds pencil in a tight grasp near the tip; rests head on forearm, lowers head almost to the tabletop when doing pencil-and-paper tasks.
- Produces letters and numbers in a deliberate and confident fashion (characters are increasingly uniform in size and shape; might run out of room on line or page when writing).

Perceptual-Cognitive Development

- Understands concepts of space and time in ways that are both logical and more practical (a year is "a long time"; a 100 miles is "far away").

7-year-olds

Figure 7-7

Is able to manipulate objects with improved accuracy.

- Begins to grasp Piaget's concepts of **conservation**; for example, the shape of a container does not necessarily reflect the quantity it can hold (Figure 7-8). (Children are now entering Piaget's stage of concrete operations.)

- Gains a better understanding of cause and effect: "If I'm late for school again, I'll be in big trouble"; "Ice cubes will melt if they get too warm."

- Tells time by the clock and understands calendar time—days, months, years, and seasons.

- Plans ahead: "I'm saving this cookie for later tonight."

Figure 7-8

Children are beginning to understand that two differently-shaped containers can hold the same amount of liquid.

(continued)

7-year-olds

---

conservation—the stage in children's cognitive development at which they understand that an object's physical qualities (e.g., weight, mass) remain the same despite changes in its appearance; for example, flattening a ball of playdough does not affect its weight.

- Shows marked fascination with magic tricks; enjoys putting on shows for family and friends.
- Finds reading easier; many seven-year-olds read for their own enjoyment and delight in retelling story details.
- Tends to have better reading than spelling skills.
- Enjoys counting and saving money.
- Continues to reverse some letters and substitute sounds on occasion; this is typical development and does not indicate a reading or learning disability.

Speech and Language Development

- Engages in storytelling; likes to write short stories and tell imaginative tales.
- Uses adult-like sentence structure and language in conversation; patterns reflect cultural and geographical differences.
- Becomes more precise and elaborate in use of language; greater use of descriptive adjectives and adverbs.
- Uses gestures to illustrate conversations.
- Criticizes own performance: "I didn't draw that right," "Her picture is better than mine."
- Verbal exaggeration commonplace: "I ate ten hot dogs at the picnic."
- Offers explanations of events in terms of own preferences or needs: "It didn't rain yesterday because I was going on a picnic."
- Describes personal experiences in great detail: "First we parked the car, then we hiked up this long trail, then we sat down on a broken tree near a lake and ate. . . ."
- Understands and carries out multiple-step instructions (up to five steps); might need to have directions repeated because of not listening to entire request the first time.
- Enjoys writing e-mail messages and simple notes to friends.

Social-Emotional Development

- Is cooperative and affectionate toward adults and less frequently annoyed with them; sees humor in everyday happenings and is more outgoing.
- Likes to be the "teacher's helper"; eager for teacher's attention and approval but less obvious about seeking it.
- Seeks out friendships; friends are important but can find plenty to do if no one is available.
- Quarrels less often, although squabbles and tattling continue to occur in both one-on-one and group play.
- Complains that family decisions are unjust; that a particular sibling might get to do more or is given more.
- Blames others for own mistakes; makes up alibis for personal shortcomings: "I could have made a better one, but my teacher didn't give me enough time."

7-year-olds

- Prefers same-gender playmates; more likely to play in groups (Figure 7-9).
- Worries about not being liked; feelings easily hurt; might cry, be embarrassed, or state adamantly, "I will never play with you again," when criticized.
- Takes responsibilities seriously; can be trusted to carry out directions and commitments; worries about being late for school or not getting work done.

Figure 7-9

Prefers same-gender playmates.

7-year-olds

VIDEO CONNECTIONS

Clip 17

Cognitive Development: Children are becoming increasingly sophisticated at understanding how things work, their causes and effects, and how various manipulations can alter the outcome. These cognitive advances pique children's curiosity and interest in undertaking many new activities.

Critical Thinking Questions:

1. Which cognitive abilities make it possible for seven-year-olds to understand Piaget's theory of conservation?
2. Which changes in children's cognitive skills are evident during Piaget's concrete operational stage?
3. In what ways do these newly emerging cognitive abilities influence children's development in other domains such as motor, speech and language, and social-emotional?
4. Do all children experience this stage of cognitive development? How might cultural or developmental differences influence this process?

• D A I L Y   R O U T I N E S •

Eating

- Eats most foods; better about sampling unfamiliar foods or taking small tastes of disliked foods, but might still refuse a few strong "hates."
- Shows interest in food; likes to help with grocery shopping and meal preparation.
- Uses table manners that adults might consider far from perfect but improving; less spilled milk and other accidents due to silliness, impulse, or haste to finish.
- Uses eating utensils with relative ease; seldom eats with fingers; some children still have trouble cutting meat.
- Is sometimes distracted during mealtimes by conversations and things going on elsewhere in the house or outdoors; at other times, is focused on eating and getting done.

Toileting, Bathing, and Dressing

- Reluctant to begin bath; however, once in the tub, seems to relax and enjoy the experience; is able to manage own bath or shower with minimal assistance.
- Dresses self although slow and distracted at times; can speed up the process when time becomes critical or there is something else they want to do.
- Buttons and zips own clothes; ties own shoes; not always careful or precise (buttons askew, zipper undone, shoelaces soon dragging).
- Shows little interest in clothes; wears whatever is laid out or available.
- Shows more interest in combing or brushing own hair.
- Has good bowel and bladder control; individual rhythm well established; might resist having bowel movements at school.
- Less likely to get up during the night to use the toilet.

Sleeping

- Averages 10–11 hours of sleep at night; children who are in bed fewer hours often have trouble getting up in the morning.
- Sleeps soundly with few if any bad dreams; instead, often dreams about their own exploits and adventures (Owens, 2005).
- Gets ready for bed independently most nights but still enjoys being tucked in or read to.
- Wakes up early most mornings; occupies self in bed with toys, counting out savings in piggy bank, looking at baseball card collection, reading, and so forth.

7-year-olds

Play and Social Activities

- Participates in organized group activities (Boys' and Girls' Clubs, Cub Scouts and Brownies, 4-H, swim and soccer teams).

- Dislikes missing school or social events; wants to keep up with friends and classmates.

- Has interest in coloring and cutting things out, with a friend or alone.

- Engages in favorite play activities such as bicycle riding, climbing activities, basketball, skating, and computer games.

- Likes to play competitive board and card games but might bend the rules when losing.

- Turns activities into challenges. "Let's see who can throw rocks the farthest." "I can run to the corner faster than you can."

Learning Activities

Tips for Families and Teachers:

- Take trips to the library for children's story time and dramatic play activities as well as for checking out books.

- Sign up for free or low-cost community offerings of interest to the child (art, science, swimming, T-ball, tumbling, yoga, or zoo and museum programs).

- Take family "collecting walks" in the neighborhood, on nearby beaches, or in parks; support the child's efforts to organize found treasures.

- Accumulate tools and equipment that really work (simple carpentry and garden tools, science materials for growing a potato vine or maintaining an ant farm or a simple aquarium).

- Gather materials for creating art projects, models, or science experiments (pieces of wood, Styrofoam, various weights and textures of cardboard and paper, beads, fabric, ribbon, yarn, and so forth) (Figure 7-10).

- Offer dress-up clothes and props for planning and staging shows; attend the performances.

- Provide a doll house, farm or zoo set, space station or airport, complete with small-scale people, animals, and equipment.

(continued)

7-year-olds

Learning Activities *(continued)*

Figure 7-10

The outdoors provides
a wealth of learning
opportunities.

7-year-
olds

Developmental Alerts

Check with a health care provider or early-childhood specialist if, by the eighth birthday, the child *does not*:

- Attend to the task at hand; show longer periods of sitting quietly, listening, and
  responding appropriately.
- Follow through on simple instructions.
- Go to school willingly most days (of concern are excessive complaints about
  stomachaches or headaches when getting ready for school).
- Make friends (observe closely to see whether the child plays alone most of the
  time or withdraws consistently from contact with other children).
- Sleep soundly most nights. (Frequent and recurring nightmares or bad dreams are
  usually at a minimum at this age.)
- Seem to see or hear adequately at times (squints, rubs eyes excessively; asks
  frequently to have things repeated).
- Handle stressful situations without undue emotional upset (excessive crying,
  sleeping or eating disturbances, withdrawal, frequent anxiety).
- Assume responsibility for personal care (dressing, bathing, feeding self) most of
  the time.
- Show improved motor skills.

Safety Concerns

Continue to implement safety practices described for the previous stages. Be aware of new safety issues as the child continues to grow and develop.

Firearms

- Store unloaded guns in a locked cabinet with ammunition kept in another location. Teach children never to pick up or touch a gun and to report immediately any that are found. Check with families of your children's friends to determine whether guns are present and properly stored in their house.

Play Environments

- Review rules for the safe use of playground equipment and safe play when away from home. Be aware of your child's friends and types of play in which they tend to engage. Remind children to wash their hands after playing, especially after touching any animals.

Tools/Equipment

- Do not let children use power mowers or other yard equipment (e.g., weed eaters, hedge trimmers); keep children away when such equipment is in use.

Water

- Continue to supervise children at all times when they are in a pool, lake, or around any body of water.
- Teach children to swim and to follow water safety rules. Insist that children wear approved floatation vests when in or around large bodies of water (fishing, boating, skiing).

8-year-olds

The Eight-Year-Old

Eight-year-olds display a great enthusiasm for life. Energy is concentrated on improving skills they already possess and enhancing what they already know. Eight-year-olds, once again, experience strong feelings of independence and are eager to make decisions about their own plans and friends. Interests and attention are increasingly devoted to peers and team or group activities rather than to family, teachers, or siblings. Sometime near midyear, boys and girls begin to go their separate ways and form new interests in same-gender groups (Rose & Rudolph, 2006).

A small percentage of children might begin to engage in aggressive, intimidating, or **bullying** behaviors (Berger, 2007). Their targets are often peers who are perceived as loners, likely to react or retaliate, lacking in self-confidence, having special needs, or unable to stand up for themselves (Veenstra et al., 2007; Van Cleave & Davis, 2006). Occasional incidences of name-calling, threatening, or hitting are not uncommon at this age. However, a pattern of intentional and hurtful behavior that escalates as children approach adolescence distinguishes bullying from typical developmental expectations (Ball et al., 2008).

Researchers continue to study why some children have more difficulty controlling aggressive behavior. Their findings suggest that bullies typically fall into two categories. The first includes children who are self-assured, impulsive, angry, and lacking in empathy and who use their physical strength to intimidate (Larsson, Viding, & Plomin, 2008). The second group consists of children who tend to be passive, less likely to initiate bullying but willing to join in after it has begun. These children often possess poor social skills, low self-esteem, and might themselves be victims of abuse or neglect. They also have difficulty knowing how to initiate appropriate social interaction and how to control their own impulsive behaviors.

Anti-bullying programs are being implemented in many schools and communities in response to state legislation and findings that demonstrate short-term and long-term consequences of bullying on children's development (Leff, 2007; Rowan, 2007). These initiatives are aimed at promoting positive social, communication, and anger management skills; boosting children's self-esteem; and reducing harassing behaviors. Prevention efforts are also focusing on the victims, helping them learn empowering behaviors such as walking away, avoiding bullies, problem-solving, informing an adult, and peaceful conflict resolution skills (Jensen, 2007).

DEVELOPMENTAL PROFILES AND GROWTH PATTERNS

Growth and Physical Characteristics

- Continues to gain 5–7 pounds (2.3–3.2 kg) per year; an eight-year-old weighs approximately 55–61 pounds (25–27.7 kg). Girls typically weigh less than boys.

- Height increases at a pace that is slow but steady, an average of 2.5 inches (6.25 cm) per year; girls are often taller (46–49 inches [115–122.5 cm]) as compared to boys (48–52 inches [120–130 cm]).

- Body shape takes on a more mature appearance; arms and legs grow longer, creating an image that is tall and lanky.

- Normal vision acuity is 20/20. Vision should be checked periodically to ensure good vision.

- Some girls might begin to develop breasts and pubic hair and experience menses (Euling et al., 2008; Golub et al., 2008).

bullying—Verbal and physical behavior that is hurtful, intentional, and repeatedly directed toward a person or child who is viewed as weaker.

- Mood swings may become more apparent as changes in hormonal activity occur.
- Overall state of health improves; fewer illnesses are typically experienced.

Motor Development

- Enjoys vigorous activity; likes to dance, inline skate, swim, wrestle, ride bikes, play basketball, jump rope, and fly kites (Figure 7-11).
- Seeks out opportunities to participate in team activities and games such as soccer, baseball, and kickball.
- Exhibits significant improvement in agility, balance, speed, and strength.
- Copies words and numbers from a blackboard with increasing speed and accuracy; has good eye–hand coordination.
- Possesses seemingly endless energy.

Perceptual-Cognitive Development

- Collects objects; organizes and displays items according to more complex systems; bargains and trades with friends to obtain additional pieces.
- Saves money for small purchases; eagerly develops plans to earn cash from odd jobs; studies catalogues and magazines for ideas of items to purchase.

Figure 7-11

Enjoys good health
and vigorous activity.

8-year-
olds

(continued)

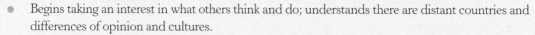

- Begins taking an interest in what others think and do; understands there are distant countries and differences of opinion and cultures.
- Accepts challenge and responsibility with enthusiasm; delights in being asked to perform tasks, both at home and in school; interested in being rewarded for efforts.
- Likes to read and work independently; spends considerable time planning and making lists.
- Understands perspective (shadow, distance, shape); drawings reflect more realistic portrayal of objects.
- Grasps the basic principles of conservation. (A tall, narrow jar might look different from one that is short and wide but they both can hold the same amount of liquid.)
- Uses more sophisticated logic in efforts to understand everyday events; for example, is systematic in looking for a misplaced jacket, backpack, or toy.
- Adds and subtracts multiple-digit numbers; learning multiplication and division.
- Looks forward to school and is disappointed when ill or unable to attend.

Speech and Language Development

- Delights in telling jokes and riddles.
- Understands and carries out multiple-step instructions (up to five steps); might need to have directions repeated because of not listening to the entire request.
- Reads with ease and understanding.
- Writes letters or sends e-mail messages to friends; includes descriptions that are imaginative and detailed (Figure 7-12).
- Uses language to criticize and compliment others; repeats slang and curse words.
- Understands and follows rules of grammar in conversation and written form.
- Is intrigued with learning secret word codes and using code language.
- Converses fluently with adults; able to think and talk about past and future: "What time is my swim meet next week?" "Where did we go on vacation last summer?"

Social-Emotional Development

- Begins to form opinions about moral values and attitudes; declares things either right or wrong (Barrett et al., 2007).
- Plays with two or three "best" friends, most often of the same age and gender; also enjoys spending some time alone (Rose, 2007).

8-year-olds

Figure 7-12

Composes stories and letters with imaginative detail.

- Seems less critical of own performance but is easily frustrated and upset when unable to complete a task or when the product does not meet expectations.
- Participates in team games and activities; group membership and acceptance by peers are important.
- Continues to blame others or makes up alibis to explain his or her own shortcomings or mistakes.
- Enjoys talking on the telephone with friends and family.
- Understands and respects the fact that some children are more talented in certain areas such as drawing, sports, reading, art, or music.
- Desires adult attention and recognition; enjoys performing for adults and challenging them in games.

8-year-olds

VIDEO CONNECTIONS

Clip 18

Social Competence: Nine- and ten-year-olds enjoy social interaction. Friends and friendships are gradually gaining importance over family members. This is an important step in the process of becoming an independent adult.

Critical Thinking Questions:

1. Why is peer acceptance important at this age?
2. What social skills are involved in making and keeping friends?
3. Which qualities are girls more likely to find attractive when making friends? What about boys?
4. Do you think television has any effect on children's concept and formation of friendships? Explain.

• DAILY ROUTINES •

Eating

- Looks forward to meals; boys are often hungry and eat more than do girls. Serving nutrient-dense foods (and limiting calorie-dense items) helps meet critical growth requirements and reduces the risk of obesity (Marotz, 2009).

- Is willing to try new foods and some of the foods previously refused.

- Takes pride in using good table manners, especially when eating out or when company is present; at home, manners are of less concern.

- Finishes meals quickly to resume previous activities; might stuff mouth with too much food or not chew food thoroughly.

Toileting, Bathing, and Dressing

- Develops a pattern for bowel and bladder functions; usually has good control but might need to urinate more frequently when under stress.

- Hurries through hand washing; dirt often ends up on the towel rather than washed down the drain.

- Enjoys bath and playing in water; easily sidetracked when supposed to be getting ready to bathe; some children are able to prepare their own bath or shower.

8-year-olds

- Takes greater interest in appearance, selecting and coordinating own outfits, brushing hair, and looking good.
- Helps care for own clothes; hangs clothes up most times, helps with laundry by folding and returning items to dresser.
- Ties own shoes skillfully but often too busy to be bothered.

Sleeping

- Sleeps soundly through the night (averages 10 hours); efforts to delay bedtime might suggest less sleep is needed.
- Begins to question established bedtime; wants to stay up later; becomes easily distracted and involved in other activities while getting ready for bed.
- Sometimes wakes early and gets dressed while family members are still sleeping.

Play and Social Activities

- Enjoys competitive activities and sports (soccer, baseball, swimming, gymnastics); eager to join a team; just as eager to quit if too much forced competition.
- Begins to adopt a know-it-all attitude toward the end of the eighth year; becomes argumentative with peers (and adults) (Barrett et al., 2007).
- Likes to play board, electronic, and card games; often interprets rules to improve her or his own chances of winning.
- Seeks acceptance from peers; begins to imitate clothing fads, hairstyles, behavior, and language of admired peers.

8-year-olds

Learning Activities

Tips for families and teachers:

- Provide (and join in) games that require a moderate degree of strategy (chess, checkers, dominoes, card games, magic sets, and appropriate computer games).
- Encourage creativity; provide materials for simple painting, crafts, cooking, gardening, or building projects.
- Make frequent trips to the library; provide books to read as well as stories on CDs and DVDs.

(continued)

Learning Activities *(continued)*

- Invest in an inexpensive camera; encourage children to experiment and to write stories about their pictures.

- Arrange for opportunities to develop skills in noncompetitive activities—swimming, dancing, tumbling, skating, basketball, karate, bowling, or playing a musical instrument; this is a time of trying out many interests; seldom is there a long-term commitment.

- Assign routine tasks, such as feeding the dog, folding laundry, dusting furniture, bringing in the mail, watering plants, or setting the dinner table, to foster a sense of responsibility.

Developmental Alerts

Check with a health care provider or early-childhood specialist if, by the ninth birthday, the child *does not*:

- Exhibit a good appetite and continued weight gain. (Some children, especially girls, might already begin to show early signs of an eating disorder.) Medical evaluation should be sought for excessive weight gains or losses.

- Experience fewer illnesses.

- Show improved motor skills in terms of agility, speed, and balance.

- Understand abstract concepts and use complex thought processes to problem-solve.

- Look forward to school and the challenge of learning on most days.

- Follow through on multiple-step instructions.

- Express ideas clearly and fluently.

- Form friendships with other children and participate in group activities.

8-year-olds

Safety Concerns

Continue to implement safety practices described for the previous stages. Be aware of new safety issues as the child continues to grow and develop.

Animals

- Remind children to respect animals (not to approach unfamiliar animals and to refrain from yelling or making sudden movements).

- Teach children to recognize poisonous snakes and to leave them alone.
- Insist on thorough hand washing after touching any animal.

Backpacks

- To prevent injury, backpacks should be worn over both shoulders, secured with a hip strap, loaded with the heaviest items against the child's back, and weigh less than 20 percent of the child's body weight. Wheeled backpacks are preferable.

Toys

- Supervise use of more advanced toys such as chemistry or woodworking sets and those that involve electricity or propellants.
- Require children to wear helmets and appropriate protective gear when biking, skating, and so forth.

Water

- Require children to wear a life jacket whenever boating, skiing, or participating in other water sports.

S U M M A R Y

The transition to formal schooling marks a distinctive change for many children. New experiences and opportunities are generally met with a combination of enthusiasm and improving abilities as well as periodic reluctance and frustration. Children often set high expectations for themselves, then falter when these standards cannot be met. However, they are eager to learn and able to accomplish many complex skills, including reading, writing, telling time, counting money, and following detailed instructions during this stage. They become imaginative storytellers, jokesters, and even "magicians." Friends and friendships are increasingly important as children's interests and independence expand. They also begin to understand the meaning and complexity of everyday events, form moral values and opinions, and recognize cultural and individual differences. By the end of this period, children are fully capable of managing their personal care and grooming needs but might still need occasional adult prompting.

8-year-olds

KEY TERMS

bullying
conservation
deciduous teeth

emerging literacy
hands-on learning
sensory

A. **Apply What You Have Learned**

Reread the brief developmental sketch about Juan and Sergio at the beginning of the chapter. How might you answer the following questions?

1. Which initial forms of screening would you arrange for Sergio to ensure that his learning delays were not being caused by a health-related condition?

2. Which motor skills would you expect Juan to exhibit if his development was typical for a seven-year-old?

3. Is it appropriate for Juan's mother to encourage his participation in a local youth soccer league? Explain your answer from a developmental perspective.

4. How might differences in environmental conditions help explain why Juan and Sergio are performing at different levels in school?

5. From a developmental perspective, explain why Juan is so persistent in asking his mother to have him tell time or the librarian to listen to his stories.

6. If you were Juan's mother, what special safety precautions should you be taking to prevent unintentional injury?

B. **Review Questions**

1. Compare and contrast the cognitive skills of a typical six-year-old and an eight-year-old.

2. Should you be concerned about a seven-year-old who weighs 75 pounds? Explain.

3. What classroom activities can a teacher plan to reinforce eight-year-olds' interest in reading and writing?

4. Describe three perceptual skills that would indicate a readiness to begin reading.

5. Identify three reasonable expectations for a six-year-old in terms of home routine.

6. Describe three developmentally appropriate activities that a parent or teacher might use to expand the language skills of seven- and eight-year-olds.

Visit the book companion website at *www.cengage.com/education/allen* for links to these websites and additional resources.

REFERENCES

American Academy of Family Physicians (AAFP). (2005). Information from your family doctor. Nightmares and night terrors in children. *American Family Physician, 72*(7), 1322. Accessed on April 20, 2008, from *http://www.aafp.org/afp/20051001/1322ph.html.*

Akande, A., Osagie, J., Mwaiteleke, P., Ababio, E., Selepe, T., & Chipeta, K. (1999). Managing children's fears and anxieties in classroom settings. *Early Child Development and Care, 158,* 51–69.

Askew, C., & Field, A. (2007). Vicarious learning and the development of fears in childhood. *Behavior Research & Therapy, 45*(11), 2616–2627.

Ball, H., Arseneault, L., Taylor, A., Maughan, B., Caspi, A., & Moffitt, T. (2008). Genetic and environmental influences on victims, bullies and bully-victims in childhood. *Journal of Child Psychology & Psychiatry, 49*(1), 104–112.

Barrett, H., Keller, M., Takezawa, M., & Wichary, S. (2007). Relationships and emotions in children's understanding of social contract violations. *Journal of Evolutionary Psychology, 5*(1), 213–234.

Berger, K. (2007). Update on bullying at school: Science forgotten? *Developmental Review, 27*(1), 90–126.

Charlesworth, R. (2007). *Understanding child development.* Clifton Park, NY: Delmar Cengage Learning.

Christian, L. (1997). Children and death. *Young Children, 52*(4), 76–80.

Dobson, V., Harvey, E., & Miller, J. (2007). Spherical equivalent refractive error in preschool children from a population with a high prevalence of astigmatism. *Optometry & Vision Science, 84*(2), 124–130.

Drew, W., Christie, J., Johnson, J., Meckley, A., & Nell, M. (2008). Constructive play: A value-added strategy for meeting early learning standards. *Young Children, 63*(4), 38–44.

Euling, S., Selevan, S., Pescovitz, O., & Skakkebaek, N. (2008). Role of environmental factors in the timing of puberty. *Pediatrics, 121*(Suppl 3), S167–171.

Gibbs, J. (2003). *Moral development and reality.* Thousand Oaks, CA: Sage.

Golub, M., Collman, G., Foster, P., Kimmel, C., Raipert-De Mevts, E., Reiter, E., Sharpe, R., Skakkebaek, N., & Toppari, J. (2008). Public health implications of altered puberty timing. *Pediatrics, 121*(Suppl 3), S218–230.

Guralnick, M., Hammond, M., Connor, R., & Neville, B. (2006). Stability, change, and correlates of the peer relationships of young children with mild developmental delays. *Child Development, 77*(2), 312–324.

Hoff, E. (2006). How social contexts support and shape language development. *Developmental Review, 26*(1), 55–88.

Honig, A. (2007). Play: Ten power boosts for children's early learning. *Young Children, 62*(5), 72–78.

Hyson, M. (2003). Putting early academics in their place. *Educational Leadership, 60*(7), 20–23.

Jensen, J. (2007). Skills-based prevention program on bullying and bully victimization among elementary school children. *Prevention Science, 8*(4), 285–296.

Ladd, G., & Burgess, K. (2001). Do relational risks and protective factors moderate the linkages between childhood aggression and early psychological and school adjustment? *Child Development, 72*(5), 1579–1601.

Larsson, H., Viding, E., & Plomin, R. (2008). Callous-unemotional traits and antisocial behavior: Genetic, environmental and early parenting characteristics. *Criminal Justice & Behavior, 35*(2), 197–211.

Leff, S. (2007). Bullying and peer victimization at school: Considerations and future directions. *The School Psychology Review, 36*(3), 406–412.

Magnuson, K., Ruhm, C., & Waldfogel, J. (2007). The persistence of preschool effects: Do subsequent experiences matter? *Early Childhood Research Quarterly, 22*(1), 18–38.

Marotz, L. (2009). *Health, safety and nutrition for the young child.* Clifton Park, NY: Thomson Delmar Learning.

NAEYC. (1997). *Developmentally appropriate practice in early childhood programs servicing children birth through age 8.* Washington, DC: Author.

NAEYC. (2002). *Early learning standards: Creating the conditions for success.* Washington, DC: Author.

Nel, E. (2000). Academics, literacy, and young children: A plea for a middle ground. *Childhood Education, 76*(3), 136–141.

Nolan, S. (2007). Young children's motivation to read and write: Development in social contexts. *Cognition and Instruction, 25*(2), 219–270.

Owens, L. (2005). Introduction: Culture and sleep in children. *Pediatrics, 115*(1 Suppl), 201–203.

Piaget, J. (1926). *The language and thought of the child.* New York: Harcourt, Brace & World.

Piaget, J. (1929). *The child's conception of the world.* New York: Harcourt Brace.

Rogoff, B. (1997). Evaluating development in the process of participation: Theory, methods, and practice building on each other. In E. Amsel & K. A. Renninger (Eds.), *Change and development: Issues of theory, method, and application.* (pp. 265–285). Hillsdale, NJ: Erlbaum.

Rose, A. (2007). Structure, content, and socioemotional correlates of girls' and boys' friendships. *Merrill-Palmer Quarterly, 53*(3), 489–506.

Rose, A., & Rudolph, K. (2006). Review of sex differences in peer relationship processes: Potential trade-offs for the emotional and behavioral development of girls and boys. *Psychological Bulletin, 132*(1), 98–131.

Rowan, L. (2007). Making classrooms bully-free zones: Practical suggestions for educators. *Kappa Delta Pi Record, 43*(4), 182–183, 185.

Singer, D., Golinkoff, R., & Hirsh-Pasek, K. (Eds.). (2006). *Play = Learning: How play motivates and enhances children's cognitive and social-emotional growth.* New York: Oxford University Press.

Slaughter, V. (2007). Death understanding and fear of death in young children. *Clinical Child Psychology and Psychiatry, 12*(4), 525–535.

Tingley, D. (2007). Vision screening essentials: Screening today for eye disorders in the pediatric patient. *Pediatrics in Review, 28*(2), 54–61.

Van Cleave, J., & Davis, M. (2006). Bullying and peer victimization among children with special health care needs. *Pediatrics, 118*(4), 1212–1219.

Veenstra, R., Lindenberg, S., Zijlstra, B., De Winter, A., Verhulst, F., & Ormel, J. (2007). The dyadic nature of bullying and victimization: Testing a dual-perspective theory. *Child Development, 78*(6), 1843–1854.

Weems, C., & Costa, N. (2005). Developmental differences in the expression of childhood anxiety symptoms and fears. *Journal of the American Academy of Child & Adolescent Psychiatry, 44*(7), 656–663.

Yugar, J., & Shapiro, E. (2001). Elementary children's school friendship: A comparison of peer assessment methodologies. *School Psychology Review, 30*(4), 568–585.

BOOK COMPANION WEBSITE

The book-specific website at *www.cengage.com/education/allen* offers students a variety of study tools and useful resources such as chapter overviews and notes, tutorial quizzes, web links, frequently asked questions, discussion questions, glossary/flashcards, internet exercises, references and more. To register or purchase access to the premium resources for this text including video clips tied to chapter content, go to *www.cengage.com/login*.

Middle Childhood: Nine-, Ten-, Eleven-, and Twelve-Year-Olds

Objectives

After reading this chapter, you should be able to:

- Describe several changes that occur during early puberty.

- Discuss how the ability to think abstractly affects learning.

- Describe the concept of friendship from the perspective of a nine-year-old and a ten-year-old.

- Plan developmentally appropriate activities for nine- and ten-year-olds and eleven- and twelve-year-olds.

- Compare and contrast the language development of nine- to ten-year-olds with that of eleven- to twelve-year-olds.

MEET JUAN AND HIS STEPSISTER, CARLIN

Juan, age eleven, and his new stepfather have enjoyed each other's companionship from the very beginning. They spend considerable time together, attending sporting events, taking camping trips in the mountains, and building model planes. Juan likes school, especially math and computer classes, and has many "best friends." His teacher considers Juan a good student and appreciates his offers to help around the classroom. Juan's parents are continually amazed by his seemingly endless appetite and energy.

Juan has slowly been adjusting to the idea of having a stepsister. Carlin, a caring and talkative nine-year-old, is somewhat less enthusiastic than Juan about school. During the last parent–teacher conference, Carlin's teachers expressed concern about her inability to remain seated and focused on assignments for longer than five or ten minutes at a time. Carlin's mother has made similar observations at home, often becoming exasperated because Carlin has difficulty following multistep directions and tends to be disorganized. Carlin often "forgets" when a book report is due, that the dog needs to be fed, or that she was supposed to bring home her list of spelling words for tomorrow's test. She has few friends and prefers to play with Juan and his friends. However, Juan finds it annoying when she tags along and frequently begs his stepfather to make her stop.

Nine-, Ten-, Eleven-, and Twelve-Year Olds

The stretch of years from age eight to early adolescence is usually an enjoyable and relatively peaceful time for all concerned. Spontaneous behavior is gradually channeled into more goal-directed efforts as children begin making the transition from a state of dependence to one of greater independence. Although they are no longer young children, they are also not yet capable adults. This tension contributes to struggles with self-concept, self-esteem, and desire for complete autonomy.

The middle years are marked by a hunger for knowledge and understanding. Most children have adjusted to being at school for six or more hours each day. The stresses, strains, and frustrations of learning to read, write, do basic arithmetic, and follow directions are long forgotten. Language usage becomes more sophisticated and adult-like. During this period, children also develop an increasingly complex ability to think in the abstract, understand cause and effect, and use **logic** for solving problems and figuring out how things work. They comprehend that things really are the same in spite of being used for alternative purposes or seen from a different perspective—a shovel can be used not only for digging but also for prying the lid off a paint can; a mixing bowl can be traced to draw a perfect circle.

Changes in physical growth and development vary greatly from child to child during this period (Figure 8-1). Girls typically experience a growth spurt (height and weight) during this period that is significantly greater than that of boys. Research finds that some girls as young as eight or nine begin to experience hormonal changes associated with puberty (Pinyerd & Zipf, 2005).

Some older children might begin to experiment with new behaviors such as wearing alternative clothing and hair styles, quitting a long-time sport or favorite musical instrument, forming associations with a "different crowd," or dieting. Although this can be

---

logic—process of reasoning based on a series of facts or events.

Figure 8-1

Children grow and develop at very different rates.

a distressing time for families, it is an important process that helps children determine what will ultimately be right for them. However, some children also begin to experiment with substances such as legal or illegal drugs, tobacco, alcohol or inhalants which can pose a serious threat to their well-being and which often require professional intervention and treatment (Steinberg, 2008).

Despite frequent protests and rejections, children still want and need their family's continued trust and support. It is important that families maintain an ongoing dialogue with children about subjects such as personal health, substance abuse (drugs, alcohol, smoking), and sex education (typical development, pregnancy, protection from sexually transmitted diseases) because many of these decisions can have serious, long-term consequences (O'Donnell et al., 2007; Park & Breland, 2007; Pluhar, Jennings, & DiIorio, 2006). When adults treat these issues in an open and nonthreatening manner, it conveys understanding and compassion to children. It also fosters their sense of self-esteem and enhances the likelihood that children will continue to seek adult input in the future.

Nine- and Ten-Year-Olds

Most nine- and ten-year-olds have entered a phase of relative contentment—sometimes described as the calm before the storm of adolescence. Although nine-year-olds might still display some emotional highs and lows, these outbursts gradually mellow by age ten. Home and family continue to serve as sources of security and comfort. Hugs and kisses are still offered as signs of affection for family members.

Most nine- and ten-year-olds also find school enjoyable. They eagerly anticipate classes and meeting with friends and are disappointed if they must miss out on school activities. Teachers are respected and their attention is highly coveted. Small homemade

Figure 8-2

Children still need ample opportunities to release excess energy.

gifts and offers of assistance are made in the hope of pleasing one's teacher. Although children's attention span is longer, they still need frequent opportunities to move about in the classroom and to participate in vigorous outdoor activity (Sit et al., 2007; Mota et al., 2005) (Figure 8-2).

DEVELOPMENTAL PROFILES AND GROWTH PATTERNS

Growth and Physical Characteristics

- Rate of growth is slow and irregular; girls begin to experience growth spurts far more dramatic than do boys; boys are more alike in size.

- Assumes a slimmer shape as fat accumulations begin to shift.

- Growth of various body parts occurs at different rates; lower half of body grows faster; arms and legs appear long and out of proportion.

- Brain increases significantly in size; almost reaches adult size by age ten.

- Height increases approximately 2 inches (5 cm) each year; increases are usually greater during growth spurts.

- Gains approximately 6 1/2 pounds (14.3 kg) per year.

- Loses remaining baby teeth; overcrowding might occur when larger, permanent teeth erupt into a yet small jaw.

- Girls might begin to experience prepubertal changes (e.g., budding breasts, appearance of pubic hair, rounding of hips, accentuated waistline; darkening of hair color); boys are less likely to undergo any sexual changes for another year or two (Cesario & Hughes, 2007).

Motor Development

- Throws a ball with accuracy; writes, sketches, and performs other fine motor skills with improved coordination. This period is marked by continued refinement of fine motor skills, especially notable among girls.

- Uses arms, legs, hands, and feet with ease and improved precision; boys tend to excel in large motor activities requiring strength and speed.

- Runs, climbs, skips rope, swims, rides bikes, and skates with skill and confidence.

- Enjoys team sports but might still need to develop some of the necessary complex skills.

- Likes to use hands for arts and crafts, cooking, woodworking, needlework, and building or taking apart objects such as a clock or telephone.

- Draws pictures in detail; takes great joy in perfecting handwriting skills.

Perceptual-Cognitive Development

- Develops ability to reason based more on experience and logic than on **intuition** (Piaget's stage of **concrete operational thought**): "If I hurry and walk the dog, I can play with my friends." Still sees some situations as either/or, with "yes" or "no" answers but is beginning to think in less concrete, more creative ways (Piaget, 1928). Understands abstract concepts if real (concrete) objects can be seen and manipulated: "If I eat one cookie now, only two will be left."

- Likes challenges in arithmetic but does not always understand mathematical relationships involved in complex operations such as multiplication or division.

- Learns best through hands-on learning; prefers to research information in books or online, conduct science experiments, build models, or put on a play rather than listen to teachers' lectures that produce the same information (Figure 8-3).

Figure 8-3

Hands-on involvement promotes learning.

(continued)

---

intuition—thoughts and ideas based on a feeling or hunch.

concrete operational thought—piaget's third stage of cognitive development; period when concepts of conservation and classification are understood.

9- to 10-year-olds

- Enjoys time at school; finds it difficult to sit still for periods longer than 30 minutes; forgets all about school as soon as it is over.
- Likes to use reading and writing skills for nonacademic activities (compiling grocery lists, composing scripts for puppet shows, drawing and labeling neighborhood maps).
- Shows improved understanding of cause and effect.
- Continues to master concepts of time, weight, volume, and distance (Harel et al., 2007).
- Traces events based on recall; able to think in reverse, following a series of occurrences back to their beginnings.
- Prefers reading books that are longer and descriptive with complex plots.

Speech and Language Development

- Talks, often nonstop and for no specific reason; sometimes used as an attention-getting device.
- Expresses feelings and emotions effectively through words.
- Understands and uses language as a system for communicating with others.
- Uses slang expressions commonly expressed by peers in conversation ("sweet," "cool," "awesome," "hey dude").
- Recognizes that some words have double meanings ("far out," "cool haircut").
- Finds humor in using illogical metaphors (play on words) in jokes and riddles (Figure 8-4).
- Shows advanced understanding of grammatical sequences; recognizes when a sentence is not grammatically correct.

Figure 8-4

Delights in telling jokes and riddles.

Social-Emotional Development

- Enjoys being with friends; seeks out friendships based on common interests and proximity (neighborhood children or classmates); is verbally critical of the opposite gender ("Boys are too rough," "Girls are babies") (Hennessey, 2007; Rose, 2007).

- Has several "good" friends and an "enemy" or two; friends and friendships often change from day to day.

- Begins to show more interest in rules and basing games on realistic play; rules should be kept simple so everyone enjoys the game (Figure 8-5).

- Responds with name-calling and teasing when provoked; less likely to use physical aggression than previously; also understands that such behavior can affect others' feelings. Still depends occasionally on adults to settle some disputes.

- Begins to develop moral reasoning; adopts social customs and moral values (understands honesty, right from wrong, fairness, good and bad, respect) (Walker, Gustafson, & Hennig, 2001).

- Develops attachments to teachers, coaches, club leaders; might see them as heroes; often goes out of way to please and gain their attention.

- Acts with considerable confidence; knows everything and can do no wrong.

- Takes criticism as a personal attack; feelings are easily hurt; has difficulty at times dealing with failure and frustration.

Figure 8-5

Begins to understand and play games by the rules.

VIDEO CONNECTIONS

Clip 19

Moral Development: Children are experiencing an important change in their moral development. Moral values and standards learned from their families are now being internalized. As a result, of this shift, children are now able to assess a situation and make judgments accordingly.

Critical Thinking Questions:

1. Explain the statement, "Younger children tend to focus on right and wrong and neglect intentions." How does this change for the nine- and ten-year-old?

2. What effects might this shift in children's moral development have on activities such as play at recess and board games and in friendships?

3. What is preconventional or conventional thinking?

4. What factors help shape children's moral beliefs?

• DAILY ROUTINES •

Eating

- Appetite can fluctuate, depending on amount and vigor of activity; eats more with increased activity; prefers to eat when hungry rather than at prescribed times.

- Eats at any time of day, yet often is still hungry at mealtime; more receptive to trying new foods. Many children also enjoy cooking and helping with meal preparations. Prefers certain favorite foods, usually pizza, French fries, tacos, ice cream, and cookies; has few dislikes but is less fond of cooked vegetables.

- Battles over posture and table manners (elbows on the table; slouched in chair; fisted grasp of forks and spoons) but usually displays good manners at friends' houses.

Toileting, Bathing, and Dressing

- Shows limited interest in personal hygiene; often needs reminders to bathe, wash hair, brush teeth, put on clean clothes.

- Requires coaxing to bathe but, after bath is started, might not want to get out.

- Shows some interest in appearance; wants to dress and look like friends; school clothes take on an important role in self-identification.

- Manages own toileting needs without reminders; seldom gets up at night unless too much liquid is consumed before bedtime.

Sleeping

- Seems unaware of fatigue and the need for sleep.
- Requires 9–10 hours of sleep to function throughout the day. Wakes up in time for school without much coaxing if getting enough sleep. Insufficient sleep has been linked to increased weight gain (Snell, Adam, & Duncan, 2007).
- Girls might have more bedtime rituals and take longer to fall asleep than do boys.
- Nightmares and fears of the dark might redevelop; some children experience sleepwalking, waking up in the middle of the night, or bed-wetting. Parents should not criticize children who develop these problems and should seek professional help if they persist.

Play and Social Activities

- Maintains activity level that fluctuates between extremes of high intensity and almost nonexistent activity; can virtually collapse following periods of intense play.
- Spends free time reading magazines, playing computer games, watching videos, listening to music, and talking with friends.
- Likes to form and join clubs with secret codes, languages, and signs.
- Offers to help with simple household chores such as dusting and sweeping, vacuuming, putting away groceries, and washing the car.
- Develops new hobbies or collections based on special interests.

Learning Activities

Tips for families and teachers:

- Take advantage of educational opportunities in the community. Plan field trips to the beach, farmers' market, library, museum, zoo, park, garden center, cabinet-maker, pet shop, or grocery store.
- Encourage children to appreciate diversity by learning about the customs and celebrations of other cultures. Obtain library books, visit Web sites, invite guests, locate musical instruments, and prepare various ethnic foods for children to taste. Teach children to be accepting and avoid prejudice through your own actions and words.
- Gather sports equipment such as balls, bats, nets, and rackets; encourage children to organize and participate in group activities.
- Provide space, seeds, and tools for planting and maintaining a garden.

(continued)

Learning Activities (continued)

- Assemble materials and provide basic instructions for conducting science experiments; science activity suggestions can be found in many good books at the public library or on child-oriented Web sites.

- Nurture children's interest in reading, writing, and friendships by locating pen pals in another state or country; encourage children to write back and forth (via letter or e-mail), read books about where their pen pal lives, and locate the state or country on a map.

- Encourage children to get at least 60 minutes of vigorous physical activity daily.

- Maintain open communication with children. Spend time doing things together, talking about their interests and friends, and being supportive.

Developmental Alerts

Check with a health care provider or early-childhood specialist if, by the eleventh birthday, the child *does not:*

- Continue to grow at a rate appropriate for the child's gender.

- Show continued improvement of fine motor skills.

- Make or keep friends.

- Enjoy going to school and show interest in learning most days. (Have children's hearing and vision tested; vision and hearing problems affect children's ability to learn and their interest in learning.)

- Approach new situations with reasonable confidence; show a willingness to try.

- Handle failure and frustration in a constructive manner; learn from mistakes.

- Sleep through the night or experiences prolonged problems with bed-wetting, nightmares, or sleepwalking.

Safety Concerns

Continue to implement safety practices described for the previous stages. Always be aware of new safety issues as the child continues to grow and develop.

Media Exposure

- Be aware of online websites that children visit; check the nature of information available on these sites. Teach children Internet safety rules and the importance of not giving out personal information (name, address, telephone number) online. Block websites that you don't want children to access.

- Know what music children listen to, what video games they play, and what movies they watch, to determine whether they are being exposed to violence, sex, or drug culture.

Firearms

- Educate children about the dangers of guns and other weapons. Stress the importance of not picking up firearms and always alerting an adult if one is found.
- Store firearms and ammunition separately and keep in locked storage.
- Never leave loaded firearms unattended.

Traffic

- Insist that children wear seat belts on every motor trip.
- Review safe practices for crossing streets, getting in and out of parked cars, riding a bicycle, skateboarding, and otherwise acting responsibly around traffic.
- Make sure children always wear helmets and appropriate protective gear when engaged in sports activities.

11- to 12- year-olds

Eleven- and Twelve-Year-Olds

For the most part, eleven- and twelve-year-olds are endearing individuals. They are curious, energetic, helpful, and happy (Figure 8-6). They assist with chores around the house, sometimes even volunteering before being asked. Their language, motor, and cognitive skills are reaching adult levels of sophistication (Jarmulowicz, 2006; Markovits & Barrouillet, 2002). By age twelve, children have developed a sense of confidence in their capabilities and approach tasks with renewed interest. Their emotional stability is generally smoother, and they encounter fewer conflicts with family and peers. Eleven- and twelve-year-olds enjoy participating in organized sports and physical activity (Rutten et al., 2003; Taras, 2005). In general, their health is good, and they begin to understand that a healthy lifestyle is not only important but also requires dedicated awareness and effort (Janssen et al., 2004). However, eleven- and twelve-year-olds also see themselves as invincible. Few children believe they will ever experience serious health conditions such as sexually transmitted diseases (STDs), lung cancer, diabetes, or heart disease despite engaging in risky behaviors (e.g., smoking, following a sedentary lifestyle, eating a high-fat diet) (Brown, Teufel, & Birch, 2007).

Figure 8-6

Eleven- and twelve-
year-olds are curious,
energetic, and confident.

*11- to 12-
year-olds*

DEVELOPMENTAL PROFILES AND GROWTH PATTERNS

Growth and Physical Characteristics

- Height and weight vary significantly from child to child; body shape and proportion are influenced by heredity and environment; birth length is tripled by the end of this period.

- Girls are first to experience a prepuberty growth spurt, growing taller and weighing more than boys at this age; might gain as much as 3.5 inches (8.75 cm) and 20 pounds (44 kg) in one year; this period of rapid growth ends around age twelve for girls; boys' growth rate is much slower (Cesario & Hughes, 2007; Lee et al., 2007).

- Bodily changes mark approaching puberty (widening hips and budding breasts [girls], enlarging testes and penis [boys], appearance of pubic hair).

- Menstruation might begin if it has not already started; some girls have vaginal discharge sooner; some might be upset if not progressing at the same rate as other girls.

- Spontaneous erections are common among eleven- and twelve-year-old boys; pictures, physical activity, talk, and daydreams can trigger these events; some will begin to have nocturnal emissions (involuntary discharge of seminal fluid).

- Muscle mass and strength increase, especially in boys; girls often reach their maximum muscle strength by age twelve.

- Posture is more erect; increases in bone size and length cause shoulders, collarbone, rib cage, and shoulder blades to appear more prominent.

- Complaints of headaches and blurred vision are not uncommon if children are experiencing vision problems; added strain of schoolwork (smaller print, computer use, long periods of reading and writing) can cause some children to request an eye examination.

Motor Development

- Displays movements that are smoother and more coordinated; however, rapid growth spurts can cause temporary clumsiness.

- Enjoys participation in activities such as dancing, karate, soccer, gymnastics, swimming, or organized games in which improved skills can be used and tested.

- Concentrates efforts on continued refinement of fine motor abilities through a variety of activities (model-building, rocket construction, drawing, woodworking, cooking, sewing, arts and crafts, writing letters, or playing an instrument); has now perfected all fundamental gross motor skills (Figure 8-7).

- Requires outlets for release of excess energy that builds during the school day; enjoys team sports, riding bikes, playing in the park, taking dance lessons, going for a walk with friends, shooting hoops.

- Has an abundance of energy but also fatigues quickly.

- Uses improved strength to run faster, throw balls farther, jump higher, kick or bat balls more accurately, and wrestle with friends.

Perceptual-Cognitive Development

- Begins thinking in more **abstract** terms; expanded memory ability enables improved long-term recall; now remembers stored information, so no longer must rely solely on experiencing an event to understand it.

11- to 12-year-olds

Figure 8-7

Children are able to accomplish new activities that require advanced fine motor skills.

(continued)

---

abstract—the ability to think and use concepts; an idea or theory.

- Succeeds in sequencing, ordering, and classifying because of improved long-term memory capacity; these are skills needed for solving complex mathematics problems.
- Accepts the idea that problems can have multiple solutions; often works through problems by talking aloud to oneself. Develops solutions or responses based on logic.
- Enjoys challenges, problem-solving, researching, and testing possible solutions; researches encyclopedias, the Internet, and dictionaries for information (Figure 8-8).
- Exhibits longer attention span; stays focused on completing school assignments and other tasks.
- Develops detailed plans and lists to reach a desired goal.
- Performs many routine tasks without having to think; increased memory sophistication makes automatic responses possible.
- Shows more complex understanding of cause and effect; identifies factors that might have contributed to or caused an event (combining baking soda with vinegar releases a gas; attaching a longer tail helps a kite fly higher in strong wind).

11- to 12-year-olds

Speech and Language Development

- Completes the majority of language development by the end of this stage; only subtle refinements are still necessary during the next few years.
- Talks and argues, often nonstop, with anyone who will listen.
- Uses longer and more complex sentence structures.

Figure 8-8

Enjoys researching and solving problems.

- Masters increasingly complex vocabulary; adds 4,000–5,000 new words each year; uses vocabulary skillfully to weave elaborate stories and precise descriptions.

- Becomes a thoughtful listener.

- Understands that word statements can have implied (intended) meanings. (When your mother asks, "Is your homework done?" she really means you had better stop playing, gather up your books, and get started.)

- Grasps concepts of irony and sarcasm; has a good sense of humor and enjoys telling jokes, riddles, and rhymes to entertain others.

- Masters several language styles, shifting back and forth based on the occasion (a more formal style when talking with teachers, a more casual style with parents, and a style that often includes slang and code words when conversing with friends).

11- to 12-year-olds

Social-Emotional Development

- Organizes group games and activities but might modify rules while the game is in progress.

- Views self-image as very important; typically defines self in terms of appearance, possessions, or activities; might also make comparisons to much admired adults (Rowley et al., 2007).

- Becomes increasingly self-conscious and self-focused; understands the need to assume responsibility for his or her own behavior and that there are consequences associated with one's actions.

- Begins to think and talk about occupational choices and career plans; daydreams and fantasizes about the future.

- Develops a critical and idealistic view of the world; realizes the world is larger than one's own neighborhood; expresses interest in other cultures, foods, languages, and customs (Figure 8-9).

- Adopts dress, hairstyles, and mannerisms of popular sports figures and celebrities.

- Recognizes that loyalty, honesty, trustworthiness, and being a good listener are prerequisites to becoming a good friend; spends more time now with peers than with family members (Cummings & Harlow, 2000).

- Handles frustration with fewer emotional outbursts; is able to discuss what is emotionally troubling; accompanies words with facial expressions and gestures for emphasis.

Figure 8-9

Expresses interest in learning about other cultures and traditions.

Clip 20

Cognitive Development: Most of the developmental skills children will need as they approach adolescence are now in place. Eleven- and twelve-year-olds are able to think abstractly, make judgments based on logic, and face challenge with a reasonable degree of competence and self-confidence.

Critical Thinking Questions:

1. Which cognitive skills are involved in children's responses to the conservation demonstration and question about "what did you do last night"?

2. What qualities did the first two children in the video clip use to describe themselves? Were they consistent with gender expectations?

3. Were you surprised by the responses of the first two children in the video clip to the questions about gender differences? What do you think accounted for the contrast in their answers?

4. What signs of stress or tension did you note while the first two children were being interviewed? If you were a teacher, how might you use this feedback?

11- to 12-year-olds

• D A I L Y   R O U T I N E S •

Eating

- Eats nonstop and is always hungry; boys in particular might consume astonishing amounts and combinations of food. Boys require approximately 2,500 calories daily; girls need 2,200 calories daily.

- Has few dislikes; willing to eat less preferred foods now and then; shows interest in trying foods from other cultures.

- Needs big snack upon arriving home from school; searches cabinets and refrigerator for anything to eat.

- Makes some connection between eating (calories) and gaining or losing weight, especially girls; for example, some girls might talk about dieting; monitor closely for signs of a developing eating disorder (Peebles, Wilson, & Lock, 2006; Neumark-Sztainer, 2005).

Toileting, Bathing, and Dressing

- Cares for most personal needs without adult assistance (Figure 8-10).

- Bathes often and willingly; keeps self clean; often prefers showers.

- Might still need occasional reminder to wash hands.

- Brushes and flosses teeth regularly; a bright smile is important for appearance. Dental checkups are recommended every 6 months to monitor rapidly erupting permanent teeth and to treat existing cavities; many children already have several decayed or filled teeth.

- Takes pride in appearance; likes to wear what is fashionable or what friends are wearing.

Figure 8-10

Children can manage their own personal care needs without adult help.

Sleeping

- Needs plenty of sleep; growth spurts and active play often leave children feeling tired.
- Heads to bed without much resistance but now wants to stay up longer on week nights and even later on weekends and nonschool days.
- Sleeps less soundly than previously; might wake up early and read or finish homework before getting up.
- Bad dreams still trouble some eleven- and twelve-year-olds.

Play and Social Activities

- Shows less interest in frivolous play; prefers goal-directed activities (money-making schemes, competing on a swim team, writing newsletters, attending summer camp).
- Gets involved in organized groups such as sports teams, 4-H Club, or Scouts or just spends time alone with a friend or two; never without something to do.
- Likes animals; offers to care for and train pets.
- Reads enthusiastically; enjoys listening to music, attending movies, watching the news, surfing on the computer, and playing video games.
- Enjoys and participates in outdoor activities such as skateboarding, inline skating, basketball, riding bikes, or walking with friends.

Learning Activities

Tips for families and teachers:

- Continue to maintain open communication with children. Spend time together, know what is going on in their lives, and be supportive (not judgmental). Provide children with information about their personal health (sexuality, drugs and alcohol, pregnancy and sexually transmitted diseases) and the importance of making sound decisions. Encourage them to come to you whenever they have questions or are experiencing problems.

- Encourage children's interest in reading; take them to the library or bookmobile.

- Read and discuss newspaper and magazine articles together; suggest that children create their own newsletter.

- Help children develop a sense of responsibility by assigning tasks they can perform on a regular basis (caring for a pet, reading stories to a younger sibling, folding laundry, loading the dishwasher, washing dishes, sweeping the garage).

- Gather a variety of large cardboard boxes, paints, and other materials; challenge children to design a structure (a store, library, train, castle, farm, space station).

- Help children stage a play; invite them to write the script, design scenery, construct simple props, and rehearse.

- Offer to help children plan and organize a pet show, bike parade, or scavenger hunt.

- Locate free or low-cost opportunities to join organized group or sporting activities; these are often available through local parks and recreation departments, YMCA / YWCAs, church youth groups, and after-school programs.

- Provide children with a variety of art materials (paints, crayons, markers, paper, old magazines and catalogues, cloth scraps); encourage children to collect natural materials such as leaves, pebbles, interesting twigs, seed pods, feathers, and grasses to use for artistic collages.

Developmental Alerts

Check with a health care provider or early-childhood specialist if, by the thirteenth birthday, the child *does not*:

- Have movements that are smooth and coordinated.

- Have energy sufficient for playing, riding bikes, or engaging in other desired activities.

- Stay focused on tasks at hand.

- Understand basic cause-and-effect relationships.
- Handle criticism and frustration with a reasonable response (physical aggression and excessive crying could be an indication of underlying problems).
- Exhibit a healthy appetite. (Frequent skipping of meals is not typical for this age group; excessive eating should also be monitored.).
- Make and keep friends.

Safety Concerns

Continue to implement safety practices described for the previous stages. Always be aware of new safety issues as the child continues to grow and develop.

Machinery

- Teach children how to operate small appliances and equipment safely.
- Provide basic first aid instruction for responding to injuries.

Sports

- Make sure proper protective equipment is available and worn; check its condition periodically.
- Provide instruction or make sure an adult is supervising any competition; check safety of area and equipment.

Substance Abuse

- Be aware of warning signs associated with "huffing" (inhaling) hazardous vapors from common household products such as hair spray, polish remover, aerosol paints, and fabric protectors. Note any unusual odor on the child's breath or clothing, slurred speech, jitteriness, poor appetite, bloodshot eyes, or reddened areas around nose or mouth.

Water

- Provide and require children to wear approved flotation devices whenever fishing, skiing, or boating.
- Teach basic water safety and continue to supervise water-related activities.

SUMMARY

Growth patterns during this stage are irregular and inconsistent. Girls tend to grow more than do boys, with fairly significant variations occurring from child to child. Most children are rather carefree, happy, energetic, industrious, and eager to learn. They spend the years between ages nine and twelve fine-tuning basic skills, many of which were already in place. Advanced cognitive abilities continue to emerge, enabling children to think in the abstract, understand concepts of weight, distance, and time, follow detailed instructions, and comprehend cause-and-effect relationships. Feelings related to self-concept gradually shift from overly harsh self-criticism to gaining considerable confidence in his or her own abilities. Although friends and friendships are very important, family ties are still valued and needed. Participation in group activities and team sports provides a necessary outlet for excess energy, competition, development of advanced motor skills, and companionship.

KEY TERMS

abstract

concrete operational thought

intuition

logic

APPLY WHAT YOU KNOW

A. Apply What You Have Learned

Reread the brief developmental sketch about Juan and Carlin at the beginning of the chapter. How might you answer the following questions?

1. Would you consider Carlin's development to be typical for a nine-year-old? Explain.

2. Would it be developmentally appropriate to expect most eleven-year-olds to like school? Why do you agree or disagree with this statement?

3. Why should Carlin's lack of friends be of concern?

4. From a developmental perspective, do you think Juan's reactions to having his sister tag along are typical or atypical? Explain.

5. What physical characteristics would you expect to observe in the "average" eleven-year-old?

6. Which of Carlin's behaviors would cause you to recommend referral to an early-childhood specialist for additional evaluation? Explain.

B. Review Questions

1. What gender differences are nine-year-olds likely to exhibit in their social-emotional development?

2. How do nine- and eleven-year-olds differ in their ability to think abstractly?

3. What are some typical changes that ten-year-olds are likely to experience in terms of their growth?

4. Describe three speech-language skills that are characteristic of most nine- and ten-year-olds.

5. Describe the cognitive abilities typical of most eleven- and twelve-year-olds.

6. Identify three qualities that are needed to make and keep friends.

HELPFUL WEBSITES

Visit the book companion website at *www.cengage.com/education/allen* for links to these websites and additional resources.

REFERENCES

Brown, S., Teufel, J., & Birch, D. (2007). Early adolescents' perception of health and health literacy. *Journal of School Health, 77*(1), 7–15.

Cesario, S., & Hughes, L. (2007). Precocious puberty: A comprehensive review of literature. *Journal of Obstetric, Gynecologic and Neonatal Nursing, 36*(3), 263–274.

Cummings, R., & Harlow, S. (2000). The constructivist roots of moral education. *The Educational Forum, 64*(4), 300–307.

Harel, B., Cillessen, A., Fein, D., & Bullard, S. (2007). It takes nine days to iron a shirt: The development of cognitive estimation skills in school age children. *Child Neuropsychology, 13*(4), 309–318.

Hennessey, B. (2007). Promoting social competence in school-aged children: The effects of the Open Circle Program. *Journal of School Psychology, 45*(3), 349–360.

Janssen, I., Katzmarzyk, P., Boyce, W., King, M., & Pickett, W. (2004). Overweight and obesity in Canadian adolescents and their associations with dietary habits and physical activity patterns. *Journal of Adolescent Health, 35*(5), 360–367.

Jarmulowicz, L. (2006). School-aged children's phonological production of derived English words. *Journal of Speech, Language and Hearing Research, 49*(2), 294–308.

Lee, J., Appugliese, D., Kaciroti, N., Corwyn, R., Bradley, R., & Lumeng, J. (2007). Weight status in young girls and the onset of puberty. *Pediatrics, 119*(3), e624–630.

Markovits, H., & Barrouillet, P. (2002). The development of conditional reasoning: A mental model account. *Developmental Review, 22*(1), 5–36.

Mota, J., Silva, P., Santos, M., Ribeiro, J., Oliveira, J., & Duarte, J. (2005). Physical activity and school recess time: Differences between the sexes and the relationship between children's playground physical activity and habitual physical activity. *Journal of Sports Science, 23*(3), 269–275.

Neumark-Sztainer, D. (2005). Preventing the broad spectrum of weight-related problems: Working with parents to help teens achieve a healthy weight and a positive body image. *Journal of Nutrition Education & Behavior, 37*(2 Suppl), S133–139.

O'Donnell, L., Wilson-Simmons, R., Dash, K., Jeanbaptiste, V., Myint-U, A., Moss, J., & Stueve, A. (2007). Saving sex for later: Developing a parent-child communication intervention to delay sexual initiation among young adolescents. *Sex Education, 7*(2), 107–125.

Park, M., & Breland, D. (2007). Starting on a healthy path: Promotion of young men's sexual health. *American Journal of Men's Health, 1*(2), 148–153.

Peebles, R., Wilson, J., & Lock, J. (2006). How do children with eating disorders differ from adolescents with eating disorders at initial evaluation? *Journal of Adolescent Health, 39*(6), 800–805.

Piaget, J. (1928). *Judgment and reasoning in the child*. New York: Harcourt, Brace & World.

Pinyerd, B., & Zipf, W. (2005). Puberty—timing is everything! *Journal of Pediatric Nursing, 20*(2), 75–82.

Pluhar, E., Jennings, T., & DiIorio, C. (2006). Getting an early start: Communication about sexuality among mothers and children 6–10 years old. *Journal of HIV/AIDS Prevention in Children & Youth, 7*(1), 7–35.

Rose, A. (2007). Structure, content, and socioemotional correlates of girls' and boys' friendships. *Merrill-Palmer Quarterly, 53*(3), 489–506.

Rowley, S., Kurtz-Costes, B., Mistry, R., & Feagans, L. (2007). Social status as a predictor of race and gender stereotypes in late childhood and early adolescence. *Social Development, 16*(1), 150–168.

Rutten, H., Ziemainz, K., Abu-Omar, K., & Groth, N. (2003). Residential area, physical education, and the health of school aged children. *Health Education, 103*(5), 264–268.

Sit, C., McManus, A., McKenzie, T., & Lian, J. (2007). Physical activity levels of children in special schools. *Preventive Medicine, 45*(6), 424–431.

Snell, E., Adam, E., & Duncan, G. (2007). Sleep and the body mass index and overweight status of children and adolescents. *Child Development, 78*(1), 309–323.

Steinberg, L. (2008). A social neuroscience perspective on adolescent risk-taking. *Developmental Review, 28*(1), 78–106.

Taras, H. (2005). Physical activity and student performance at school. *Journal of School Health, 75*(6), 214–215.

Walker, L., Gustafson, P., & Hennig, K. (2001). The consolidation/transition model in moral reasoning development. *Developmental Psychology, 37*(2), 187–197.

BOOK COMPANION WEBSITE

The book-specific website at *www.cengage.com/education/allen* offers students a variety of study tools and useful resources such as chapter overviews and notes, tutorial quizzes, web links, frequently asked questions, discussion questions, glossary/flashcards, internet exercises, references and more. To register or purchase access to the premium resources for this text including video clips tied to chapter content, go to *www.cengage.com/login*.

When and Where to Seek Help

MEET ANDREY AND HIS MOTHER

Andrey, at four years, nine months of age, was new to the Head Start class in the urban area where his family was now living. The teachers were immediately concerned about his overall development. Andrey seemed unable to follow directions, his language skills were limited, and his speech was unintelligible to everyone but his family. When he attempted to interact with other children, he often hit them, apparently to gain their attention. During entire free play periods, he seemed incapable of playing with a specific toy or child for longer than two or three minutes at a time. There was one exception: block building held his attention for fifteen minutes or more.

When asked about Andrey's health history, his mother spoke vaguely of earaches and "runny ears," "hot spells," and "twitches." Andrey's mother, who recently celebrated her twenty-first birthday, had attended special education

Objectives

After reading this chapter, you should be able to:

- Discuss five or more legislative acts passed on behalf of children with exceptionalities and their families.

- Explain the purpose of developmental screening tests and the reasons for exercising caution when interpreting results.

- Describe several factors that can complicate the developmental picture when deciding whether a child is developing normally.

- Defend this statement: Observing and recording a child's behavior is an essential first step in determining whether there is a developmental problem.

- Explain why a Family Service Coordinator is essential to successful implementation of intervention recommendations for the child and family.

programs for most of her school years. She was a thin, pale woman, midway into her third pregnancy. She worked part-time as a waitress and was the sole breadwinner because her husband was currently unemployed.

She expressed warmth and concern for Andrey and his two-year-old sister but apparently had never understood the importance of medical care or nutrition for herself or her children. It appeared that she had been unable to follow through on whatever medical assistance she had been offered. The fact that the family had moved seven times since Andrey was born quite likely accounted, in part, for the family having fallen through the cracks of the social service system.

Is my child all right? Most parents, at one time or another, have asked this question during their child's infancy and growing-up years (Figure 9-1) (Johnson, 2008; Dewey, Crawford, & Kaplan, 2003). Many caregivers and teachers ask a similar question about a child who seems "different" from other children with whom they work. Such questions are a positive sign because they indicate awareness and concern. Children, as emphasized in Chapters 1 and 2, vary greatly in their development. Many factors, including genetics, culture, family structure and values, nutrition, health, and poverty can influence the rate and nature of children's development. It is the rare child who is truly typical in every way. Many children with developmental irregularities of one kind or another do not experience any long-term negative effects. Other children with irregularities that appear no more serious or threatening might be considered at developmental risk. In both instances, the child needs to be seen by a health care professional or child-development specialist and perhaps referred for evaluation and intervention services.

Figure 9-1

Families often wonder if their child is developing "normally."

Public Policy and Social Attitudes

Supporting children's optimal development has become a major social and legislative focus. Much of the initial impetus came in the 1960s as part of the antipoverty movement (often referred to as the "war on poverty"). Many precedent-setting research studies provided conclusive evidence that we could significantly reduce developmental disabilities in infants and children. As a result, several major strategies have evolved. One is based on the prevention of atypical development through improved prenatal care and nutrition. Another is the early identification of children with, or are at risk for, developmental problems. If a potential problem is identified, the next step is to establish an intervention program as soon as is feasible, thus minimizing the effects on a child's overall development (Holstrum et al., 2008; Matson, Wilkins, & González, 2008). Throughout this process, a critical factor involves supporting the child's family by helping them understand and participate in the intervention recommendations.

LEGISLATION SUPPORTING OPTIMUM DEVELOPMENT

Beginning in the mid-1960s, several pieces of legislation led to the implementation of programs that supported child and family health and helped reduce developmental risks.

- **PL 88-452 Head Start (1965)**   This act, part of the antipoverty movement, established the Head Start program and its supplemental services, including developmental screening, medical and dental care, nutrition, parent training, and early education for income-eligible children 3–5 years of age. Amendments in 1972 and 1974 mandated Head Start to also serve children with disabilities. Reauthorization in 1994 created Early Head Start programs, which serve infants and toddlers from low-income families.

- **PL 101-239 Early and Periodic Screening, Diagnosis, and Treatment Act (EPSDT) (1967)**   This national program was added to Medicaid and continues to serve the health and developmental needs (diagnosis and treatment) of income-eligible children at risk.

- **PL 94-105 Supplemental Nutrition Program for Women, Infants, and Children (WIC) (1975)**   This act created a program aimed at improving maternal health during pregnancy, promoting full-term fetal development, and increasing newborn birth weight. Medical supervision, food vouchers, and nutrition education are provided to low-income pregnant and nursing women and their children under age five to ensure a healthy start.

Legislation that specifically addressed the needs of children with developmental differences has also been enacted, including:

- **PL 89-10 Elementary and Secondary Education Act (ESEA) (1965)**   This act established federal requirements and funding for U.S. public schools (K–12).

Additional funds and resources were authorized for schools and districts (preschool through high school) serving a high proportion of children from low-income families; these programs are designated as Title I programs.

- **PL 90-538 The Handicapped Children's Early Education and Assistance Act (HCEEAA) (1968)**   This law provided funding for the establishment of model classrooms to serve preschool children with disabilities.

- **PL 94-142 (1975)**   Originally called the **Education for All Handicapped Children Act (EHA),** this law, now known as Part B, mandates states to provide comprehensive evaluation, "free and appropriate" education, and intervention services for all children ages 3–5 years who have, or are at-risk for, developmental problems. Amendments in 1990 and 1997 reauthorized the bill, renaming it the Individuals with Disabilities Education Act (IDEA) (PL 101-476).

- **PL 99-457 Education of the Handicapped Act Amendments (1986)** Because the original initiative (PL 94-142) had proven so successful, it was amended to extend early intervention services to infants, toddlers, and their families through the Individualized Family Service Plan (IFSP). This portion of the bill (now known as Part C of IDEA) is not mandated or fully funded and, therefore, is not available in all communities. Additional features of this act include an emphasis on multidisciplinary assessment, a designated service coordinator, a family-focused approach, and a system of service coordination.

- **PL 101-336 Americans with Disabilities Act (ADA) (1990)**   This national civil rights law protects against discrimination on the basis of a disability. The intent is to remove barriers that interfere with full inclusion in every aspect of society—education, employment, and public services. Implications for children and their families are clear: child care programs are required to adapt their settings and programs to accommodate children with disabilities.

- **PL 108-446 The Individuals with Disabilities Education Improvement Act of 2004 (2004)**   This reauthorization of the original act (PL 94-142) increased accountability for children's educational outcomes, improved identification methods, enhanced family involvement, and reduced the amount of required paperwork. Guidelines for appropriate discipline of students with disabilities were also included.

- **PL 107-110 No Child Left Behind Act (2002)**   This legislation, a reauthorization of the Elementary and Secondary Education Act, addressed the problems of academic inequity and failure in this country. Its aim is to improve the quality of educational opportunities for all children and to increase academic success rates by making schools and teachers accountable.

EARLY IDENTIFICATION AND INTERVENTION PROGRAMS

As a result of legislation and changes in public policy, several avenues are now available for getting children with suspected developmental problems into appropriate evaluation and early-intervention programs.

INFANTS AND CHILDREN AT MEDICAL RISK

Family physicians and pediatricians are becoming increasingly aware of the importance of monitoring infants and young children for developmental and behavioral problems (Crane & Winsler, 2008; Shulman, Meringolo, & Scott, 2007) (Figure 9-2). Many pediatric practices today ask parents to complete a developmental screening tool such as the Abbreviated Denver Developmental Screening Test, the Revised Parent Developmental Questionnaire, or the Ages and Stages Questionnaire during each office visit so that children's progress can be monitored more closely (Hix-Small et al., 2007; Lipkin & Gwynn, 2007; AAP, 2001). Physicians are also paying more attention to the early detection of deviations in infants' neurological development that might indicate a potential problem and are referring families to genetic, neurological, and child-development specialists for evaluation. These trends have contributed to the earlier detection of high-risk conditions often associated with developmental delays.

Another group of children at medical risk for developmental problems includes infants discharged from premature nurseries and neonatal intensive care units. Many communities in urban areas now have follow-up clinics for this high-risk group. Continued monitoring of children born prematurely permits the early detection of any developmental delays. Children with suspect development are typically referred to early-childhood screening and intervention programs where they can receive needed services.

Older children's development can also be affected at any time by a variety of medical conditions such as diabetes, hearing loss, communicable diseases, or arthritis. Daily observations become especially important in these situations so that any changes

Figure 9-2

Developmental delays associated with certain medical conditions and syndromes are better understood today.

in a child's behavior or classroom performance are noted right away. Measures can then be implemented in the early stages and, thus, lessen the negative impact a medical condition might otherwise have on children's learning and development.

COMMUNITY SCREENING

The majority of young children who will benefit from early identification and intervention do not always come from medically high-risk groups. These children might be located most effectively through a variety of community screening services.

Screening programs are designed to identify children who have or might be at risk for developmental problems. The primary emphasis is on evaluating a child's hearing and vision, general health, speech and language, motor skills, and overall developmental progress. Screening tests are designed so they are easy to administer locally to large numbers of children. Some forms of testing can be accessed through public health departments, Head Start programs, community colleges and universities, local clinics, public schools, and early-education programs. Teachers and volunteers can be trained to conduct certain types of screenings such as measurements of children's height and weight and vision. More advanced training is often required to administer other forms of assessment such as hearing, speech and language, and developmental progress. Early screening and detection of developmental delays allows children to receive intervention services before they reach school age. Delays in identifying children's special needs can result in conditions that require more extensive therapies and special education services and are more difficult to overcome.

Child Find is a nationwide system of screening programs mandated by IDEA and administered by individual states (Jackson & Needelman, 2007). Their purpose is twofold. One is to raise public awareness about developmental disabilities and to locate eligible infants and young children who have undiagnosed developmental problems or are at risk for the onset of such problems. The second purpose is to help families locate appropriate diagnostic screenings and intervention programs and services. Each state is required by law (IDEA) to establish a Child Find system. They also determine their own eligibility criteria and definition of what qualifies as a disability.

Is There a Problem?

Deciding whether a developmental delay or irregularity is of serious concern might not be easy. The signs can be so subtle, so hard to pinpoint, that it is often difficult to distinguish clearly between children who have a definite problem, the definite *yeses*, and those who definitely do not have a problem, the definite *nos*. Identifying the *maybes*—is there or is there not a problem—can be an even more complex issue.

Child Find—a screening program designed to locate children with developmental problems through improved public awareness.

In determining whether a delay or deviation is of real concern, several factors can complicate the matter. For example:

- Children who exhibit signs of developmental problems in certain areas often continue to develop like a typical child in every other way; such children present a confusing developmental profile. (See Developmental Checklists in Appendix B)

- Great variation exists in the range of an individual child's achievements within developmental areas. The rate of maturation is uneven, and conditions in the child's environment are continually changing. Both maturation and environment interact to exert a strong influence on every aspect of development.

- Family beliefs, values, and cultural background have significant influence on how children are raised (Trawick-Smith, 2006). Developmental milestones are not universal; how they are perceived varies from culture to culture, even from family to family. Respect for diverse family and community lifestyles must always be taken into consideration when gathering and interpreting information about a child's development (Figure 9-3).

- Developmental delays or problems might not be immediately apparent. Many children learn to compensate for a deficiency. For example, children who have a mild to moderate hearing loss might position themselves closer to the teacher during story time so they can hear. Children who experience difficulty learning to read might depend on other cognitive strategies to overcome their disability. Sometimes deficiencies do not become apparent until the child is placed in structured and more demanding situations (as in a first-grade reading class) (Allen & Cowdery, 2008).

- Intermittent health problems can affect children's performance. For example, a child might have severe and recurring bouts of **otitis media** that appear to

Figure 9-3

Diversity of family and community values, beliefs, and cultural differences must be considered and treated with respect and dignity.

otitis media—an infection of the middle ear.

clear up completely between episodes. A hearing test administered when the child is free of infection might reveal no hearing loss, although the same child might be quite deaf during an acute infection. Intermittent periods of hearing loss, sometimes lasting a week or more, can result in language and cognitive delays and even in severely challenging behaviors in some children (Tharpe, 2007; Roberts, Burchinal, & Zeisel, 2002). During these periods, children's perception of word and letter sounds are often distorted and can result in learned mispronunciations over time. Children can also unknowingly misbehave or disregard requests and instructions simply because they cannot hear. Unfortunately, adults can misinterpret this behavior as problematic instead of recognizing it as a medical problem that is interfering with a child's ability to learn.

WHEN TO SEEK HELP

At what point should a hunch or uncomfortable feeling about a child be a call for action? The answer is clear: whenever families or teachers are concerned about a child's development or behavior. Any such uneasiness needs to be discussed with a pediatrician, health care provider, or child development specialist.

Concern about a developmental irregularity also demands investigation anytime it interferes with a child's participation in everyday activities. The frequent occurrence or repetition of a troublesome behavior is often a reliable sign that professional help should be sought. However, seldom is a single incidence of a questionable behavior cause for concern. What is of concern, however, is a child's *continuing* reluctance to attempt a new skill or to acquire a basic developmental skill fully. For example, a ten-month-old who tries to sit alone but still must use both hands for support might or might not have a problem. On the other hand, clusters of developmental differences are always significant—a ten-month-old who is not sitting without support, not smiling, and not babbling in response to others is likely to be at developmental risk.

What do teachers and caregivers do when a family fails to express concern or denies the possibility of a problem? Although it can be difficult, it is the teacher's responsibility to discuss any concerns in a conference with the family. In that setting, every effort must be made to be straightforward and objective. Teachers must report only what has been observed and what they would expect to see based on the child's developmental stage. Teachers must also refrain from making a diagnosis or labeling the child's behavior. For example, a teacher should say, "Danesha avoids eye contact and often responds inappropriately to questions," rather than "Danesha is probably autistic." Teachers should work closely with the family to help them understand and accept the child's need for further evaluation. Under no circumstances should a teacher or administrator bypass family members and make referrals without their permission. However, teachers can offer their support and willingness to assist families in making the necessary arrangements.

VIDEO CONNECTIONS

Clip 21

Developmental Disabilities: The importance of early identification and intervention services has been stressed throughout the book. The lives of many children have been changed significantly as a result of this knowledge and the dedication of their families and early childhood educators.

Critical Thinking Questions:

1. Why must first-person language always be used when referring to children with a disability?
2. After watching this video clip, can you justify the importance of early identification and intervention? Explain.
3. What social skills does each of the children in the video have that are similar to their typically developing counterparts? How do they differ?
4. What basic needs do all children share in common?

Information Gathering

Multiple levels of information gathering must be included in a developmental evaluation: observation and recording, screening, and diagnostic assessment. Diagnostic assessment includes in-depth testing and clinical interpretation of results. Clinicians from various disciplines should participate in the diagnosis. It is their responsibility to provide detailed information about the specific nature of the child's problems. For example, a four-year-old's delayed speech might be observed by family members and noted during routine screening procedures. Subsequent diagnostic testing by clinicians might pinpoint several other conditions: a moderate, **bilateral** hearing loss, poor production of many letter sounds, and an expressive vocabulary typical of a three-year-old. These clinical findings can be translated into educational strategies and intervention procedures that will benefit the child's overall development.

OBSERVING AND RECORDING

The evaluation process always begins with systematic observation (see Chapter 1.) Noting and recording various aspects of a child's behavior enables the evaluator—whether a family member, a teacher, or a clinician—to focus on what is actually

---

bilateral—affecting both sides, as in loss of hearing in both ears.

occurring. In other words, observations yield objective information about what the child can and cannot do at the time of the observation.

An effective evaluation is also based on multiple observations, conducted over a period of days and in a variety of natural settings that are familiar to the child. Direct observation often confirms or rules out impressions or suspicions regarding a child's abilities (Layton & Lock, 2007). For example, a child might not count to five when asked to do so in a testing situation. That same child, however, might be observed counting seven or eight objects spontaneously and correctly while at play in the block area. A child thought to have attention deficit/hyperactivity disorder (ADHD) might be observed sitting quietly for five to ten minutes when given more interesting and challenging activities, thereby ruling out concerns about hyperactivity. *Note:* The term *hyperactive* is greatly overused and misused. A child should not be so labeled unless specifically diagnosed by a multidisciplinary team. Focusing on a child at play, alone or with other children, can be especially revealing. Again, no evaluation is valid without direct and objective observations of a child in familiar their surroundings.

A family's observations are an especially valuable component of the assessment process (Figure 9-4). They often can provide information that is not available from other sources. Their observations also give insight into unique family attitudes, perceptions, and expectations concerning the child. Involving families in the observation phase of evaluation also helps reduce their anxiety. Furthermore, direct observation often points out unrecognized strengths and abilities. When family members actually see their child engaged in appropriate activities, it can encourage them to focus more on the child's strengths and abilities instead of on his or her limitations.

Figure 9-4

Information contributed by families adds insight and meaning to the evaluation process.

SCREENING TESTS

A number of screening tests are useful for gathering information about children's developmental problems. They are designed to assess a child's current abilities as well as potential delays in fine and large motor skills, cognition, speech and language development, and personal and social responsiveness. The findings are used to determine whether more comprehensive evaluation is needed.

If problems or suspected problems are noted during screening, further in-depth clinical assessment by a child-development specialist is needed before a final diagnosis can be reached. *Note:* Results obtained from screening tests are neither conclusive nor diagnostic. They do not predict a child's future abilities or achievement potential and should not be used as a basis for planning intervention programs.

Several questions should be asked when choosing or interpreting a screening instrument:

- Is it appropriate for the child's age?
- Is it free of bias related to the child's economic, geographic, or cultural background (Sternberg, 2007)?
- Can it be administered in the child's native language (Xu & Drame, 2008; Santos, 2004)? If not, is a skilled interpreter available to assist the child and family?
- Is it reliable for identifying children who should be referred for further testing from those who do not require additional evaluation at this time (Kohl, McLaughlin, & Nagle, 2006)?

A sample of widely used screening tests and assessment instruments is provided in Appendix D. Included are examples of ecological evaluations of home and school; information about the child's everyday surroundings is essential to gather and use in interpreting testing results and planning prevention and intervention programs.

Interpreting Screening Results

The widespread availability of community-based screening programs has contributed to the early detection of potential developmental problems among young children. However, the findings are always open to question. In some cases, the screening process itself might have a negative effect on the outcome. Children's attention spans, especially those of young children, are often short and inconsistent from day to day and from task to task. Illness, fatigue, anxiety, hunger, lack of cooperation, irritability, or restlessness can also lead to unreliable results. Children might perform poorly when they are unaccustomed to being tested or unfamiliar with the person conducting the test. They are also more likely to cooperate and perform reliably when they are in familiar surroundings. Consequently, results derived from screening assessments must be regarded with caution. The following points are intended as reminders for both families and teachers.

- Avoid conclusions based on limited information or a single test score. The results might not be an accurate representation of the child's actual development or developmental potential. Only repeated and periodic observation can provide a complete picture of the child's developing abilities (Dodge et al., 2004).
- Never underestimate the influence of home and family on a child's performance (Venn, 2007). Newer screening procedures make a greater effort to promote family

participation and to evaluate family concerns, priorities, and resources. There also is growing emphasis on screening in familiar or naturalistic environments and everyday situations where children feel more secure.

- Recognize the dangers of labeling a child as having a learning disability, mental retardation, speech impairment, or behavior disorder, especially on the basis of single test results. Labels can have a negative effect on expectations for both the child and the way in which adults respond to the child unless they have been validated through appropriate testing (Figure 9-5).

- Question test scores. Test results can easily be misinterpreted. One test might suggest that a child has a developmental delay when actually nothing is wrong. Such conclusions are called *false positives*. The opposite conclusion can also be reached. A child might have a problem that does not show up in the screening process and so might be incorrectly identified as normal. This is a *false negative*. The first situation leads to unnecessary anxiety and disappointment and might change the way the family responds to their child. The latter situation, the false negative, can lull a family into not seeking further help, so the effect of the child's problem worsens. Both situations can be avoided through careful interpretation of test scores.

- Understand that results from screening tests *do not* constitute a diagnosis. Additional information must be collected and in-depth clinical testing completed before a diagnosis is given or confirmed (Silverstein et al., 2006). Even then,

Figure 9-5

Labels are inappropriate unless a disability has been documented.

errors can occur. There are many reasons for misdiagnosis, such as inconsistent and rapid changes in a child's growth or changing environmental factors such as divorce or family relocation.

- Do not use failed items on a screening test as curriculum items or skills to be taught; a test item is simply one isolated example of a broad range of skills to be expected in a given developmental area at an approximate age. For example, a child who cannot stand on one foot for five seconds will not overcome a developmental problem by being taught to stand on one foot for a given time period. *Screening test items are not a suitable basis for constructing curriculum activities.*

- Recognize that test results do not predict the child's developmental future, nor do they necessarily correlate with subsequent testing. There is always the need for *ongoing* observation, assessment, and in-depth clinical diagnosis when screening tests indicate potential problems and delays.

IQ TESTS: ARE THEY APPROPRIATE FOR YOUNG CHILDREN?

Intelligence tests, such as the Wechsler Intelligence Scale for Children (WISC) and the Stanford Binet Intelligence Scales, were not designed or intended to be used as screening instruments (Mindes, 2006). Neither are they regarded by most early childhood specialists as appropriate to use with young children for any purpose. IQ tests administered during the early years are not valid predictors of future or even current intellectual performance. Especially, they do not predict subsequent academic performance. IQ tests do not take into account the opportunities a child has had to learn, the quality of those learning experiences, or what the *dominant culture* says a child should know at a given age. Children raised in poverty or in non-English-speaking homes often do not have the same opportunities to acquire specific kinds of information represented by the test items. For example, studies have identified maternal education as an important predictor of children's academic achievement, especially among ethnically diverse and low-income families (Magnuson, 2007; Suizzo & Stapleton, 2007). Therefore, an IQ test score used as the sole determinant of a child's cognitive or intellectual development must be challenged.

ACHIEVEMENT TESTS

The administration of formal **achievement tests** in elementary and secondary schools has become a widespread practice since the passage of No Child Left Behind (Figure 9-6). These tests are designed to measure how much the child has been learning in school about specific subject areas (Kohl, McLaughlin, & Nagle, 2006). Depending on the results, each child is assigned a percentile ranking, based on a comparison with other children of the same grade level. For example, a child in the 50th percentile in mathematics is doing as well as 50 percent of the children in the same grade.

---

achievement tests—tests used to measure a child's academic progress (what the child has learned).

Figure 9-6

Achievement tests are often administered to assess student learning.

Test results are also increasingly being used to determine children's placement, assess teacher performance, and evaluate a school's overall academic effectiveness (Driscoll, Halcoussisand, & Svorny, 2008; Reback, 2008). Again, test scores should be backed up by observations of children and by collected samples (portfolios) of their work to have valid meaning.

Diagnosis and Referral

Information obtained from authentic assessment, including direct observations and samples of children's products, combined with screening test results provides the basis for the next question: Are comprehensive diagnostic procedures required? Not all children will require an in-depth clinical assessment, but many will if they and their family are to receive the best possible referral for intervention services. Families can be directed to early-childhood intervention services (Child Find) in their community for evaluation and services offered under Part B for preschool-age children and Part C for infants and toddlers. Diagnoses and referrals are most effective and meaningful when based on a team process that combines the input of clinicians, child development specialists, and the child's family.

THE DEVELOPMENTAL TEAM

Federal law (PL 105-17, IDEA) requires families to be involved in all phases of the assessment and intervention process. They become important members of the child's **developmental team** when they work collaboratively with early-childhood professionals. A family-centered approach improves information sharing and enables family members to learn and implement therapy recommendations at home (Trohanis, 2008; Sylva, 2005). Sustained interest and participation in the child's intervention program can be achieved when the developmental team:

- Keeps families informed.
- Explains rationales for treatment procedures.
- Uses terms that families can understand and takes time to explain those that are unfamiliar.
- Emphasizes the child's progress.
- Teaches family members how to work with their child at home.
- Provides families with positive feedback and supports their continued efforts and advocacy on the child's behalf.

Best practice suggests that the pooling of knowledge and multidisciplinary expertise is required to manage children's developmental disabilities effectively—in other words, a team approach. For example, a team effort provides the most accurate picture of how a delay in one area can affect development in other areas, just as progress in one area supports progress in others. A two-year-old with a hearing loss could experience delays in language as well as in the areas of cognitive and social development. Thus, appropriate intervention strategies for this child might require the services of an audiologist, speech and language therapist, early childhood teacher, nurse, and, perhaps, social worker. If a team approach is to benefit the child's overall development, effective communication and cooperation among specialists, service providers, and the family is essential. This process is facilitated by the inclusion of an Individual Family Service Plan (IFSP for infants and toddlers) or an Individualized Educational Plan (IEP for preschool through school-age children).

FAMILY SERVICE COORDINATOR

Many families are overwhelmed by the process of approaching multiple agencies and dealing with bureaucratic red tape. As a result, they often fail or are unable to complete the necessary arrangements unless they receive assistance. This supportive role was viewed as

---

developmental team—a team of qualified professionals such as special educators, speech pathologists, occupational therapists, social workers, audiologists, nurses, and physical therapists who evaluate a child's developmental progress and together prepare an intervention plan that addresses the child's special needs.

so crucial to successful intervention that the position of **Family Service Coordinator** was written into federal legislation (PL 99-457, Part C) to help families address their infant's and toddler's developmental problems. A Family Service Coordinator works closely with families, matching their needs and their child's needs with appropriate community services and educational programs. The coordinator also assists the family in establishing initial contacts and provides continued support.

REFERRAL

The referral process involves a multiple-step approach. As described earlier, the child's strengths, weaknesses, and developmental skills are evaluated. The family's needs and resources (such as financial, psychological, physical, and transportation capabilities) must also be taken into consideration. For example, if a family cannot afford special services, has no knowledge of financial assistance programs, and does not own a car, it is unlikely that they will be able to follow through on professional recommendations. However, such problems are seldom insurmountable. Most communities have individuals and social service agencies available to help families locate and use early-childhood intervention services.

Placement in an appropriate educational setting is frequently recommended as part of the intervention plan. In these settings, classroom teachers, child-development specialists, and other members of the developmental team conduct ongoing assessments of the child's progress (Figure 9-7). In addition, the developmental team reviews the appropriateness of both the placement and the special services on a regular basis to determine whether the child's and family's needs are being met. This step is especially critical with infants and toddlers, whose development progresses quickly. Throughout, there must be effective communication and support among teachers, practitioners, and families to ensure that the child is receiving individually appropriate services and benefiting from the prescribed program.

Figure 9-7

Family Service Coordinators assist families in arranging intervention services for children with disabilities.

Family Service Coordinator—an individual who serves as a family's advocate and assists them with identifying, locating, and making final arrangements with community services.

S U M M A R Y

Beginning in the mid-1960s, a series of federal laws changed public attitudes and policies related to persons with developmental disabilities. Several of the laws focus on infants and children with, or who are at risk for, developmental problems. Mandated specifically are programs concerned with prevention, early identification, and intervention where there is an obvious or potential problem. The role of the family is formally recognized as essential when addressing the child's needs, as is the clinical expertise from a variety of disciplines. Integral to the family–team collaboration is a designated Family Service Coordinator who orchestrates child, family, and team members' needs, concerns, and recommendations.

Any concern about a child's development demands immediate attention. The starting point is firsthand observation of the child in a familiar, everyday environment. A series of screening tests, appropriate to the child's age, language, and culture, can be administered concurrently. The results obtained from a single test are likely to yield an outcome that can be misleading. Several screening instruments should be administered, and all results interpreted with caution. In-depth clinical diagnosis is the next step if observation and screening results indicate the likelihood of a problem. Therapeutic intervention for infants, toddlers, and preschoolers often includes placement in an early education program. A Family Service Coordinator works with the child, family, and early-intervention program on an ongoing basis as needed.

KEY TERMS

achievement tests
bilateral
Child Find

developmental team
Family Service Coordinator
otitis media

APPLY WHAT YOU KNOW

A. Apply What You Have Learned

Reread the brief developmental sketch about Andrey and his mother at the beginning of the chapter. How might you answer the following questions?

1. Which specific behaviors led Andrey's teachers to be concerned that he might be at risk developmentally?

2. Prior to holding a first conference with Andrey's mother, what observations and information do his teachers need to gather and prepare?

3. Why is it imperative that the teachers' initial evaluation of Andrey's development include a series of firsthand observations (and recorded notes) conducted in a familiar setting such as the classroom and play yard?

4. Describe three pieces of legislation discussed in this chapter that could be of benefit to a high-risk family such as Andrey's.

5. What role and what forms of assistance might a Family Service Coordinator provide for Andrey's family?

B. Review Questions

1. Identify and discuss three concerns that might prevent families from seeking help for their child.

2. Describe three qualities that should be considered when deciding whether a screening test is appropriate for young children.

3. Discuss three methods that a developmental team can use to foster family involvement.

4. Identify and discuss three reasons why it is important to encourage family involvement in a child's intervention program.

5. Describe three aspects of early development that can make it difficult to pinpoint a potential problem.

6. Describe three reasons why the results of screening tests should be interpreted with caution.

HELPFUL WEBSITES

Visit the book companion website at *www.cengage.com/education/allen* for links to these websites and additional resources.

REFERENCES

American Academy of Pediatrics (AAP). (2001). Developmental surveillance and screening of infants and young children. Policy statement. *Pediatrics, 108*(1), 192–195.

Allen, K. E., & Cowdery, G. (2008). *The exceptional child: Inclusion in early childhood education.* Clifton Park, NY: Delmar Cengage Learning.

Crane, J., & Winsler, A. (2008). Early autism detection: Implications for pediatric practice and public policy. *Journal of Disability Policy Studies, 18*(4), 245–253.

Dewey, D., Crawford, S., & Kaplan, B. (2003). Clinical importance of parent ratings of everyday cognitive abilities in children with learning and attention problems. *Journal of Learning Disabilities, 36*(1), 87–95.

Dodge, D., Heroman, C., Charles, J., & Maiorca, J. (2004). Beyond outcomes: How ongoing assessment supports children's learning and leads to meaningful curriculum. *Young Children, 59*(1), 20–28.

Driscoll, D., Halcoussisand, D., & Svorny, S. (2008). Gains in standardized test scores: Evidence of diminishing returns to achievement. *Economics of Education Review, 27*(2), 211–220.

Hix-Small, H., Marks, K., Squires, J., & Nickel, R. (2007). Impact of implementing developmental screening at 12 and 24 months in a pediatric practice. *Pediatrics, 120*(2), 381–389.

Holstrum, W., Gaffney, M., Gravel, J., Oyler, R., & Ross, D. (2008). Early intervention for children with unilateral and mild bilateral degrees of hearing loss. *Trends in Amplification, 12*(1), 35–41.

Jackson, B., & Needelman, H. (2007). Building a system of Child Find through a 3-tiered model of follow-up. *Infants & Young Childen, 20*(3), 255–265.

Johnson, C. (2008). Recognition of autism before age 2 years. *Pediatrics in Review, 29*(3), 86–96.

Kohl, F., McLaughlin, M., & Nagle, K. (2006). Alternate achievement standards and assessments: A descriptive investigation of 16 states. *Exceptional Children, 73*(1), 107–123.

Layton, C., & Lock, R. (2007). 20 Ways to use authentic assessment techniques to fulfill the promise of No Child Left Behind. *Intervention in School and Clinic, 42*(3), 169–173.

Lipkin, P., & Gwynn, H. (2007). Improving developmental screening: Combining parent and pediatrician opinions with standardized questionnaires. *Pediatrics, 119*(3), 655–656.

Lopez, E., Salas, L., & Flores, J. (2005). Hispanic preschool children: What about assessment and intervention? *Young Children, 60*(6), 48–54.

Magnuson, K. (2007). Maternal education and children's academic achievement during middle childhood. *Developmental Psychology, 43*(6), 1497–1512.

Matson, J., Wilkins, J., & González, M. (2008). Early identification and diagnosis in autism spectrum disorders in young children and infants: How early is too early? *Research in Autism Spectrum Disorders, 2*(1), 75–84.

Mindes, G. (2006). *Assessing young children.* (3rd ed.). Upper Saddle River, NJ: Merrill Prentice Hall.

Reback, R. (2008). Teaching to the rating: School accountability and the distribution of student achievement. *Journal of Public Economics, 92*(5–6), 1394–1415.

Roberts, J., Burchinal, M., & Zeisel, S. (2002). Otitis media in early childhood in relation to children's school-age language and academic skills. *Pediatrics, 110*(4), 696–706.

Roberts, J., Hunter, L., Gravel, J., Rosenfeld, R., Berman, S., Haggard, M., Hall, J., Lannon, C., Moore, D., Vernon-Feagans, L., & Wallace, I. (2004). Otitis media, hearing loss, and language learning: Controversies and current research. *Journal of Development & Behavioral Pediatrics, 25*(2), 110–122.

Santos, R. (2004). Ensuring culturally and linguistically appropriate assessment of young children. *Young Children, 59*(1), 48–50.

Shulman, L., Meringolo, D., & Scott, G. (2007). Early intervention: A crash course for pediatricians. *Pediatric Annals, 36*(8), 463–439.

Silverstein, M., Sand, N., Glascoe, F., Gupta, V., Tonniges, T., & O'Connor, K. (2006). Pediatrician practices regarding referral to early intervention services: Is an established diagnosis important? *Ambulatory Pediatrics, 6*(2), 105–109.

Sternberg, R. (2007). Who are the bright children? The cultural context of being and acting intelligent. *Educational Researcher, 36*(3), 148–155.

Suizzo, M., & Stapleton, L. (2007). Home-based parental involvement in young children's education: Examining the effects of maternal education across U.S. ethnic groups. *Educational Psychology, 27*(4), 533–556.

Sylva, J. (2005). Issues in early intervention: The impact of cultural diversity on service delivery in natural environments. *Multicultural Education, 13*(2), 26–29.

Tharpe, A. (2007). Unilateral hearing loss in children: A mountain or a molehill? *The Hearing Journal, 60*(7), 10–16.

Trawick-Smith, J. (2006). *Early childhood development: A multicultural perspective.* (4th ed.). Upper Saddle River, NJ: Merrill Prentice Hall.

Trohanis, P. (2008). Progress in providing services to young children with special needs and their families. *Journal of Early Intervention, 30*(2), 140–151.

Venn, J. (2007). *Assessing students with special needs.* Upper Saddle River, NJ: Prentice Hall.

Xu, Y., & Drame, E. (2008). Culturally appropriate context: Unlocking the potential of response to intervention for English language learners. *Early Childhood Education Journal, 35*(4), 305–311.

BOOK COMPANION WEBSITE

The book-specific website at *www.cengage.com/education/allen* offers students a variety of study tools and useful resources such as chapter overviews and notes, tutorial quizzes, web links, frequently asked questions, discussion questions, glossary/flashcards, internet exercises, references and more. To register or purchase access to the premium resources for this text including video clips tied to chapter content, go to *www.cengage.com/login.*

Recommended Immunization Schedule

Recommended Immunization Schedule for Persons Aged 0–6 Years—UNITED STATES • 2008

For those who fall behind or start late, see the catch-up schedule

Vaccine ▼ Age ►	Birth	1 month	2 months	4 months	6 months	12 months	15 months	18 months	19–23 months	2–3 years	4–6 years
Hepatitis B[1]	HepB	HepB		see footnote 1		HepB					
Rotavirus[2]			Rota	Rota	Rota						
Diphtheria, Tetanus, Pertussis[3]			DTaP	DTaP	DTaP	see footnote 3	DTaP				DTaP
Haemophilus influenzae type b[4]			Hib	Hib	*Hib*[4]	Hib					
Pneumococcal[5]			PCV	PCV	PCV	PCV				PPV	
Inactivated Poliovirus			IPV	IPV		IPV					IPV
Influenza[6]						Influenza (Yearly)					
Measles, Mumps, Rubella[7]						MMR					MMR
Varicella[8]						Varicella					Varicella
Hepatitis A[9]						HepA (2 doses)				HepA Series	
Meningococcal[10]										MCV4	

Range of recommended ages

Certain high-risk groups

This schedule indicates the recommended ages for routine administration of currently licensed childhood vaccines, as of December 1, 2007, for children aged 0 through 6 years. Additional information is available at www.cdc.gov/vaccines/recs/schedules. Any dose not administered at the recommended age should be administered at any subsequent visit, when indicated and feasible. Additional vaccines may be licensed and recommended during the year. Licensed combination vaccines may be used whenever any components of the combination are indicated and other components of the vaccine are not contraindicated and if approved by the Food and Drug Administration for that dose of the series. Providers should consult the respective Advisory Committee on Immunization Practices statement for detailed recommendations, including for **high-risk conditions:** http://www.cdc.gov/vaccines/pubs/ACIP-list.htm. Clinically significant adverse events that follow immunization should be reported to the Vaccine Adverse Event Reporting System (VAERS). Guidance about how to obtain and complete a VAERS form is available at **www.vaers.hhs.gov** or by telephone, **800-822-7967.**

1. Hepatitis B vaccine (HepB). *(Minimum age: birth)*
At birth:
- Administer monovalent HepB to all newborns prior to hospital discharge.
- If mother is hepatitis B surface antigen (HBsAg) positive, administer HepB and 0.5 mL of hepatitis B immune globulin (HBIG) within 12 hours of birth.
- If mother's HBsAg status is unknown, administer HepB within 12 hours of birth. Determine the HBsAg status as soon as possible and if HBsAg positive, administer HBIG (no later than age 1 week).
- If mother is HBsAg negative, the birth dose can be delayed, in rare cases, with a provider's order and a copy of the mother's negative HBsAg laboratory report in the infant's medical record.

After the birth dose:
- The HepB series should be completed with either monovalent HepB or a combination vaccine containing HepB. The second dose should be administered at age 1–2 months. The final dose should be administered no earlier than age 24 weeks. Infants born to HBsAg-positive mothers should be tested for HBsAg and antibody to HBsAg after completion of at least 3 doses of a licensed HepB series, at age 9–18 months (generally at the next well-child visit).

4-month dose:
- It is permissible to administer 4 doses of HepB when combination vaccines are administered after the birth dose. If monovalent HepB is used for doses after the birth dose, a dose at age 4 months is not needed.

2. Rotavirus vaccine (Rota). *(Minimum age: 6 weeks)*
- Administer the first dose at age 6–12 weeks.
- Do not start the series later than age 12 weeks.
- Administer the final dose in the series by age 32 weeks. Do not administer any dose later than age 32 weeks.
- Data on safety and efficacy outside of these age ranges are insufficient.

3. Diphtheria and tetanus toxoids and acellular pertussis vaccine (DTaP). *(Minimum age: 6 weeks)*
- The fourth dose of DTaP may be administered as early as age 12 months, provided 6 months have elapsed since the third dose.
- Administer the final dose in the series at age 4–6 years.

4. *Haemophilus influenzae* type b conjugate vaccine (Hib). *(Minimum age: 6 weeks)*
- If PRP-OMP (PedvaxHIB® or ComVax® [Merck]) is administered at ages 2 and 4 months, a dose at age 6 months is not required.
- TriHIBit® (DTaP/Hib) combination products should not be used for primary immunization but can be used as boosters following any Hib vaccine in children age 12 months or older.

5. Pneumococcal vaccine. *(Minimum age: 6 weeks for pneumococcal conjugate vaccine [PCV]; 2 years for pneumococcal polysaccharide vaccine [PPV])*
- Administer one dose of PCV to all healthy children aged 24–59 months having any incomplete schedule.
- Administer PPV to children aged 2 years and older with underlying medical conditions.

6. Influenza vaccine. *(Minimum age: 6 months for trivalent inactivated influenza vaccine [TIV]; 2 years for live, attenuated influenza vaccine [LAIV])*
- Administer annually to children aged 6–59 months and to all eligible close contacts of children aged 0–59 months.
- Administer annually to children 5 years of age and older with certain risk factors, to other persons (including household members) in close contact with persons in groups at higher risk, and to any child whose parents request vaccination.
- For healthy persons (those who do not have underlying medical conditions that predispose them to influenza complications) ages 2–49 years, either LAIV or TIV may be used.
- Children receiving TIV should receive 0.25 mL if age 6–35 months or 0.5 mL if age 3 years or older.
- Administer 2 doses (separated by 4 weeks or longer) to children younger than 9 years who are receiving influenza vaccine for the first time or who were vaccinated for the first time last season but only received one dose.

7. Measles, mumps, and rubella vaccine (MMR). *(Minimum age: 12 months)*
- Administer the second dose of MMR at age 4–6 years. MMR may be administered before age 4–6 years, provided 4 weeks or more have elapsed since the first dose.

8. Varicella vaccine. *(Minimum age: 12 months)*
- Administer second dose at age 4–6 years; may be administered 3 months or more after first dose.
- Do not repeat second dose if administered 28 days or more after first dose.

9. Hepatitis A vaccine (HepA). *(Minimum age: 12 months)*
- Administer to all children aged 1 year (i.e., aged 12–23 months). Administer the 2 doses in the series at least 6 months apart.
- Children not fully vaccinated by age 2 years can be vaccinated at subsequent visits.
- HepA is recommended for certain other groups of children, including in areas where vaccination programs target older children.

10. Meningococcal vaccine. *(Minimum age: 2 years for meningococcal conjugate vaccine [MCV4] and for meningococcal polysaccharide vaccine (MPSV4))*
- Administer MCV4 to children aged 2–10 years with terminal complement deficiencies or anatomic or functional asplenia and certain other high-risk groups. MPSV4 is also acceptable.
- Administer MCV4 to persons who received MPSV4 3 or more years previously and remain at increased risk for meningococcal disease.

The Recommended Immunization Schedules for Persons Aged 0–18 Years are approved by the Advisory Committee on Immunization Practices (www.cdc.gov/vaccines/recs/acip), the American Academy of Pediatrics (http://www.aap.org), and the American Academy of Family Physicians (http://www.aafp.org).

DEPARTMENT OF HEALTH AND HUMAN SERVICES • CENTERS FOR DISEASE CONTROL AND PREVENTION • SAFER • HEATHIER • PEOPLE™

CS103164

Source: *www.cdc.gov/nip/recs/child-schedule*

NOTE: Immunization recommendations are reviewed and updated annually.

Developmental Checklists

A simple checklist, one for each child, is a useful observation tool for anyone working with infants and young children. Questions on the checklists that follow can be answered during the course of a child's everyday activities and over a period of one week or more. "No" answers signal that further investigation might be in order. Several "No" answers indicate that additional investigation is a necessity.

The "Sometimes" category is an important one. It suggests what the child can do at least part of the time or under some circumstances. The "Sometimes" category provides space where brief notes and comments can be recorded about how and when a behavior occurs. In many cases, a child might simply need more practice, incentive, or adult encouragement. Hunches often provide a good starting point for working with the child. Again, if "Sometimes" is checked a number of times, further investigation is recommended.

The observation checklists may be duplicated and used as part of the assessment process. They are based on detailed information provided in each of the preceding chapters. The items represent a sampling of developmental milestones associated with each approximate age. When completed, a checklist contains information about a child that members of a developmental team will find useful in evaluating a his or her development status and in determining an intervention program. However, it is important to interpret these findings cautiously because children's development can be influenced by variations in cultural, linguistic, family background, or in all these categories.

Child's Name _____ Age _____

Observer _____ Date _____

DEVELOPMENTAL CHECKLIST

BY SIX MONTHS *Does the child . . .*	Yes	No	Sometimes
Show continued gains in height, weight, and head circumference?			
Reach for toys or objects when they are presented?			
Begin to roll from stomach to back?			
Sit with minimal support?			
Transfer objects from one hand to the other?			
Rise up on arms, lifting head and chest, when placed on stomach?			
Babble, coo, and imitate sounds?			
Turn to locate the source of a sound?			
Focus on an object and follow its movement vertically and horizontally?			
Exhibit a blink reflex? Enjoy being held and cuddled?			
Recognize and respond to familiar faces?			
Begin sleeping 6 to 8 hours through the night?			
Suck vigorously when it is time to eat?			
Enjoy (splash, coo) playing in water during bath time?			

Child's Name _____   Age _____

Observer _____   Date _____

DEVELOPMENTAL CHECKLIST

BY TWELVE MONTHS *Does the child . . .*	Yes	No	Sometimes
Walk with assistance?			
Roll a ball in imitation of an adult?			
Pick objects up with thumb and forefinger?			
Transfer objects from one hand to the other?			
Pick up dropped toys?			
Look directly at an adult's face?			
Imitate gestures: peek-a-boo, bye-bye, pat-a-cake?			
Find object hidden under a cup?			
Feed oneself crackers (munching, not sucking on them)?			
Hold cup with two hands; drink with assistance?			
Smile spontaneously?			
Turn head or come when name is called?			
Respond to "no"?			
Show hesitation with strangers; want to be picked up only by familiar persons?			
Respond differently to sounds: vacuum, phone, door?			
Look at person who speaks to him or her?			
Respond to simple directions accompanied by gestures?			
Make several consonant–vowel combination sounds?			
Vocalize back to person who has talked to him or her?			
Use intonation patterns that sound like scolding, asking, exclaiming?			
Say "da-da" or "ma-ma"?			

Child's Name _____ Age _____

Observer _____ Date _____

DEVELOPMENTAL CHECKLIST

	Yes	No	Sometimes

BY TWO YEARS
 Does the child . . .
 Walk alone?
 Bend over and pick up a toy without falling over?
 Seat oneself in child-size chair? Walk up and down stairs with assistance?
 Place several rings on a stick?
 Place five pegs in a pegboard?
 Turn pages two or three at a time?
 Scribble?
 Follow one-step direction involving something familiar:
     "Give me _____,"
     "Show me _____,"
     "Get a _____"?
 Match familiar objects?
 Use a spoon with some spilling?
 Drink from cup holding it with one hand unassisted?
 Take off coat, shoe, sock?
 Zip and unzip large zipper?
 Name and point to oneself in a mirror?
 Refer to self by name?
 Imitate adult behavior in play—for example, feeds "baby?"
 Help put things away?
 Respond to specific words by showing what was named: toy, pet, family member?
 Ask for desired items by name: (cookie)?
 Answer with name of object when asked "What's that?"
 Make and maintain eye contact when asking or responding to questions?
 Make some two-word statements: "Daddy bye-bye?"			

Child's Name _____   Age _____

Observer _____   Date _____

DEVELOPMENTAL CHECKLIST

	Yes	No	Sometimes
BY THREE YEARS *Does the child . . .* Run with coordination in a forward direction; avoid running into objects or people?			
Jump in place, two feet together?			
Walk heel to toe (not on tiptoe)?			
Throw ball (but without direction or aim)? Kick ball forward?			
String four large beads?			
Turn pages in book singly?			
Hold crayon: imitate circular, vertical, horizontal strokes?			
Match shapes?			
Demonstrate number concepts of 1 and 2? (Can select 1 or 2; can tell if one or two objects.)			
Use a spoon without spilling?			
Drink from a straw?			
Put on and take off coat?			
Wash and dry hands with some assistance?			
Watch other children; play near them; sometimes join in their play?			
Defend own possessions?			
Use symbols in play (tin pan on head becomes helmet and crate becomes a spaceship)?			
Respond to "Put _____ in the box," "Take the _____ out of the box"?			
Select correct item on request (big versus little; one versus two)?			
Identify objects by their use (show their own shoe when asked "What do you wear on your feet?")?			
Ask questions and make eye contact?			
Tell about something with functional phrases that carry meaning ("Daddy go airplane," "Me hungry now")?			

Child's Name _____ Age _____

Observer _____ Date _____

DEVELOPMENTAL CHECKLIST

BY FOUR YEARS *Does the child . . .*	Yes	No	Sometimes
Walk on a line?			
Balance on one foot briefly? Hop on one foot?			
Jump over an object 6 inches high and land on both feet together?			
Throw ball with direction?			
Copy circles and Xs?			
Match six colors?			
Count to 5?			
Pour well from a pitcher? Spread butter, jam with a knife?			
Button, unbutton large buttons?			
State own gender, age, last name?			
Use toilet independently and when needed?			
Wash and dry hands unassisted?			
Listen to stories for at least 5 minutes?			
Draw head of a person and at least one other body part?			
Play with other children?			
Share, take turns (with some assistance)?			
Engage in dramatic and pretend play?			
Respond appropriately to "Put it beside," "Put it under"?			
Respond to two-step directions: "Give me the sweater and put the shoe on the floor"?			
Respond by selecting the correct object (hard versus soft object)?			
Answer "if," "what," and "when" questions?			
Answer questions about function: "What are books for?"			
Make and maintain eye contact?			

Child's Name _____   Age _____

Observer _____   Date _____

DEVELOPMENTAL CHECKLIST

BY FIVE YEARS *Does the child . . .*	Yes	No	Sometimes
Walk backward, toe to heel?			
Walk up and down stairs, alternating feet?			
Cut on line?			
Print some letters?			
Point to and name three shapes?			
Group common related objects: shoe, sock, and foot; apple, orange, and plum?			
Demonstrate number concepts to 4 or 5?			
Cut food with a knife: celery, sandwich?			
Lace shoes?			
Read from story picture book (tell story by looking at pictures)?			
Draw a person with three to six body parts?			
Play and interact with other children; engage in dramatic play that is close to reality?			
Build complex structures with blocks or other building materials?			
Respond to simple three-step directions: "Give me the pencil, put the book on the table, and put your feet on the floor"?			
Respond correctly when asked to show penny, nickel, and dime?			
Ask "How" questions?			
Respond verbally to "Hi" and "How are you?"			
Tell about event using past and future tenses?			
Use conjunctions to string words and phrases together ("I saw a bear and a zebra and a giraffe at the zoo")?			

Child's Name _____   Age _____

Observer _____   Date _____

DEVELOPMENTAL CHECKLIST

BY SIX YEARS *Does the child . . .*	Yes	No	Sometimes
Walk across a balance beam?			
Skip with alternating feet?			
Hop for several seconds on one foot?			
Cut out simple shapes?			
Copy his or her own first name?			
Show well-established handedness; demonstrate consistent right- or left-handedness?			
Sort objects on one or more dimensions (color, shape, or function)?			
Name most letters and numerals?			
Count by rote to 10; know what number comes next?			
Dress self completely; tie bows?			
Brush teeth unassisted?			
Have some concept of clock time in relation to daily schedule?			
Cross street safely, holding an adult's hand?			
Draw a person with head, trunk, legs, arms, and features; often add clothing details?			
Play simple board games?			
Engage in cooperative play with other children, involving group decisions, role assignments, rule observance?			
Use construction toys such as Legos and blocks to make recognizable structures?			
Do fifteen-piece puzzles?			
Use all grammatical structures: pronouns, plurals, verb tenses, conjunctions?			
Use complex sentences; carry on conversations?			

Child's Name _____   Age _____

Observer _____   Date _____

DEVELOPMENTAL CHECKLIST

BY SEVEN YEARS *Does the child . . .*	Yes	No	Sometimes
Concentrate on completing puzzles and board games?			
Ask many questions?			
Use correct verb tenses, word order, and sentence structure in conversation?			
Correctly identify right and left hands?			
Make friends easily?			
Show some control of anger, using words instead of physical aggression?			
Participate in play that requires teamwork and rule observance?			
Seek adult approval for efforts?			
Enjoy reading and being read to?			
Use a pencil to write words and numbers?			
Sleep undisturbed through the night?			
Catch a tennis ball, walk across a balance beam, hit a ball with a bat?			
Plan and carry out simple projects with minimal adult help?			
Tie his or her own shoes?			
Draw pictures with greater detail and sense of proportion?			
Care for own personal needs with some adult supervision? Wash hands? Brush teeth? Use toilet? Dress self?			
Show some understanding of cause-and-effect concepts?			

Child's Name _____ Age _____

Observer _____ Date _____

DEVELOPMENTAL CHECKLIST

BY EIGHT AND NINE YEARS *Does the child . . .*	Yes	No	Sometimes
Have energy to play, continue to grow, experience few illnesses?			
Use a pencil in a deliberate and controlled manner?			
Express relatively complex thoughts in a clear and logical fashion?			
Carry out multiple four- or five-step instructions?			
Become less easily frustrated with his or her own performance?			
Interact and play cooperatively with other children?			
Show interest in creative expression (telling stories, jokes, writing, drawing, singing)?			
Use eating utensils with ease?			
Have a good appetite? Show interest in trying new foods?			
Know how to tell time?			
Have control of bowel and bladder functions?			
Participate in some group activities (games, sports, plays)?			
Want to go to school? Seem disappointed if he or she must miss a day?			
Demonstrate beginning skills in reading, writing, and mathematics?			
Accept responsibility and complete work independently?			
Handle stressful situations without becoming overly upset or aggressive?			

Child's Name _____ Age _____

Observer _____ Date _____

DEVELOPMENTAL CHECKLIST

BY TEN AND ELEVEN YEARS *Does the child . . .*	Yes	No	Sometimes
Continue to increase in height and weight?			
Exhibit improving coordination (running, climbing, riding a bike, writing)?			
Handle stressful situations without losing control or becoming overly upset or violent?			
Construct sentences using reasonably correct grammar (nouns, adverbs, verbs, adjectives)?			
Understand concepts of time, distance, space, volume?			
Have one or two "best friends?"			
Maintain friendships over time?			
Approach challenges with a reasonable degree of self-confidence?			
Play cooperatively and follow group instructions?			
Begin to show an understanding of moral standards (right from wrong, fairness, honesty, good from bad)?			
Look forward to and enjoy school most days?			
Appear to hear well, listen attentively, respond appropriately?			
Enjoy reasonably good health with few episodes of illness or health-related complaints?			
Have a good appetite and enjoy mealtimes?			
Take care of own personal hygiene without assistance?			
Sleep through the night, waking up refreshed and energetic?			

Child's Name _____ Age _____

Observer _____ Date _____

DEVELOPMENTAL CHECKLIST

BY TWELVE AND THIRTEEN YEARS *Does the child . . .*	Yes	No	Sometimes
Appear to be growing (increasing height and maintaining a healthy weight, not too thin or too heavy)?			
Understand changes associated with puberty or have an opportunity to learn and ask questions?			
Have good vision or wear glasses; not complain of headaches or blurred vision?			
Have straight posture (no curving of the spine or other abnormality)?			
Seem energetic and not chronically fatigued?			
Stay focused on a task and complete assignments?			
Remember and carry out complex instructions?			
Sequence, order, and classify objects?			
Use longer and more complex sentence structure?			
Engage in conversation; tell jokes and riddles?			
Enjoy playing organized games and team sports?			
Respond to anger-invoking situations without resorting to violence or physical aggression?			
Begin to understand and solve complex mathematical problems?			
Accept blame for actions on most occasions?			
Participate in, and enjoy, competitive activities?			
Accept and carry out responsibility in a dependable manner?			
Go to bed willingly and wake up refreshed?			
Take pride in appearance; keep self reasonably clean?			

Child Health History

SAMPLE FORM

The information provided on this form is intended to serve only as a guideline. You are encouraged to modify the questions according to the needs and goals of your individual program.

GENERAL INFORMATION

1. Child's Name _____   _____
   (First)   (Last)

2. Child's Address _____
   (Street)

   _____
   (City, State, Zip)

3. Home Telephone Number ( )_____-_____

4. Child's Gender _____ Female _____ Male

5. Child's Date of Birth _____ _____ _____
   Month   Date   Year

6. Mother (Guardian's) Name _____

7. Father's (Guardian's) Name _____

BIRTH HISTORY

8. Length of pregnancy _____ 6 _____ 7 _____ 8 _____ 9 months

9. Child's weight at birth _____ lb. _____ oz. or _____ kilograms

10. Were there any unusual factors or complications during this pregnancy?

    _____ yes _____ no   Please describe: _____

11. Did your child have any medical problems at birth (i.e., jaundice, difficulty breathing, birth defects)? _____ yes _____ no   Please describe: _____
_____

12. Name of child's doctor: _____
Doctor's telephone number ( ) _____

13. Does your child take any medications on a regular basis? _____ yes _____ no
If yes, provide the medication name and dosage:_____

14. Has your child had any of the following illnesses (dates)?

_____ measles   _____ rheumatic fever   _____ chicken pox

_____ mumps   _____ pneumonia   _____ meningitis

_____ whooping cough   _____ hepatitis   _____ middle ear infection
                                                        (otitis media)

15. Were there any complications with these illnesses, such as high fever, seizures, muscle weaknesses, hearing loss, or others? _____ yes _____ no
Please describe: _____

16. Has your child ever been hospitalized? _____ yes _____ no
Number of times _____ Length of time _____
Reasons: _____

17. Has your child had any other serious illness or injuries that did not involve hospitalization? _____ yes _____ no   Please describe: _____
_____

18. How many colds has your child had during the past year? _____

19. Does your child have:
Allergies? _____ yes _____ no (Please specify which allergies):
Foods _____
Animals _____
Medicine _____
Asthma? _____ yes _____ no   Hay fever? _____ yes _____ no

20. Has your child had any problems with earaches or ear infections?
_____ yes _____ no   If yes, how often in the past year? _____

21. Has your child's hearing been tested? _____ yes _____ no
Month/year of test: _____
Was there any evidence of hearing loss? _____ yes _____ no
If yes, describe: _____

22. Does your child currently have tubes in his or her ears? _____ yes _____ no

23. Do you have any concerns about your child's speech or language development? _____ yes _____ no   If yes, describe: _____

24. Has your child's vision been tested? _____yes _____ no
    Month/year of test: _____

25. Was there any evidence of vision loss? _____ yes _____ no
    Please describe: _____

26. Does your child do things that you find troublesome?
    Please describe: _____

27. Has your child ever participated in out-of-the-home child care services (for example, baby sitter, play group, preschool)? _____ yes _____ no
    Please describe: _____

CHILD'S PLAY ACTIVITIES

28. Where does your child usually play (for example, backyard, kitchen, bedroom)?
    _____

29. Does your child usually play: _____ alone? _____ with one to two other children?
    _____ with brothers/sisters? _____ with older children? _____ with younger children?
    _____ with children of the same age?

30. Is your child usually _____ cooperative? _____ shy? _____ aggressive or hurtful?

31. What are some of your child's favorite toys and activities?
    Please describe: _____

32. Do you have any particular concerns about your child's behavior or interactions with other children?
    Please describe: _____

CHILD'S DAILY ROUTINE

33. Do you have any concerns about your child's: _____ eating habits? _____ sleeping habits? _____ toilet training?
    If yes, please describe: _____

34. Is your child toilet trained? _____ yes _____ no   If yes, how often does your child have an accident? _____

35. What word(s) does your child use or understand for:
    urination? _____ bowel movement? _____

36. How many hours does your child sleep at night? _____
    Goes to bed at: _____ P.M.   Wakes up at: _____ A.M.   Afternoon nap: _____

37. When your child is upset, how do you comfort him or her? _____
    _____

38. The term *family* has many different meanings. Because the topic of families and family members is often included in classroom discussions, please list or describe who your child considers to be "family" at home. _____

_____

39. How many brothers and or sisters does your child have?

Brothers (ages): _____   Sisters (ages): _____

_____   _____

40. What language(s) is/are most commonly spoken in your home?

English _____ Other _____

41. Is there any additional information that would help us understand or work more effectively with your child? _____

_____

Selected Screening and Assessment Instruments

Examples of Screening Tests

Ages and Stages Questionnaires (ASQ) is a monitoring system for assessing children's development in five areas: communication, personal-social, problem-solving, fine motor, and gross motor. Questionnaires are available for children 4, 6, 8, 10, 12, 14, 16, 18, 20, 22, 24, 27, 30, 33, 36, 42, 48, 54, and 60 months of age. Families complete the questionnaires based on their observations. Forms require 2 to 3 minutes to score. Spanish, French, Korean, and other language versions of the questionnaires are available.

GS Early Screening Profiles test children 2 to 7 years of age for cognitive, language, social, self-help, and motor skills; includes information provided by families, teachers, and child care providers.

Battelle Developmental Screening Test is a screening tool that includes 96 items from the Battelle Developmental Inventory that can be used to assess children, birth to 8 years, in five domains: communication, cognitive, personal-social, motor, and adaptive. This instrument is effective for assessing typical development, school readiness, and identification of children with disabilities.

Denver Developmental Screening Test (Denver II) is appropriate for testing children from birth to 6 years of age in four developmental areas: personal-social, language, fine motor, and gross motor. Ratings of the child's behavior during testing can be recorded.

Developmental Activities Screening Inventory (DASI II) screens children 1 month to 5 years; a nonverbal test especially useful for children with hearing or language disorders; also offers adaptations for children with vision problems.

Developmental Indicators for the Assessment of Learning, 3rd Edition (DIAL-3) is designed to screen children ages 3 to 6 years, 7 months, in five developmental domains: motor, concepts, communication, self-help, and social. A Spanish language version is available. *Speed DIAL-3* is an abbreviated version of the test that includes items for motor, language, and concepts development and can be administered in less than 15 minutes. New versions of these tests are currently being tested.

First Steps: Screening Test for Evaluating Preschoolers can be used with children 2 years, 9 months, to 6 years, 2 months, on cognitive, communication, and motor skills; an Adaptive Behavior Checklist and a Social-Emotional Scale are included as well as a Parent–Teacher Scale related to the child's behavior at home and at school.

Examples of Assessment Instruments

APGAR Scoring System is administered at 1 minute and again at 5 minutes after birth; the APGAR assesses muscle tone, respiration, color, heartbeat, and reflexes for a maximum score of 10. The information is used to determine which infants need special care.

Assessment, Evaluation, and Programming Systems (AEPS) for Infants and Children, 2nd Edition (volume 2, birth to three, three to six; volumes 3 and 4, curriculum interventions for birth to three, three to six) is an authentic, family-friendly system for assessing very young children. It ties together assessment outcomes with early intervention strategies that are activity-based and family-centered. Test results can be used to determine a child's eligibility for services, establishment of IEP/IFSP goals, and evaluation of intervention effectiveness.

Audiology, that is, hearing assessment of infants and children, requires clinical testing by a trained technician. It is *imperative*, however, in terms of early identification, for teachers and families to record and report their observations whenever they suspect a child is not hearing well. Warning signs include:

- Pulling or banging on an ear.
- Drainage from the ear canal.
- Failing to respond or looking puzzled when spoken to.
- Requesting frequent repetitions—What? Huh?
- Speaking in too loud or too soft of a voice.
- Articulating or discriminating sounds poorly.

Bayley Scales of Infant Development II Assessment evaluates both motor and cognitive development. The age range has been expanded to cover children from 1 month to 3½ years. The Mental Scales and the Motor Scales are separate instruments.

Brigance Diagnostic Inventory of Early Development II (IED-II) is a criterion-referenced instrument for assessing children, birth through 6 years, in multiple developmental domains: fine and gross motor, speech and language, knowledge and comprehension, self-help, and pre-academic skills (basic reading, mathematics, and writing readiness).

Test results can be used for goal-setting and curriculum planning but are not intended for determining a child's eligibility for special services.

Early Childhood Environmental Rating Scale-Revised (ECERS-R) is a well-respected, culturally sensitive assessment tool for evaluating classroom environments, including space, materials, activities, language, personal care routines, communication, program structure, and family/staff interaction. Additional versions are available for assessing infant/toddler (ITERS-R), family home child care (FDCRS), and school-age care environments (SACERS).

Hawaii Early Learning Profile (HELP) is a user- and family-friendly assessment instrument designed for monitoring children's (birth through age 3) developmental progress and developing play-based interventions. Developmental milestones for each of the six domains are outlined on an easy-to-read chart. HELP fosters an interdisciplinary and family-centered approach.

Home Observation for Measurement of the Environment (HOME) is the best known and most widely used in-home inventory. Scales range from infancy to middle childhood; each version assesses the physical environment as well as the social, emotional, and cognitive support available to the child. A modified version, *Supplement to the HOME for Impoverished Families (SHIF)*, is available for assessing the home environment of children who live in poverty.

Kaufman Assessment Battery for Children, 2nd Edition (KABC-II) is a "culturally fair" test developed to assess the cognitive abilities of children ages 3 to 18 years. Test items are designed to minimize the effects of verbal, gender, and ethnic bias.

Kaufman Survey of Early Academic and Language Skills (K-SEALS) assesses 3–7-year-olds' reception and expressive language skills as well as concepts related to numbers, counting, letters, and words; includes an articulation survey.

Learning Accomplishment Profile—Diagnostic Edition (LAP-D) assesses children aged 2½ to 6 years on fine motor (writing and manipulative skills), gross motor (body and object movement), matching and counting (viewed as cognitive tasks), and language skills (comprehension and object naming).

Learning Accomplishment Profile—Revised (LAP-R) is a criterion-referenced instrument designed to assess children's development across seven domains. A modified version, the *Early Learning Accomplishment Profile (Early LAP)*, is available for use with children whose functional development ranges from birth to 3 years.

Neonatal Behavioral Assessment Scale (NBAS—often referred to as the Brazelton) assesses behavioral responses in full-term infants up to 28 days of age. A significant modification of the NBAS is the *Kansas Supplement (NBAS-K)*. It adds a number of critical parameters as well as assessing the infant's typical behavior (state) and optimal behavior (the only focus of the original NBAS).

Peabody Developmental Motor Scales (PDMS-2) assess children from birth through 5 years of age in fine motor (grasping, eye–hand coordination, and manual dexterity) and gross motor development (reflexes, balance, locomotion, throwing, and catching). Strategies for remediation are also included.

Peabody Picture Vocabulary Test, 4th Edition (PPVT-IV) is a norm-referenced test that can be administered in 10 to 15 minutes to evaluate receptive language and verbal ability; appropriate for use with children 30 months and older. A Spanish version is also available.

Preschool Language Scale-4 (*PLS-4*) can be used to assess children, birth through 6 years, on auditory comprehension, articulation, grammatical forms, and basic concept development. A Spanish version based on cultural variations is also available.

The Snellen E or *Illiterate E* eye test is an instrument commonly used for assessing the visual acuity of young children (knowing the alphabet is not required). As with hearing, screening young children for vision problems also relies heavily on adult observations for indicators such as:

- Rubbing eyes frequently or closing or covering one eye.
- Constantly stumbling over or running into things.
- Complaining of frequent headaches.
- Blinking excessively when looking at books or reading.
- Brushing hand over eyes as if trying to get rid of a blur.

Healthy eye development has important long-term implications. A nationwide public health program called InfantSEE® was initiated in 2005 to promote early detection and treatment of vision problems. Infants can receive free screening and eye care provided by participating optometrists. Observations are also useful for noting early signs of potential vision problems:

- Observing the infant's ability to focus on an object.
- Watching for uncoordinated eye movements such as crossed or wandering eyes.
- Checking for a blink reflex.
- Seeing if the infant can visually follow (track) an object, such as a toy, as it is moved in a 180-degree arc.

Work Sampling System (*WSS*) is a unique approach for documenting authentic and ongoing evaluation of children's developmental progress; it uses a combination of portfolio development (with samples of child's work) and checklists for data collection. Assessments are conducted three times during the course of one year and provide teachers with feedback on effective instructional strategies as well as on how children are responding; appropriate for children preschool to fifth grade.

Resources for Families and Professionals

Many resources are available to families, teachers, and service providers who work with young children. These resources are provided at the community, state, and national levels and fall into two major categories: direct services and information sources.

Direct Services

Developmental screenings are available through a number of local agencies and organizations. In addition, most communities offer an array of services and programs designed to help families cope with and meet the special needs and challenges of caring for a child with developmental disabilities. Some agencies also provide technical assistance to educators and other professionals who are working with these children. Often, the agencies themselves serve as a valuable resource because they are familiar with other community-based services, assistance programs, and trained specialists.

EXAMPLES OF COMMUNITY SERVICES AND RESOURCES FOR FAMILIES

- Child Find screening programs
- Interagency Coordinating Councils (ICCs)
- Early childhood centers and therapeutic programs for exceptional children
- Public health departments at city, county, and state levels
- Local public school districts, especially the special services divisions

- Hospitals, medical centers, and well-child clinics
- University-Affiliated Programs (UAPs)
- Head Start and Even Start programs
- Mental health centers
- State-supported low-cost health insurance for children
- Parent support groups
- Service groups that provide respite care, transportation, or financial assistance
- Marriage counseling programs
- Philanthropic organizations such as the Lion's Club (glasses), Shriners, and Make a Wish Foundation
- Professional practitioners: pediatricians, nurses, psychologists, audiologists, ophthalmologists, early childhood specialists, educators, speech-language therapists, occupational and physical therapists, and social workers

EXAMPLES OF NATIONAL AND PROFESSIONAL ORGANIZATIONS

There are also many national organizations that offer extensive information as well as direct assistance to children and families with specific needs. Contact information can usually be found in local telephone directories, the *Encyclopedia of Associations* (at the library), or on the Internet. For example:

- Allergy and Asthma Foundation *www.aafa.org*
- American Council for the Blind *www.acb.org*
- American Diabetes Association *www.diabetes.org*
- The American Foundation for the Blind *www.afb.org*
- American Heart Association *www.americanheart.org*
- American Society for Deaf Children *www.deafchildren.org*
- The Autism Society of America *www.autism-society.org*
- Children's Craniofacial Association *www.ccakids.org*
- Cleft Palate Foundation *www.cleftline.org*
- Council for Exceptional Children *www.cec.sped.org*
- Down Syndrome Children *www.downsnet.org*
- Epilepsy Foundation of America *www.efa.org*
- Learning Disabilities Association *www.ldanatl.org*
- National Down Syndrome Society *www.ndss.org*
- National Easter Seals *www.easter-seals.org*
- The United States Cerebral Palsy Athletic Association *www.uscpaa.org*

EXAMPLES OF TECHNICAL ASSISTANCE PROGRAMS

There are also a number of programs and organizations whose purpose is to provide direct, technical assistance to educational programs and agencies serving young children with developmental disabilities. Many of these groups also offer instructional material. A sample of such agencies includes:

- American Printing House for the Blind at *www.aph.org*. This group produces materials and services for children with visual impairments, including talking books, magazines in Braille, and large-type books as well as materials intended for educators of blind or visually impaired children.

- Head Start Resource Access Projects (RAPs). Their purpose is to assist Head Start programs in providing comprehensive services to children with developmental problems.

- National Early Childhood-Technical Assistance Center (NECTAC) at *www.nectac.org*. This agency provides many forms of assistance to federally funded early-childhood programs and projects (IDEA) serving children with disabilities.

- National Information Center for Children and Youth with Disabilities at *www.nichcy.org*. This organization serves as a central source for information about disabilities, early intervention, research, law, and parent materials. A bilingual site is also provided.

Information Sources

A wealth of information is published for families, teachers, and professionals who work with children with developmental problems. Many professional journals, government publications, CD-ROMs, and reference books are available in most public and university libraries. Special-interest groups and professional organizations also produce a wealth of printed and online material focused on high-risk children and children with developmental delays.

SELECTED EXAMPLES OF INFORMATION RESOURCES

- Professional journals and periodicals such as the *Journal of the Division for Early Childhood, Topics in Early Childhood Special Education, Young Exceptional Children, Teaching Exceptional Children, Child Development, Early Childhood Research Quarterly, Early Childhood Digest,* and *Young Children.*

- Trade magazines for families, such as *Parents of Exceptional Children, Parenting,* and *Parents Magazine.*

- Government documents, reports, and pamphlets. These cover almost any topic related to child development, child care, early intervention, nutrition, parenting, and specific developmental problems. Publications can be obtained through the Superintendent of Documents, U.S. Government Printing Office, Washington, DC, 20402; many are available in local government buildings, including public libraries, and on the Internet.

- Bibliographic indexes and abstracts usually located in university, college, and large public libraries. These are particularly useful to students and practitioners who need to locate information quickly on a specific topic. Examples of several include:

  - *The Review of Child Development*
  - *Current Topics in Early Childhood Education*
  - Electronic journals and serials such as *Early Childhood Research & Practice*, *Networks* (online journal for teacher research), *Parent News*, *Contemporary Issues in Early Childhood*, *Future of Children*, *Health Child Care*, and *Bulletin of the World Association of Early Childhood Educators*

EXAMPLES OF PROFESSIONAL ORGANIZATIONS THAT FOCUS ON CHILDREN'S ISSUES

- American Academy of Pediatrics *www.aap.org*
- American Association on Mental Retardation (AAMR) *www.aamr.org*
- American Public Health Association *www.apha.org*
- American Speech, Language, Hearing Association (ASHA) *www.asha.org*
- Association for Childhood Education International *www.acei.org*
- Association for Retarded Citizens (ARC) *www.thearc.org*
- Children's Defense Fund *www.childrensdefense.org*
- Council for Early Childhood Professional Recognition (formerly CDA) *www.cda.org*
- Council for Exceptional Children (CEC), especially the Division for Early Childhood (DEC) within the Council *www.cec.sped.org*
- Early Childhood Resource Center *www.rti.org*
- Early Head Start National Resource Center *www.ehsnrc.org*
- Head Start Bureau *www.acf.dhhs.gov*
- March of Dimes *www.modimes.org*
- National Association for the Education of Young Children (NAEYC) *www.naeyc.org*
- National Association for Family Child Care *www.nafcc.org*
- National Association of Child Care Resource & Referral Agencies *www.naccrra.org*
- The National Information Center for Children and Youth with Disabilities *www.nichcy.org*
- National Parent Information Network (NPIN) *www.npin.org*
- National Parent Network on Disabilities *www.npnd.org*
- Parents Helping Parents *www.php.org*
- Special Olympics International *www.specialolympics.org*

Conclusion

Finding help for children with developmental delays and disabilities is not a simple matter. The issues are often complex; some children present tangles of interrelated developmental problems that tend to become more complex when not addressed during the crucial first 5 years of life. Therefore, effective intervention must begin early and be comprehensive, integrated, ongoing, and family-centered. It must also take into account multiple developmental areas at the same time. This effort requires teamwork on the part of specialists from many disciplines, service providers, and agencies working cooperatively with the child and the family. It also requires an awareness of legislative acts and public policies that affect services for children with developmental problems and their families, as well as available resources and effective means of collaboration. Only then will children and families fully benefit from an early intervention team approach.

Additional Reading Resources

Child Development

Bee, H. (2006). *The developing child.* (11th ed.). Boston: Allyn & Bacon.
This comprehensive child development text is highly readable. It provides psychologically sound yet conversational coverage of all aspects of child development. Research findings are reported in a way that readily relates to everyday home and school settings.

Berk, L. A. (2008). *Infants, children and adolescents.* (5th ed.). Boston: Allyn & Bacon.
The fundamentals of child development are presented in a clear and chronological manner. Many contemporary topics are addressed, with special emphasis on the influence of culture on children's development and the application of research to practice and social policy as it affects children and families.

Berns, R. (2007). *Child, family, school, community: Socialization and support.* Belmont, CA: Thomson/Wadsworth.
Written by a sensitive child developmentalist, this insightful text combines theory and research to describe the influential forces that home, school, peers, and communities exert on shaping children's behavior and development.

Charlesworth, R. (2008). *Understanding child development.* (7th ed.). Clifton Park, NY: Thomson Delmar Learning.
An excellent book for teachers and families; the focus is on growth and development in the infant, toddler, and preschool child. A wealth of basic information is skillfully combined with numerous suggestions for working with young children.

Cobb, N. (2001). *The child.* Mountain View, CA: Mayfield.

> A comprehensive introductory textbook that examines development from pre-birth through adolescence. The material addresses many contemporary social issues in a reader-friendly style.

Cole, M., & Cole, S. (2004). *The development of children.* New York: Worth Publishing.

> This child development text presents the fundamental theories and contemporary issues, inclusive of birth through adolescence, in a thorough and readable style with a strong emphasis on the influence of culture.

Flavell, J. H., Miller, P. H., & Miller, S. (2001). *Cognitive Development.* (4th ed.). Upper Saddle River, NJ: Prentice Hall.

> No text on cognitive development can completely escape technical complexity, but this one, written by a leading researcher on cognitive development and developmental theory, is one of the best yet least difficult because of its easy, anecdotal style.

Fogel, A. (2000). *Infancy: Infant, family and society.* New York: Wadsworth.

> A comprehensive overview of child development, conception through age 3, that examines a number of contemporary factors that influence individual differences, including intelligence, sociability, and temperament.

Santrock, J. W. (2007). *Children.* (8th ed.). Boston: McGraw-Hill.

> An appealing and easily read textbook that addresses contemporary topics in child development in a culturally sensitive manner. Extensive research findings, with emphasis on everyday application, are incorporated throughout the book. Content covers birth through adolescence with an emphasis on family education, culture, and gender influence.

Trawick-Smith, J. (2006). *Early childhood development: A multicultural perspective.* (3rd ed.).

> The author examines children's development from a multicultural perspective and provides numerous examples to illustrate cultural differences. Anyone who works with children and their families will find this insightful book an exceptional resource.

Observation and Assessment

Bagnato, S. (2007). *Authentic assessment for early childhood intervention: Best practices.* New York: Guilford Press.

> The author has written an excellent resource book that focuses on the developmentally appropriate assessment of young children. Multiple tools and methods are described for gathering information about children in their natural settings and interpreting the results for intervention planning.

Bentzen, W. R. (2008). *Seeing young children: A guide to observing and recording behavior.* (6th ed.). Clifton Park, NY: Thomson Delmar Learning.

> A practical book on observing young children, recording their developmental

progress, and using the information to foster each child's development in multiple areas.

Gronlund, G., & James, M. (2005). *Focused observations: How to observe children for assessment and curriculum planning.* St. Paul: Redleaf Press.

This hands-on guide reflects the author's years of experience in the field. It is written to help educators conduct assessments that are authentic and developmentally appropriate and to use the results to improve learning experiences. Teachers new to the field will especially appreciate the practical suggestions and illustrations included in this book.

Losardo, A., & Notari-Syverson, A. (2001). *Alternative approaches to assessing young children.* Baltimore: Paul H. Brookes.

The authors suggest a variety of nontraditional methods for assessing young children from cultural, linguistic, or developmentally diverse backgrounds. Sample forms, a discussion of the advantages and disadvantages of each approach, and implementation suggestions are included.

McAfee, O., & Leong, D. (2006). (4th ed.). *Assessing and guiding young children's development and learning.* Boston: Allyn & Bacon.

This is an excellent book that covers authentic assessment and screening strategies in easily understood detail; many examples are also included. The authors stress assessment as a process, sensitivity to individual differences, and professional responsibility.

McLean, M., Bailey, D., & Wolery, M. (2003). *Assessing infants and preschoolers with special needs.* (2nd ed.). Columbus, OH: Prentice-Hall.

An excellent book written for early childhood educators and allied health professionals. The authors stress the importance of observation in natural settings, a family-centered approach, and sensitivity to cultural differences.

Mindes, G. (2006). *Assessing young children.* Upper Saddle River, NJ: Prentice Hall.

This book provides valuable information about a range of assessment strategies and includes a review of screening tools and suppliers. Appropriate use of assessment findings for making sound decisions that affect children, birth through 8 years, and planning developmentally appropriate practices are emphasized throughout. The author also addresses many contemporary issues relative to assessment in early childhood education.

Nilsen, B. A. (2005). *Week by week: Observing and recording young children.* (2nd ed.). Clifton Park, NY: Thomson Delmar Learning.

The author presents a systematic yet feasible plan for documenting children's behavior. Various methods of observing and recording are featured along with principles of child development and appropriate classroom practices. Teacher trainers, practicum students, and classroom teachers will find this text most useful.

Venn, J. (2007). *Assessing students with special needs.* Upper Saddle River, NJ: Merrill/ Prentice Hall.

An excellent book that includes easy-to-understand explanations of basic statistical concepts for interpreting assessment testing outcomes. The author also provides extensive descriptions of the full range of assessment options and instruments, including the pros, cons, cultural considerations, technology, and limitations of each.

Children with Special Needs

Allen, K. E., & Cowdery, G. (2008). *The exceptional child: Inclusion in early childhood education.* (6th ed.). Clifton Park, NY: Thomson Delmar Learning.

A comprehensive text based on developmental principles as they apply to the inclusion and appropriate education of children of all developmental capabilities in early childhood programs. The authors also discuss the legal aspects of developmentally appropriate interventions.

Batshaw, M., Pellegrino, L., & Roizen, N. (Eds.). (2007). *Children with disabilities.* (6th ed.). Baltimore: Paul H. Brookes.

An excellent multidisciplinary text edited by three noted physicians and written for professionals working with children who have special needs, including cognitive, communication, autism spectrum, chromosomal, neural tube, and seizure disorders. Invited chapters, prepared by experts in their respective areas, provide the latest developments and applications in practice. Numerous case studies, illustrations, and resources are included.

Deiner, P. (2005). *Resources for educating children with diverse abilities.* Clifton Park, NY: Thomson Delmar Learning.

Teachers will find information about IDEA, the IEP process, detailed descriptions of specific disabilities, and an overview of giftedness as well as resources for working with children in inclusionary programs.

Fuller, M., & Olsen, G. (2007). *Home-school relations.* Needham Heights, MA: Allyn & Bacon.

An excellent introduction to the fundamental principles underlying effective family involvement. Particularly good are the chapters on communication, advocacy, school violence, fathers, and research-based family involvement models. Many resources (e.g., videos, organizations, Web sites) are also provided.

Noonan, M., & McCormick, L. (2006). *Young children with disabilities in natural environments.* Baltimore: Paul H. Brookes.

A book devoted to professionals who work with children 0 to 5 years. Cultural competence is a theme emphasized throughout the text as the authors discuss practical approaches to serving children in naturalistic environments.

Pianta, R., Cox, M., & Snow, K. (Eds.). (2007). *School readiness and the transition to kindergarten in the era of accountability.* Baltimore: Paul H. Brookes.

Experts discuss many issues of critical interest to families, educators, and professionals dedicated to helping children achieve their personal and academic potentials. Topics included in this book range from educational policies and program opportunities in the United States to development across domains and family involvement.

Shonkoff, J., & Meisels, S. (Eds.). (2000). *Handbook of early childhood intervention.* New York: Cambridge University Press.

> Written by noted professionals in the field, this book examines key issues and challenges associated with early intervention services for young children and their families. A strong commitment to professional collaboration and a transdisciplinary team approach are evident throughout this book.

Turnbull, H. R., Huerta, N., & Stowe, M. (2006). *Explanation of the Individuals with Disabilities Education Act as amended 2004.* (2nd ed.). Columbus, OH: Prentice Hall.

> This handbook is designed to help special educators and administrators understand, interpret, and implement changes established by this most recent set of amendments.

Diversity

deMelendez, W., & Beck, V. (2007). *Teaching young children in multicultural classrooms: Issues, concepts and strategies.* (2nd ed.). Clifton Park, NY: Delmar Cengage Learning.

> The authors describe themselves as newcomers to the United States, but they obviously are not newcomers to the cultural diversity represented in schools and early-childhood programs. This well-organized text lays out plans for developing a functional, multicultural curriculum. In addition, it provides an insightful perspective on the history as well as the future of multiculturalism in our schools and country.

Eggers-Piérola, C. (2005). *Connections and commitments: Reflecting Latino values in early childhood programs.* Washington, DC: NAEYC.

> Teachers will find this book valuable for learning about the Latino culture and designing learning environments that support children, families, and cultural values.

Gonzalez-Mena, J. (2008). *Diversity in early care and education: Honoring differences.* (4th ed.). New York: McGraw-Hill.

> This book celebrates the rich diversity that young children and their families bring to early-childhood programs and helps teachers understand how differences in cultural background and ability can be addressed in a respectful manner.

Isenberg, J. P., & Jalongo, M. R. (Eds.). (2003). *Major issues and trends in early childhood education.* New York: Teachers College Press.

> This publication includes a series of articles in which the authors examine current issues and challenges in the field with respect to public policy, inclusion, diversity, family involvement, DAP, assessment, and technology.

Klein, M., & Chen, D. (2000). *Working with children from culturally diverse backgrounds.* Clifton Park, NY: Thomson Delmar Learning.

> A good resource book that addresses cultural influences on children's development and offers suggestions for modifying learning experiences and instructional methods to meet children's unique needs.

Lynch, E. W., & Hanson, M. J. (2004). *Developing cross-cultural competence: A guide to working with young children and their families.* Baltimore: Paul H. Brookes.

Cultural, language, and developmental diversity among children and their families is the focus of this well-researched text. Chapters 4–11 offer detailed insights into seven of the most common cultures represented in schools and child care centers today. Cultural differences are described and analyzed by the authors, each native to his or her respective culture.

Trawick-Smith, J. (2006). *Early childhood development: A multicultural perspective.* (4th ed.). Columbus, OH: Prentice Hall.

Anyone who works with children will find one of the most comprehensive treatments of children's development, by stages, and the cultural variations and expectations typical of diverse populations included in this book. Additional concerns, such as poverty, special needs, advocacy, and facilitation of children's skill development are woven throughout.

York, S. (2003). *Roots and wings: Affirming culture in early childhood programs.* (revised ed.). St. Paul: Redleaf Press.

This proven book provides early-childhood teachers with a wealth of valuable suggestions and updated resources for creating culturally responsive classrooms. The author has addressed several new topics, including children and racial prejudice, bilingual education, empowering children, and working with children and families from diverse backgrounds.

Parenting

Bigner, J. (2006). *Parent-child relations: An introduction to parenting.* (7th ed.). Upper Saddle River, NJ: Prentice Hall.

This research-based text addresses the concept of family from a developmental perspective and examines significant issues that confront today's contemporary families. Teachers and practitioners will find this book helpful in understanding and developing effective working relationships with families.

Brooks, J. B. (2006). *The process of parenting.* New York: McGraw-Hill.

A comprehensive book that addresses many contemporary parenting issues. Information on behavior management and developmentally appropriate expectations is included for children at all stages along the developmental continuum. Special attention is also given to issues of working families, the single parent, stepparenting, and children with specific needs.

Christopherson, E. R. (1998). *Beyond discipline: Parenting that lasts a lifetime.* (2nd ed.). Kansas City, KS: Westport.

This respected authority on child development and behavior management tackles a universal concern of families and teachers with his usual wit and humor. His techniques have evolved from extensive research and years of clinical experience with young children.

Eisenberg, A., Murkoff, H., & Hathway, S. (1996). *What to expect: The toddler years.* New York: Workman.

(2003). *What to expect: The first year.* New York: Workman.

Both of these books provide a wealth of down-to-earth information about very young children for new as well as experienced parents and caregivers. Excellent coverage of child development and caregiving routines is provided in an easy-to-understand manner. These just might be the owner's manuals about baby for which every family searches.

Heath, P. (2005). *Parent-child relations: History, theory, research and context.* Columbus, OH: Prentice Hall.

The author examines the lifespan and cultural perspectives of parenting, including the historical evolution of parenting roles and the influence of child-development theories.

Hamner, T., & Turner, P. (2008). *Parenting in contemporary society.* Needham Heights, MA: Allyn & Bacon.

The authors discuss the diversity of traditional and nontraditional family patterns in the United States, along with cultural differences, socioeconomic variations, working families, high-risk families, and adoption and foster care as well as families of exceptional children. Throughout this book, emphasis is placed on effective parenting strategies.

Luster, T., & Okagaki., L. (Eds.). (2005). *Parenting: An ecological perspective.* Hillsdale, NJ: Erlbaum.

An up-to-date compilation of research findings on a variety of contemporary issues related to differences in parenting behavior. These multidisciplinary studies were undertaken in an effort to improve the understanding of parental behavior and how to enhance parent–child relationships effectively.

Marotz, L. (2009). *Health, safety, and nutrition for the young child.* (7th ed.). Clifton Park, NY: Thomson Delmar Learning.

A comprehensive treatment of children's health and development, including preventive practices, environmental causes of illness, nutrition, and health education. The book also includes the latest research findings and numerous suggestions for its practical application in homes and classroom settings.

Wilson, L., & Swim, T. (2007). *Infants and toddlers curriculum and teaching.* (6th ed.). Clifton Park, NY: Thomson Delmar Learning.

Families and teachers will find this book particularly useful in understanding developmental sequences, creating enriching environments, and providing appropriate learning experiences for infants and toddlers based on their developmental needs. New information has been included on brain research and its application in learning environments.

GLOSSARY

A

abstract   The ability to think and use concepts; an idea or theory.

achievement tests   Tests used to measure a child's academic progress (what the child has learned).

acquisition   The process of learning or achieving objectives (e.g., walking, counting, reading).

amniocentesis   Genetics-screening procedure in which a needle is inserted through the mother's abdomen into the sac of fluid surrounding the fetus to detect abnormalities such as Down syndrome or spina bifida; usually performed between the twelfth and sixteenth weeks.

anencephaly   A birth defect resulting in malformation of the skull and brain; portions of these structures might be missing at birth.

at risk   Term describing children who might be more likely to have developmental problems due to certain predisposing factors such as low birth weight, neglect, or maternal drug addiction.

authentic assessment   A process of collecting and documenting information about children's developmental progress; data is gathered in children's naturalistic settings and from multiple sources.

autonomy   A sense of self as separate from others.

B

bilateral   Affecting both sides, as in loss of hearing in both ears.

binocular vision   Both eyes working together, sending a single visual image to the brain.

bonding   The establishment of a close, loving relationship between an infant and an adult, usually the mother and father; also called *attachment*.

bullying   Verbal and physical behavior that is hurtful, intentional, and repeatedly directed toward a person or child who is viewed as weaker.

C

cephalocaudal   Bone and muscular development that proceeds from head to toe.

cervix   The lower portion of the uterus that opens into the vagina.

cesarean section   The delivery of a baby through an incision in the mother's abdomen and uterus.

Child Find   A screening program designed to locate children with developmental problems through improved public awareness.

chronological   Events or dates in sequence in the passage of time.

cleft lip/cleft palate   Incomplete closure of the lip, palate (roof of the mouth), or both, resulting in a disfiguring deformity.

conception   The joining of a single egg or ovum from the female and a single sperm from the male.

concrete operational thought   Piaget's third stage of cognitive development; period when concepts of conservation and classification are understood.

conservation   The stage in children's cognitive development when they begin to understand that an object's physical qualities (e.g., weight, mass) remain the same despite changes in its appearance; for example, flattening a ball of playdough does not affect its weight.

constructivism   A learning approach in which a child forms his or her own meaning through active participation.

cumulative   An add-on process, bit by bit or step by step.

CVS   Chorionic villus sampling; a genetics-screening procedure in which a needle is inserted and cells are removed from the outer layer of the placenta; performed between the eighth and twelfth weeks to detect some genetic disorders, such as Down syndrome.

D

deciduous teeth   Initial set of teeth that eventually fall out; often referred to as baby teeth.

depth perception   Ability to determine the relative distance of objects from the observer.

descriptive praise   Words or actions that describe to a child specifically what she or he is doing correctly or well.

development   Refers to an increase in complexity, from simple to more complicated and detailed.

developmental sequence   A continuum of predictable steps along a developmental pathway of skill achievement.

developmental team   A team of qualified professionals, such as special educators, speech pathologists, occupational therapists, social workers, audiologists, nurses, and physical therapists, who evaluate a child's developmental progress and together prepare an intervention plan that addresses the child's special needs.

developmentally appropriate   A term used to describe learning experiences that are individualized based on a child's level of skills, abilities, and interests.

discrete behaviors   Behaviors that can clearly be observed and described: hitting, pulling hair, spitting.

domains   A term describing an area of development, such as physical, motor, social-emotional, or speech and language.

dysfluency   Repetition of whole words or phrases uttered without frustration and often at the beginning of a statement such as, "Let's go, let's go get some cookies."

E

ecology   In terms of children's development, refers to interactive effects between children and their family, child care situation, school, and everything in the wider community that affects their lives.

egocentricity   Believing that everything and everyone is there for your purpose.

embryo   The cell mass from the time of implantation through the eighth week of pregnancy.

emerging literacy   Early experiences, such as being read and talked to, naming objects, and indentifying letters, that prepare a child for later reading, writing, and language development.

essential needs   Basic physical needs such as food, shelter, and safety as well as psychological needs such as love, security, and trust, required for survival and healthy development.

expressive language   Words used to verbalize thoughts and feelings.

F

Family Service Coordinator   An individual who serves as a family's advocate and assists them with identifying, locating, and making final arrangements with community services.

fine motor   Also referred to as manipulative skills; includes stacking blocks, buttoning and zipping, and toothbrushing.

fontanels   Small openings (sometimes called soft spots) in the infant's skull bones, covered with soft tissue. Eventually, they close.

food jag   A period when only certain foods are preferred or accepted.

functional language   Language that enables children to get what they need or want.

G

gender   Reference to being either male or female.

genes   Genetic material that carries codes, or information, for all inherited characteristics.

gross motor   Large muscle movements such as locomotor skills (walking, skipping, swimming) and nonlocomotive movements (sitting, pushing, pulling, squatting).

growth   Physical changes leading to an increase in size.

H

hand dominance   Preference for using one hand over the other; most individuals are said to be either right- or left-handed.

hands-on learning   A curriculum approach that involves children as active participants, encouraging them to manipulate, investigate, experiment, and solve problems.

head circumference   Measurement of the head taken at its largest point (across forehead, around back of head, returning to the starting point).

holophrastic speech   Using a single word to express a complete thought.

I

implantation   The attachment of the blastocyst to the wall of the mother's uterus; occurs around the twelfth day.

in utero   Latin term for 'in the mother's uterus.'

inclusion programs   Community child care, school, and recreational facilities in which all children from the most gifted to the most disabled participate in the same activities. Inclusion is a federal law mandated by the Congress of the United States. Originally, it was referred to as *mainstreaming*.

intelligible   Language that can be understood by others.

interdependent   Affecting or influencing development in other domains.

intuition   Thoughts or ideas based on feelings or a hunch.

J

jargon   Unintelligible speech; in young children, it usually includes sounds and inflections of the native language.

L

linguistic code   Verbal expression that has meaning to the child.

logic   Process of reasoning based on a series of facts or events.

low birth weight (LBW)   An infant who weighs less than 5.5 pounds (2500 grams) at birth regardless of age.

N

naturalistic settings   Environments that are familiar and part of children's everyday experiences, such as classrooms, care arrangements, and home.

nature-nurture   Refers to whether development is primarily due to biological and genetic forces (heredity/nature) or to external forces (environment/nurture).

neurological   Refers to the brain and nervous system.

norms   Age-level expectancies associated with the achievement of developmental skills.

normal (typical) development   Achievement of certain skills according to a fairly predictable sequence, although with many individual variations.

nurturing   Includes qualities of warmth, loving, caring, and attention to physical needs.

O

object permanence   Piaget's sensorimotor stage when infants understand that an object exists even when it is not in sight.

otitis media   An infection of the middle ear.

P

parallel play   Playing alongside or near another person but not involved in their activity.

placenta A specialized lining that forms inside the uterus during pregnancy to support and nourish the developing fetus.

premature infant An infant born before 37 weeks following conception.

proximodistal Bone and muscular development that begins closest to the trunk, gradually moving outward to the extremities.

pruning Elimination of neurons and neural connections that are not being used; this process strengthens developing connections the child is using.

pupil The small, dark, central portion of the eye.

R

receptive language Ability to understand words that are heard.

reciprocal Exchanges between individuals or groups that are mutually beneficial (or hindering).

refinement Progressive improvement in ability to perform fine and gross motor skills.

reflexive Movements resulting from impulses of the nervous system that cannot be controlled by the individual.

respite care Child care assistance given to families to allow them temporary relief from the demands of caring for a child with disabilities.

S

self-esteem Feelings about one's self-worth.

sensory Refers to the five senses: hearing, seeing, touching, smelling, and tasting.

sensory information Information received through the senses: eyes, ears, nose, mouth, and touch.

sonogram Visual image of the developing fetus created by directing high-frequency sound waves (ultrasound) at the mother's uterus; used to determine fetal age and physical abnormalities.

sphincter The muscles necessary to accomplish bowel and bladder control.

spina bifida A birth defect caused by a malformation of the baby's spinal column.

stammering To speak in an interrupted or repetitive pattern; not to be confused with stuttering.

strabismus Condition in which one or both eyes appear to be turned inward (crossed) or outward.

stranger anxiety A cross-cultural phenomenon in which infants begin to show distress or fear when approached by persons other than their primary caregivers.

T

telegraphic speech Uttering two-word phrases to convey a complete thought.

temperament An individual's characteristic manner or style of response to everyday events, including degree of interest, activity level, and regulation of her or his own behavior.

teratogens Harmful agents that can cause fetal damage (e.g, malformations, neurological, and behavioral problems) during the prenatal period.

transactional process The give-and-take relationship between children, their primary caregivers, and daily events that influences behavior and developmental outcomes.

tripod grasp Hand position whereby an object, such as a pencil, is held between the thumb and first and second fingers.

typical Achievement of certain skills according to a fairly predictable sequence, although with many individual variations.

V

voluntary Movements that can be willed and deliberately controlled and initiated by the individual.

Z

zygote The cell formed as a result of conception; called a zygote for the first 14 days.

INDEX